GERONTOLOGICAL
HOME HEALTH CARE

GERONTOLOGICAL
HOME HEALTH CARE

A GUIDE FOR THE SOCIAL WORK PRACTITIONER

Goldie Kadushin and Marcia Egan

COLUMBIA UNIVERSITY PRESS   NEW YORK

COLUMBIA UNIVERSITY PRESS
Publishers Since 1893
New York   Chichester, West Sussex

Library of Congress Cataloging-in-Publication Data
Kadushin, Goldie.
Gerontological home health care : a guide for the social work practitioner /
Goldie Kadushin and Marcia Egan.
   p. cm.
  Includes bibliographical references and index.
  ISBN 978-0-231-12464-5 (cloth : alk. paper) — ISBN 978-0-231-12465-2 (pbk. : alk. paper)
1. Social work with older people—United States. 2. Home care services—United states.
I. Egan, Marcia.   II. Title.

HV1461.K33   2008
362.6'3   dc22   2007053053

Columbia University Press books are printed on permanent
    and durable acid-free paper.
This book is printed on paper with recycled content.

Printed in the United States of America
c 10 9 8 7 6 5 4 3 2 1
p 10 9 8 7 6 5 4 3 2 1

References to Internet Web sites (URLs) were accurate at the
time of writing. Neither the author nor Columbia University
Press is responsible for URLs that may have expired or changed
since the manuscript was prepared.

To Steven Morrison with love, respect, and admiration

and

to my parents, Alfred and Sylvia, whose dignity and resilience inspired this book

—GK

This book is dedicated to those older adults, including my parents and grandparents, and older adult clients and their families who generously, though often unknowingly, informed my understanding of the challenges and treasures of the aging process, and collectively motivate my research. I also dedicate the book to my sons, Todd and Dean, whose steadfast support and encouragement enrich both my work and my own experience of aging.

—ME

CONTENTS

PREFACE

DEMOGRAPHIC CHANGES such as the aging of the baby boomer cohort and the lengthening of the average life span are increasing the number and proportion of older adults in the American population. As age increases, the prevalence of chronic health conditions rises, affecting quality of life and utilization of health care services. The majority of older adults with disabilities related to chronic conditions live in the community. Home health care is one of the health services that these older adults with chronic and disabling health conditions use to maintain their safety and well-being. The demand for home health care is illustrated by the fact that home health care was the fastest-growing category of health spending between 2003 and 2005, a period of overall lower health spending.

The typical home health care recipient is age 65 or older, has a chronic health condition that results in impairment of ADL/IADL (activities of daily living/instrumental activities of daily living), is female, not married, non-Hispanic, and lives in a private residence with family. Psychosocial problems experienced by home care users are low income, disability, chronic health conditions, and stressors related to family caregiving as family members are required to provide more care for a longer duration as the life expectancy of older adults increases. In general, home health care users experience multiple psychosocial risk factors that require social work services.

However, a labor force shortage of social workers to provide direct services to older adults is predicted because of the projected retirement of older front-line social workers, along with the increase in demand for health and social services for this age group. Retention and recruitment strategies will be needed to meet this challenge in home health care, as well as in other settings that serve older adults. Obstacles to both goals include the lack of content that addresses aging-related issues in the most frequently used foundational social work textbooks and a need to expand teaching, research, and practicum resources within social work education to increase the number of social workers who have specific expertise in aging and to enhance the level of competency among generalist social workers.

This textbook is intended to provide a comprehensive discussion of social work practice with older adults in home health care. The book was motivated by the gap in the availability of social work textbooks on health care and home health care that synthesized and applied empirical research to practice. Consistent with this goal, the book integrates and applies research to home health social work practice with older adults from the disciplines of social work, nursing, psychology, and other social sciences. It was necessary to review research from disciplines outside of social work because of a shortage of empirically based social work research on the topic of gerontological home health care. Sources cited in the book were selected according to the criterion of the "best available" research.

Decisions about the "best available" research were based on the following:

- Sampling strategy: review of the databases Social Sciences Full Text, PubMed, PsycINFO, and Social Work Abstracts Plus; relevant Web sites (e.g., Centers for Medicare and Medicaid Services, U.S. Census Bureau, Centers for Disease Control and Prevention, Alliance of Family Caregivers, AARP); relevant books from a variety of disciplines; several unpublished dissertations and article manuscripts by colleagues with expertise in a particular area.
- Criteria for inclusion/exclusion: priority given to research conducted in the United States, empirical research (some exceptions to this rule were conceptual articles authored by recognized experts and referenced as "classic" examples of scholarship), the most current research available (exceptions were made for studies considered "classic" or groundbreaking). Only research relevant to home care social work with older adults was included.
- Methodological quality and weighting: when available, recent systematic reviews from the Cochrane Database, controlled clinical trials, meta-analyses, and empirical research by recognized experts were included and weighted more heavily.
- Data extraction: authors' judgment of content most relevant to the social work practice in home health care.
- Data analysis: no formal analysis; data were combined by organizing research and other sources of information to logically address topics discussed.

Throughout the text, the quality of the "best available" research applying these criteria is indicated.

The text is not a workbook, but it attempts to discuss practice in enough detail to give the reader knowledge and skill in the "how-to" of gerontological social work practice in home health care. Consistent with this objective, directions for accessing rapid-assessment instruments are provided whenever possible.

The book can be used in graduate-level foundation courses at the university level to infuse gerontological content, as well as in elective upper-level graduate courses in aging and health care concentrations. It is also a potential resource for continuing education courses directed to social work practitioners, supervisors, or human services personnel. Because the content is relevant to social work practice in community-based settings generally, this text would also be useful for social work practice courses on aging. Disciplines that overlap social work, such as nursing, counseling, health care administration, and rehabilitation therapy, may also find the chapters on the context of home care, cultural competence, engagement, assessment, and intervention useful. Case managers in any discipline are also a possible audience for this content.

The book is organized to first address contextual issues that influence gerontological social work home care practice. Chapter 1 defines home care and discusses goals, clients, providers, history, and major funding programs. Chapter 2 presents the social work role in gerontological home care, including history, the parameters of the social work role, contemporary challenges, and ethical concerns. Chapter 3 focuses on culturally competent practice in home care with older adults, including an understanding of client spiritual orientation, family system and values, and health care beliefs and practice.

Chapter 4 begins the second part of the book, which presents knowledge and skills for practice. This chapter discusses engagement of the older client in home health care, including clarification of the purpose of the meeting, orienting the client to the helping process, exploration of the client's view of helping, collaboration on goals, and clarification of unrealistic expectations. Chapter 5 presents knowledge and skills relevant to assessment of the older adult in home care, including assessment of characteristics of the client's disease with psychosocial implications, medication management, advance directives, health beliefs, self-efficacy, depression, suicide, anxiety, and substance abuse. Chapter 6 concerns assessment of social systems, including clients' unmet needs, social networks and resources, family caregiving, family conflict, elder maltreatment, and nursing home placement. Chapter 7 is concerned with social work interventions with the individual older home care client, such as medication management, advance directives, alternative health care beliefs, depression, anxiety, and substance abuse. Chapter 8 discusses interventions with social systems, such as reduction of unmet needs, reduction of caregiver burden and family conflict, and assistance for clients/families during relocation to a nursing home.

The final chapter addresses practice evaluation, including the need to prove the "added value" and cost efficiency of social work to the organization, and evaluation of the effectiveness of social work interventions on patient outcomes. An afterword and an appendix highlighting resources complete the book.

The need for a specialized social work workforce to improve the quality of life for older adults requires a new curriculum and the integration of gerontological content across that curriculum. We hope that this book can make a contribution toward achieving those goals.

ACKNOWLEDGMENTS

THE CONTRIBUTIONS of several people must be acknowledged. We want to express our gratitude and fondness for John Michel, our editor at Columbia University Press, whose mentoring and guidance were essential during the early period of writing this book. Our current editor, Lauren Dockett, provided skillful support and guidance to expedite the book's completion. Jan McInroy's copyediting and sharp eye for detail improved the readability and accuracy of the text. The library reference skills of Kristin Beebe made it possible to meet deadlines, and her kindness and friendship were a welcome respite from the pressures of writing. The collaboration and friendship of Marcia Egan have been a source of intelligence, wit, and companionship in writing this book and for the past seventeen years.

While I always loved and respected my parents, these feelings intensified as I had the opportunity to hear new parts of their life stories that have revealed the complex nature of their experiences and personalities. Their courage, resilience, and dignity, as we have gone through the life cycle together, are reassuring and inspiring. This book would not exist without my husband, Steven Morrison, who shopped, cooked, did laundry, provided computer consultation, and patiently tolerated hours of solitude while I was locked in my study. His belief in me and his encouragement, intelligence, and love sustained me during the most difficult periods and made a "place" of connection from the work and solitude.

—Goldie Kadushin

❖ ❖ ❖

I have to acknowledge the gifts of collaboration with Goldie in developing this text—a process of hard work and learning liberally sprinkled with good humor.

—Marcia Egan

GERONTOLOGICAL
HOME HEALTH CARE

1

THE CONTEXT OF SOCIAL WORK PRACTICE
IN HOME HEALTH CARE

THE FIRST chapter is intended to provide a context for thinking about practice by discussing:

- the definition of home care
- the goals of home care
- who receives and provides home care
- the history of home health care
- trends influencing the expansion of home care
- funding for home health care

What is most obvious about this discussion is the extent to which home care has been and is currently a rapidly changing field of practice, characterized by a lack of consensus regarding goals, and affected by changing reimbursement regulations, demographics, and technology. In order to adapt to this constantly shifting environment, social workers must have a clear sense of their professional role.

THE DEFINITION OF HOME CARE

The definition of *home care* initially seems to be obvious, suggested by the term itself (Kane 1995). There is some agreement that home care is health-related care received from paid personnel by people with physical impairments and medical conditions (Cox and Ory 2000; R. A. Kane 1999). *Disability* is defined as a major limitation in a primary life activity. It is generally measured as impairment in performing activities of daily living (ADLs) (for example, eating, bathing, dressing, toileting), instrumental activities of daily living (IADLs) (for example, preparing meals, shopping, doing housework, using the telephone, managing personal finances), or more general mobility-related activities (Wan et al. 2005). Problems related to a lack of money or health insurance, mental health difficulties, lack of knowledge about or difficulty in accessing concrete resources, or lack of adequate help from family and friends may affect the ability of a client to maintain or recover health. Consequently, "health-related" care includes medical services such as nursing and physical, speech, and occupational therapy, as well as services provided by social workers and paraprofessionals, like chore workers and personal care assistants (personal care provides help with hygiene-related tasks such as bathing and dressing), that focus on meeting the social and psychological needs of clients (Cowles 2003; Cox and Ory 2000; National Association of Social Workers 1987).

While there is some agreement about the definition of home care, a changing issue is the limits of the concept of *home*. Currently, home care may be provided to people in group residential settings such as board and care homes and adult foster homes. An individual can receive room and board and housekeeping from the residential staff in the setting and personal or home health care from an outside agency (Kane 1995). Those residing in assisted-living facilities or apartment complexes that provide housekeeping and group meal services may also receive personal care and home health services from facility staff or from an outside agency. According to Cox and Ory (2000) "home" may refer to any residential setting that does not provide formal medical services but may or may not offer supportive services. Therefore, while nursing homes and out-of-home day care are excluded, "home" may include a detached home, an apartment in a family member's home, a unit in a congregate housing arrangement with or without supportive services, or a board and care arrangement (Cox and Ory 2000).

Formal home care, then, is health-related care provided to people with physical disabilities and medical conditions; it includes both medical (nursing, physical, speech, and occupational therapies) and non-medical services (e.g., social work and personal care). Recipients of care may or may not be totally homebound. Care may occur in a variety of settings including private homes, group residential, and assisted-living facilities.

THE GOALS OF HOME CARE

Home care goals may be defined from the perspective of the individual, the provider, and/or the community or society. The choice of goals will also depend on the physical, social, and psychological condition of the individual receiving services (Benjamin 1999; Cox and Ory 2000).

In general, from the perspectives of the individual and the provider, the goal of home care is to improve or stabilize the client's medical condition. Services conform to a medical model that emphasizes professional assessment of clinical problems and guidelines for treatment. Medicare-certified home care agencies are dominated by therapeutic goals such as client recovery from illness and rehabilitation (Bishop 1999; Kane 1995; Kane, Kane, and Ladd 1998; R. A. Kane 1999; R. L. Kane 1999).

SOCIETAL VALUES RELATED TO HOME HEALTH CARE

From the perspective of society, the provision of efficient and cost-effective home care is an important goal (Bishop 1999; R. L. Kane 1999; Wolf 1999). Concerns about cost-effectiveness and efficient use of resources are the result of a recent dramatic growth in Medicare expenditures for home care, combined with pressures to control public spending for home care services (R. L. Kane 1999; Shaughnessy 2000; Wolf 1999). Until recently, home health care agencies evaluated the process, not the outcome, of home health care. Evaluation measured only whether care was provided, not how much it cost or whether it achieved positive outcomes for clients; it was therefore difficult to determine whether resources were being used efficiently (Bishop 1999; Sperling and Humphrey 1999).

Since the late 1990s, home care agencies have been required to collect outcome data to measure the effect of the types and amount of care provided in producing beneficial outcomes for patients, using a tool called OASIS (Outcome and Assessment Information Data Set). While OASIS does not completely address the many difficulties in determining whether home care is efficient, its implementation represents a paradigm shift in the evaluation of care (R. L. Kane 1999).

A second goal for home health care at the societal level is to strengthen and support families who are providing informal or unpaid care (Cox and Ory 2000). The majority of caregiving for chronically ill or physically disabled elders is provided by family and friends (Ory et al. 2000). In the United States the assumption expressed in legislation and policies is that the family has an inherent obligation to carry primary responsibility for caring for a dependent member (Montgomery 1999). The family is regarded as the "natural" source of such care because it is a nurturing environment, characterized by relationships based on love, morality, and duty.

However, legislation and policies are ambivalent about the extent to which society is willing to support family caregiving. While families are valued as important ends in themselves, they are also valued because they provide uncompensated care that represents an economic benefit, thereby allowing society to avoid the cost of replacing family care with paid formal care.

Finally, a very specific goal that is unanimously endorsed is to allow the consumer to remain in the community, living in the least-restrictive environment possible (Cox and Ory 2000). According to this goal, no person would be required to receive care in a setting that restricts freedom and choice more than is necessary (Kane, Kane, and Ladd 1998). Different settings are presumed to be appropriate for clients, according to their need for care, and represent different levels in terms of "restrictiveness" (e.g., a small group home or a foster home is more restrictive than home care but less restrictive than a nursing home) (Kane, Kane, and Ladd 1998).

This goal is supported by the 1999 Supreme Court decision in *Olmstead v. L.C.*, which found that states may be in violation of the Americans with Disabilities Act (ADA) if they provide community-based care and do not make it available to all disabled persons, including older adults, who are capable of living in a less-restrictive setting with appropriate services. The priority accorded to care in the least-restrictive setting was expected to result in an expansion of home care, but to date states have not implemented the law consistently (Palley and Rozario 2007).

WHO RECEIVES AND PROVIDES HOME CARE?

The data on demographic characteristics of the older home health care population cited in this discussion were collected in 1996 for the last published National Home and Hospice Survey (Haupt 1998; Munson 1999). Only a small proportion of the total population uses home care (Kane, Kane, and Ladd 1998). Among these recipients, the majority (66 percent), are age 65 or older (Haupt 1998).

Older adults are more likely to use home care for a variety of reasons. First, as people age, the probability that they will develop multiple chronic illnesses increases. A chronic illness is differentiated from an acute illness by three criteria:

- it lasts more than three months
- it interferes with ordinary physical, social, and psychological functioning
- it is incurable (Sidell 1997)

The primary admitting diagnosis to home care in 1996 for both older men and older women was diseases of the circulatory system (e.g., hypertension, heart disease, and cerebrovascular accident). Heart disease is the most frequent diagnosis in this category (Munson 1999). Comorbidity (having two or more illnesses) is common among home care clients—three out of four have two or more diagnoses when they are admitted to care (Haupt 1998). The increase in chronic diseases is associated with an increasing incidence and prevalence of disability with age (He et al. 2005).

The typical older home care user is a woman, age 75–84 years at admission to care, non-Hispanic white, widowed, and living in a private residence with family. A larger percentage of these older women live alone than older men (Munson 1999). The profile described here is consistent with general demographic trends. Currently, disability rates are higher for females at older ages than for males (He et al. 2005). Since women have a longer life expectancy than men do, they spend more years living with disability than men do (He et al. 2005). Women are more likely to live alone as they age than men are, since they outnumber men in the population at older ages (He et al. 2005). Longer life expectancy, higher disability rates, and a higher probability of living alone for older women compared to older men may combine to contribute to an ongoing trend in the predominance of older unmarried females as users of home care.

According to the latest available data, 70 percent of older home care users were white. Approximately 11 percent were black, 12 percent were black and other, 3 percent were Hispanic, and 18 percent were classified as "unknown" (Munson 1999). Current data indicate that older African Americans and Hispanics experience higher disability rates than non-Hispanic whites. African Americans have a lower life expectancy than non-Hispanic whites. Non-Hispanic whites own more private life insurance coverage, experience lower poverty rates, and achieve higher education levels than African Americans and Hispanics. These demographics suggest that older African Americans and Hispanics are exposed to higher levels of social stressors than non-Hispanic whites, a factor that may complicate the course of illnesses and contribute to negative health outcomes (Wan et al. 2005). Among Medicare beneficiaries in 2002, home health care use was higher among those with lower incomes (Kaiser Family Foundation 2005).

As the previous discussion indicates, family members or informal caregivers provide the majority of care for their disabled relatives. When we discuss "home health care," however, we are referring to care provided by "formal" providers— that is, professionals and paraprofessionals who are compensated for the services they provide. At the same time, it should be noted that this distinction between "formal" and "informal" caregivers is becoming somewhat blurred, since in some states family members can now be paid with public money for caregiving (Kane, Kane, and Ladd 1998). Bureau of Labor Statistics data suggest that the majority of home care employees are home care aides, with nurses being the next largest group. Social workers are a minority of the home care labor force (U.S. Department of Labor, Bureau of Labor Statistics 1998). In 1996, 11 percent of older home care patients reported receiving social services; 84 percent, nursing services; and 28 percent, homemaker-household services (Munson 1999).

The fact that home care is dominated by aides and nurses suggests that social workers are employed in "host settings" or organizations whose mission and decision making are defined and dominated by other disciplines (Dane and Simon 1991).

THE HISTORY OF HOME HEALTH CARE

According to Benjamin (1993), home health care has been characterized by an absence of consensus about its principal goals. Consensus has been difficult to achieve because of the coexistence of two different models of home care: the medical post-acute model and the social-supportive model. The medical post-acute model is based on the assumption that home care is necessary to reduce utilization and costs of institutional care. Home care is residual care, to be provided to people for whom mainstream medical interventions have not been effective (Benjamin 1993). Home care in this model is short-term medical care focused on achieving rehabilitation. The social-supportive model, by contrast, has not been as clearly defined. In that model, in addition to medical intervention, home care provides personal care services and, less often, homemaker and case management assistance. While it is concerned with rehabilitation, it also focuses on maintenance, providing services to slow the client's decline or to give comfort when decline is inevitable (Benjamin 1993).

As the following discussion will demonstrate, the passage of Medicare and Medicaid legislation in 1965 institutionalized this dual approach to home care, with Medicare providing post-acute skilled care to homebound individuals, while Medicaid emphasized preventive, skilled, and unskilled care to low-income, chronically ill individuals (Benjamin 1993; Hudson 1996). However, changes during the 1980s and 1990s in the volume and type of home care services provided under Medicare, and the concomitant increase in Medicare expenditures for home care, suggested that Medicare was becoming a program focused on providing long-term care, an intent clearly excluded from covered benefits in the original legislation (Leon, Neuman, and Parente 1997; Welch, Wennberg, and Welch 1996). As a result of this trend, the Balanced Budget Act was passed in 1997 to limit home care expenditures and refocus the home care benefit on the provision of post-acute services (McCall et al. 2001).

HOME CARE BEFORE 1965

Before the twentieth century most medical care was provided in the home, largely by female relatives and/or private nurses (Reverby 1987). Early home care programs originated in the public health nursing programs of the mid-nineteenth century. Boston University started the first hospital-based home care program in 1885 (Keenan and Fanale 1989). From the beginning of these early home care programs until the 1940s, home visits by doctors were a regular part of care provided in the home (Reverby 1987).

In the late nineteenth century medical care shifted away from the home and into the hospital (Benjamin 1993; Reverby 1987). In the early 1900s, as a consequence of improvements in public health, increasing numbers of the chronically ill, particularly the older chronically ill, began to present problems for society. Beginning in the 1920s, new interest in home care was stimulated because of a concern that care of the chronically ill was compromising the ability of hospitals to treat patients with acute illnesses. A great deal of study and debate at this time addressed the question of which setting(s) to recommend as the appropriate alternative to the acute care hospital for treatment of the chronically ill. There were conflicting opinions about the appropriateness of the home as a location for care for the chronically ill. It was argued that visiting nurses were more focused on providing medical care than the custodial care (for example, homemaker services) required by chronic patients. The homes of the chronically ill were also criticized as sites for care because they were poorly ventilated and lacked space and proper lighting. Another factor was that the ability of the family to learn care routines was frequently compromised by language, cultural barriers, and poor education. However, proponents of home care embraced it as a less expensive alternative to hospitalization and promoted it by suggesting that chronic patients preferred to receive care at home (Benjamin 1993).

Until the 1950s, home care was financed through some combination of public funds, private philanthropy, or, less frequently, on a fee-for-service basis (a sliding fee scale, adjusted according to the patient's ability to pay) (Follman 1963). During the late 1950s and early 1960s private insurance in the form of Blue Cross plans began to reimburse for home care. Coverage was generally limited to skilled medical services and excluded homemaker and social work services. An objective of Blue Cross coverage was to substitute home care for expensive hospital care by discharging patients from the hospital earlier. There was also concern that home care coverage could be costly, particularly for the chronically ill, and some plans attempted to limit home care benefits by tying the number of home care days to the number of "unused" hospital days (Benjamin 1993; Follman 1963).

At the same time, there was growing interest in the federal role in financing health insurance. The Social Security Administration (SSA) reviewed two existing models for providing home care: (1) the organized home care program, which provided comprehensive home care (medical care, social services, homemaker services, and physical and occupational therapies) and (2) the Blue Cross plans. While the organized home care program was regarded as admirable, SSA officials were concerned about the administrative feasibility and cost of providing comprehensive home care coverage and feared that such programs would lead to the substitution of publicly funded care for informal care (Benjamin 1993). Ultimately, the emphasis of the Blue Cross plans on limited post-acute care designed to contain hospital costs was attractive to SSA officials concerned with the cost of publicly financed health insurance.

PASSAGE OF MEDICARE AND MEDICAID: 1965

Amendments to the Social Security Act, creating Medicare and Medicaid, both of which contained provisions for home health services, were passed in 1965 (Benjamin 1993). To qualify for services, individuals had to be homebound, in need of skilled nursing or therapy services (physical therapy, speech therapy) or continuing occupational therapy, and under the care of a physician who prescribed the plan of care. A beneficiary needing personal care did not qualify. Once a beneficiary was determined to be eligible, Medicare paid for care from any home health service disciplines (i.e., nursing, physical therapy, speech therapy, occupational therapy, medical social work, and home health aide services). Consistent with Medicare's emphasis on post-acute care, eligibility was limited to patients recovering from an acute illness following a hospitalization (Keenan et al. 1990; Vladeck and Miller 1994).

Medicaid originally covered home health care as an optional service; in 1970 coverage of home health services became mandatory (Stevens and Stevens 1974). Eligibility for home care under Medicaid included no prior hospitalization or need-for-skilled-care requirements (Benjamin 1993). Medicaid requirements for home health care were changed in 1981 when Congress authorized the waiver of certain federal requirements to allow states to provide home health and other community-based services to Medicaid recipients who would otherwise require nursing home care.

The Medicaid model of home care implied longer-term services for people with both chronic and acute conditions. By contrast, the Medicare model was designed to provide short-term post-acute care, primarily through the provision of skilled medical services. In practice, however, beneficiaries had difficulty accessing Medicaid home care because of restrictive reimbursement and benefit limits that curbed the availability of care (Dombi 1991).

HOME CARE AS AN ALTERNATIVE TO INSTITUTIONALIZATION: 1970S AND 1980S

During the 1970s and early 1980s increasing amounts of public money were spent on nursing home care. Home care was viewed by some policymakers as a less costly alternative to nursing home care. Eligibility and reimbursement requirements were liberalized in the Omnibus Budget Reconciliation Act of

1980 to facilitate access to home care. Most significantly, this legislation permitted for-profit agencies to become Medicare-certified providers. By mid-decade, the number of for-profit agencies receiving Medicare reimbursement increased sixfold (Benjamin 1993). Research has suggested that for-profit agencies provide more visits than nonprofits, leading to an expansion in the use and cost of care (Ellenbecker 1995; Leon, Neuman, and Parente 1997; Williams 1994; Williams, McKay, and Torner 1991). It is unclear, however, whether this increased use is because these agencies attract sicker patients or because they "induce demand" for their services (Leon, Neuman, and Parente 1997).

In 1983 a prospective payment system (DRG) was instituted to control the growth of Medicare hospital reimbursement. Before this change, hospitals and physicians had less incentive to discharge patients to home care because they were reimbursed by Medicare for the entire hospital stay, irrespective of number of days. Under DRG, Medicare paid hospitals a flat rate prospectively for an "episode" of care. Payment was determined by the patient's disease category (Diagnostic Related Group, or DRG). Patients who consumed more resources than the flat-rate payment cost the hospital money. Prospective payment contributed to the expansion of home care by creating an impetus to move patients out of the hospital and into home care more quickly (Benjamin 1993; Leon, Neuman, and Parente 1997; Spohn, Bergthold, and Estes 1988).

EXPANSION OF HOME CARE: 1990S

In 1988 the *Duggan v. Bowen* court decision liberalized eligibility requirements for home care. As a result of this new ruling, spending for home care increased at an unprecedented pace as more beneficiaries used it and the average number of visits per beneficiary increased. This trend continued throughout the 1990s (Bishop and Skwara 1993). Most of this spending was attributed to an increase in the number of visits by home health aides (Bishop and Skwara 1993). It became apparent that a large share of home health care expenditures went for a small proportion of beneficiaries who received long-term (one hundred visits or more) personal care (U.S. General Accounting Office 2000a).

Thus, the 1988 regulations made home health care more available to beneficiaries who had ongoing medical problems requiring skilled nursing but whose primary needs were for long-term personal care and assistance with activities of daily living. This trend represented a shift toward a social-supportive model of care, and away from the original short-term, post-acute medical care emphasis of the Medicare home health benefit.

Incentives related to the payment system may have also contributed to the increase in visits and the shift from skilled care to personal care. During this time, Medicare reimbursement for home care agencies was cost-based and subject to a limit. Agencies could balance high-cost medical services with low-cost paraprofessional services (e.g., home health aides) and still remain within the allowable amount (Komisar and Feder 1998). This cost-based system may have led to the provision of unnecessary services and in some instances to fraud and abuse (MedPac 1999).

As a result of these factors, between 1990 and 1996 Medicare spending increased 29 percent per year, from $3.9 billion to $18.3 billion. Research conducted on the Medicare home health care population during the mid-1990s concluded that only a small proportion of home health care visits were linked to post-acute recovery from hospitalization and that the Medicare home health benefit had become a form of long-term care for a significant proportion of home health care users (Leon, Neuman, and Parente 1997; Welch, Wennberg, and Welch 1996). These findings provided more evidence that home health care was being substituted for long-term care, though that had not been the original intent of the Medicare legislation establishing the benefit (Leon, Neuman, and Parente 1997).

THE BALANCED BUDGET ACT: 1997

The increase in spending for Medicare home health care resulted in concern among policymakers and contributed to the passage of the Balanced Budget Act in 1997. The BBA legislated the development of a prospective payment system (PPS) for home health care reimbursement that was preceded by an interim payment system (IPS), which was in effect from 1997 until 2000, when PPS was implemented. The objective of the BBA was to refocus Medicare home health care from the provision of long-term care to the original goal of providing short-term acute medical care.

PPS, a form of managed care, attempts to reduce home care costs by paying agencies a flat rate for a sixty-day "episode of care," irrespective of the number of services delivered. The capitated payment is determined at the time of admission, by the patient's clinical and functional status. This information is assumed to predict anticipated resource use and is used to classify the patient into one of eighty Home Health Resource Groups (HHRGs) (Goldberg and Delargy 2000; Murtaugh et al. 2003). However, psychological (e.g., patient cognitive and mental status) and social (e.g., presence of an informal caregiver) factors are omitted from the formula that determines the flat-rate payment for each patient (Ferry 2001).

This review of the history of home care reveals a lack of consensus about the principal goals. The confusion continues today, as evidenced by the 1997 shift in Medicare home care from a program focused on providing long-term care to a program focused on meeting acute medical needs. Medicaid home care continues to provide long-term care through Medicaid waiver programs (these services are not provided through Medicare-certified home health care agencies and therefore are not a primary focus of the discussion) and personal care programs that are available in some states.

TRENDS INFLUENCING THE EXPANSION OF HOME CARE

DISABILITY RATES

More-sophisticated scientific knowledge of the causes of disease, regular immunizations, availability of antibiotics, better nutrition, improved medical technology, and pharmaceuticals have led to a decreased risk of death from acute illnesses, accidents, and congenital conditions and have contributed to an increasing number of disabled individuals (Harris 1997).

Disability among older adults may result from the progression of a chronic health condition or an impairment in a specific body system (Verbugge and Jette 1994). As noted, as individuals age, the incidence and prevalence of disability increase (He et al. 2005). For example, among the working-age population (16–64), 6.4 percent reported difficulty going outside the home alone to shop or visit the doctor, but 20.4 percent of older adults (65 and older) reported such difficulties (Waldrop, Stern, and U.S. Census Bureau 2003). Self-care disability was more than five times greater (9.5 percent) among older adults than among individuals of working age (1.8 percent) (Waldrop, Stern, and U.S. Census Bureau 2003). Memory problems and sensory impairment exhibit a similar pattern of increase with advancing age (Waldrop, Stern, and U.S. Census Bureau 2003). The projected growth in the older population in the next fifty years will likely mean an increase in the prevalence of disability and will contribute to an expansion of home care (Berke 2000; He et al. 2005).

FUTURE DEMOGRAPHIC CHANGES

Experts agree that the aging of the "baby boom" generation (the 75 million babies born in the United States between 1946 and 1964) will increase the number of disabled elderly needing home care and other forms of long-term care over the next several decades (U.S. General Accounting Office 1998), with the most significant increase expected between 2011 and 2030, as baby boomers reach 65 years of age. According to U.S. Census Bureau projections, between 2000 and 2030 the population of those who are 65 and older will more than double, from 35 million to 72 million (He et al., 2005). The growth will continue between 2030 and 2050 at a slower pace (15 percent), as individuals born during the 1960s and 1970s turn 65.

The number of oldest-old (85 and older) is expected to increase gradually in the beginning of the twenty-first century but then accelerate between 2010 and 2030 as the baby boomers enter this group. In 2000, 12.1 percent of the population were age 85 and older; this group is expected to increase to 15 percent by 2010. By 2050, when the baby boomers start to enter this category, one out of every four older individuals will be 85 or older (24 percent) (He et al. 2005). The old, and particularly the oldest-old, and their families will require formal social supports to remain in the community; thus an expansion of all long-term care, including home care, will be needed (Berke 2000).

This group will also become more racially diverse as a result of demographic shifts in the population as a whole over the coming decades. In 2003, the racial distribution in the older population was approximately 83 percent non-Hispanic white, 8 percent African American, 6 percent Hispanic, and 3 percent Asian. It is projected that by 2030, this group will be 72 percent non-Hispanic white, 11 percent Hispanic, 10 percent African American, and 5 percent Asian. By 2050 the non-Hispanic white group is projected to decrease to 61 percent, while the Hispanic group will increase to almost 18 percent and the Asian to 8 percent (He et al. 2005). The increasing diversity of the population suggests that home health care social workers will need to acquire additional knowledge and skills in order to become culturally competent practitioners.

TECHNOLOGY-BASED HOME CARE

Acutely and chronically ill people once cared for only in hospitals and other institutions can now remain in their own homes because technology-based home care is possible. This approach encompasses three general categories of home care. First, the application of engineering and ergonomic principles that promote safety, such as grab bars in bathrooms and showers, ramps, canes, and railings, and assistive devices for cooking, dressing, and grooming, reduces the impact of impairments in the ability to perform ADLs and IADLs. Second, medical technology such as artificial hydration and nutrition, mechanical ventilation, intravenous infusion of medications, home dialysis, and chemotherapy enables clients to receive treatment at home rather than in the hospital. Finally, information technology such as in-home computer systems can provide instruction in taking medications, maintaining proper nutrition, and promoting self-care. Another form of information technology is telehealth—the use of telecommunications to provide health care services to clients in separate locations when they cannot receive face-to-face services (Kaye and Davitt 1999; Kropf and Grigsby 1999). Telehealth has been used to monitor the health conditions of patients via remote video systems that allow patients and providers to interact in real time and via emergency response systems that signal a need for help in a medical crisis (Johnston 2000; Kropf and Grigsby 1999). It is predicted that home-based technology will become the fastest-growing segment of the home care industry (Kaye and Davitt 1999).

FUNDING FOR HOME HEALTH CARE

In order to provide effective services to clients and to understand the influence of reimbursement policies and programs on social work practice, social workers must be familiar with programs that fund home health care This section will identify and provide basic information about sources of reimbursement for home care. The discussion is intentionally broad, however, because program specifics vary from state to state and reimbursement regulations undergo constant revision. To provide competent services, workers will need to become knowledgeable about the specific regulations and programs that are relevant to the populations they serve within their geographic area.

Currently, home health care funding by the two largest public payers, Medicare and Medicaid, is dominated by managed care (Kaye 2005; Lee and Rock 2005). Managed care has primarily relied on capitated payments, a single payment to a provider for coverage of each patient's treatment for a specific time period (Bodenheimer and Grumbach 2002). Home health care agencies can remain profitable only if they treat the majority of their patients within the limits of the flat-rate payment. While managed care is a good fit for a healthier patient, whose care costs less, it may be a poor fit for the chronically ill frail older home care patient who consumes medical and psychosocial resources beyond the limitations of the capitation fee (Haupt 1998; Kraus, Stoddards, and Gilmartin 1996; Murtaugh et al. 2003; U.S. Office of Strategic Planning, Health Care Financing Administration 1999). Initial research shows that under PPS, home health visits declined by 25 percent, with the sharpest drop registered in the number of visits by home health aides, suggesting a shift in the proportion of total visits toward skilled medical care and away from social care (Murtaugh et al. 2003). One hypothesis is that under PPS home care agencies avoid admitting chronically ill frail elders with complex medical and social needs in favor of patients with simple medical problems (Murtaugh et al. 2003).

PUBLIC THIRD-PARTY PAYERS

MEDICARE

Medicare is a health insurance program for people aged 65 and older and for some younger people with disabilities, regardless of income or assets, provided they have paid into the Social Security system. In addition to providing coverage for inpatient and outpatient hospital services, physician services, and skilled nursing care, Medicare pays for home health care (U.S. Department of Health and Human Services, Centers for Medicare and Medicaid Services 2001b). The largest proportion of publicly funded home care is paid by Medicare (Heffler et al. 2001).

Beneficiaries are eligible for Medicare coverage of home health care if:

- care is authorized by a physician
- it is needed on an intermittent basis (not full time)
- there is a need for at least one skilled service (nursing or physical, speech, or continuing occupational therapy)
- the individual is homebound
- the home care agency is Medicare-certified

The homebound requirement is interpreted to mean that a beneficiary cannot leave home without a major effort. However, a beneficiary is permitted to leave home for a short time to receive medical care or to attend religious services (U.S. Department of Health and Human Services, Centers for Medicare and Medicaid Services 2001a).

Beneficiaries who meet all five conditions receive skilled nursing care, physical, speech, or occupational therapy, medical social services, home health aide services, and certain medical supplies like wound dressings and medical equipment (for example, a wheelchair or walker). Services provided by professionals, including social workers, are fully covered (i.e., there is no copayment or deductible); 80 percent of the cost of durable medical equipment is covered if authorized as medically necessary by a physician (U.S. Department of Health and Human Services, Centers for Medicare and Medicaid Services 2001a).

Medicare does not cover home-delivered meals or homemaker services (such as shopping, cooking, cleaning). Personal care services provided by a home health aide (e.g., help with bathing or toileting) are not covered unless a patient is also receiving skilled services.

As noted, Medicare payments to home health care agencies are in the form of capitated payments, and Medicare can be considered a form of managed care with regard to payment policies (Murtaugh et al. 2003).

MEDICAID

The Medicaid program, a means-tested federal-state program administered by the states, is responsible for financing long-term care for people with low incomes or people who become poor as a result of medical or long-term-care expenses (Feder, Komisar, and Niefeld 2000). Each state has different eligibility requirements for Medicaid. Approximately two-thirds of states enroll the older adult population in managed-care plans (Kaye 2005).

Federal law mandates that home health care provided by states include part-time nursing, home health aide services, and medical supplies and equipment. At the state's option, Medicaid may also cover audiology, physical, occupation-al, and speech therapies, as well as personal care and medical social services (Smith et al. 2000). All nonmedical services are provided whether or not the patient is receiving skilled medical services (Smith et al. 2000).

There is wide variation in state plans, depending on the optional services available and who receives them (U.S. Department of Health and Human Ser-vices, Centers for Medicare and Medicaid Services 2005a). Medicaid-eligible older recipients receive Medicaid-funded home care if:

- services are ordered by a physician as part of a regular plan of care
- the individual is "entitled" to nursing home care in the state (this is not the same as being "eligible" or meeting the state's nursing facility level of care; it simply means that the individual is part of a covered group)
- a Medicare-certified home care agency is providing the service

Individuals are not required to be homebound to receive services, but services must be delivered in the home and not in the community (U.S. Department of Health and Human Services 2000).

MEDICAID WAIVER PROGRAMS

The Medicaid waiver program grants states the authority to provide services not usually covered by Medicaid as long as these services are required to keep a person from being institutionalized. Many Medicaid clients in waiver programs are enrolled in managed-care organizations (U.S. Department of Health and Human Services, Centers for Medicare and Medicaid Services 2005a). Services covered under waiver programs relevant to home health care for older adults include case management, homemaker services, home health aide, personal care, adult day health, and respite. All states have waiver programs. Unlike ser-vices in the state plan, services under the waiver program can be targeted to specific populations (such as individuals age 65 and older who have Parkinson's disease) (Smith et al. 2000).

OTHER FEDERAL SOURCES OF FUNDING

Public programs that pay a smaller proportion of the cost of home health care than Medicare and Medicaid are summarized below. The U.S. Administration on Aging provides federal funds for home and community-based services to states through the National Aging Services Network, a consortium of local and national aging organizations and agencies. Anyone who is age 60 and older is eligible to receive services, but "vulnerable" older adults (for example, the poor, members of minority groups, and residents of rural areas) are priority clients. In-home services include chore, homemaker, and personal care services, as well as home-delivered meals (U.S. Department of Health and Human Services, Administration on Aging 2005).

The National Family Caregiver Support Program, created through the Older Americans Act Amendments of 2000, covers services to assist caregivers, including respite and supplemental services, such as home modification and transportation on a limited basis. The Eldercare Locator is a service offered through the program to help clients access resources (www.eldercare.gov or 1-800-677-1116). Further information is available at http://www.aoa.gov/aoa/pages/state.html (U.S. Department of Health and Human Services, Administration on Aging 2004).

The Social Services Block Grant, authorized by Title 20 of the Social Security Act, provides federal funding to states to help low-income individuals and families maintain self-sufficiency and independence. The funds assist low-income individuals with household or personal care activities (U.S. Department of Health and Human Services 1999).

Finally, the Department of Veterans Affairs has three programs that provide in-home care, home-based primary care, contract home care, and homemaker and home health aide care (U.S. Department of Veterans Affairs 2005). Veterans who have a 50 percent service-connected disability and/or who are unemployable because of a service-connected disability are given the highest priority in enrolling in any type of health care. Among the three programs, contract home care most closely resembles the model of home care presented in this book. Under the contract home care program, the Department of Veterans Affairs contracts with private-sector home care agencies to provide medically necessary skilled home care in the community. Speech, physical, and occupational therapy, nursing, and social work are reimbursable services (U.S. Department of Veterans Affairs 1998, 2005).

PRIVATE THIRD-PARTY PAYERS AND OUT-OF-POCKET PAYMENTS

PRIVATE LONG-TERM-CARE INSURANCE

While sales of private long-term-care insurance policies are increasing, a minority of the older adult population own such policies. Higher income and assets distinguish policy owners from those without this type of insurance (Cohen 2003). The primary attraction of long-term-care insurance is that it provides custodial care not available from Medicare and Medicaid (LifePlans 1999). While Medicaid provides limited custodial care, eligibility is established by the applicant "spending down" assets to qualify. Insurance in most cases provides sufficient custodial care to protect older adults from Medicaid application. Finally, in combination with other health care expenses, cost of insurance is tax deductible when medical expenses exceed 7.6 percent of income (Cohen 2003).

OUT-OF-POCKET PAYMENT

When home care services do not meet the eligibility requirements of third-party payers, the client is responsible for payment of fees. Out-of-pocket payments covered a little over one-third of home care fees in 1999 (Heffler et al. 2001).

CONSUMER-DIRECTED HOME CARE

Consumer-directed home care is based on a model of putting consumers of home care and their families in control of choices about what supportive services they use to meet their needs for care in the community. At a minimum, the consumer-directed model permits individuals with disabilities across the life span or others, such as family members who are their representatives, to make decisions about selecting and dismissing service providers—generally referred to as personal attendants, aides, or attendants—who are paid to provide supportive services (i.e., help with ADL/IADLs) (Doty and Flanagan 2002).

Medicaid is the primary source of funding for consumer-directed services. In 2001, 65 percent of such programs were funded through state home and community-based waiver programs and 15 percent through the Medicaid state plan personal care services benefit (Doty and Flanagan 2002). A little more than half of all consumer-directed programs are funded entirely or partly through state revenues (other than the state's share of Medicaid). Other sources of funding are the Family Caregiver Support Act, the Social Services Block Grant, and private long-term-care insurance (Doty 2004; Doty and Flanagan 2002).

The majority of programs have rules restricting participation. The most common are that the individual must be able to self-direct care (that is, have physical but not cognitive impairments) or that if the individual does have cognitive impairments, he or she has a representative (most often a family member) who assists in directing care (Doty and Flanagan 2002). Most states offering consumer-directed options for caregivers include respite care (i.e., in-home, adult day care and overnight stays in long-term-care facilities) and supplemental services (i.e., home modification, yardwork, chore services, assistive devices, etc.). Some states allow consumers to choose from a list of approved providers, others allow the caregiver to hire someone privately, and others provide both options) (Feinberg, Wolkwitz, and Goldstein 2006).

In summary, publicly funded home health care is currently dominated by managed-care arrangements, whether patients are covered by Medicare or

Medicaid or both. Preliminary research suggests that PPS agencies may restrict access to home care when frail elderly patients have complex medical and social needs. Medicare and Medicaid are the largest publicly funded sources of home health care. While Medicare coverage is available to the eligible elderly irrespective of income or assets, provided that they have contributed to the Social Security system, Medicaid is a means-tested program with strict income and asset eligibility requirements that vary from state to state. Other sources of funding for home care are channeled through the Older Americans Act and the National Family Caregiver Support Program. The Veterans Administration provides another source of publicly funded home health care for individuals who served in the armed forces. A small percentage of affluent older individuals own long-term-care insurance, primarily to provide custodial care. Private out-of-pocket spending contributes a significant amount to funding home care services. A recent innovation in home care is consumer-directed care, funded primary through Medicaid home and community-based waiver programs.

❖ ❖ ❖

The intention of this chapter has been to provide an overview of the context for social work practice in home health care. Home health care has been defined as health-related care received from paid personnel by people with disabilities and medical conditions. "Health-related care" includes both medical services and social services provided by social workers and home health aides. Recipients of home care may or may not be homebound. Care can be provided in a variety of settings, including private homes, group residential facilities, and assisted-living facilities.

The goals of home care are to improve or stabilize the condition of the patient, to help consumers pursue their own lives independently, to provide efficient and cost-effective services, to strengthen and support families, and to enable the consumer to remain in the community in the least-restrictive environment possible.

Home care recipients are primarily older non-Hispanic white, low-income, widowed women living in private residences with family. While family members provide the majority of informal home care, formal home care is provided primarily by home health aides and skilled medical personnel (e.g., nurses and physical, speech, and occupational therapists). Similar to the work environment in hospitals and other "host settings," social workers constitute a minority of the agency employees.

The history of home health care has been characterized by a lack of consensus about its principal goals. The intention of the original Medicare home care program, instituted in 1965, was the provision of short-term acute medical care.

Following a brief period in the 1980s and 1990s when a home care model focusing on the provision of long-term personal care was dominant, the post-acute care medical model was reinstituted with the implementation of the Medicare prospective payment system in 2000.

The expansion of home care in recent years has resulted from an increasing number of chronically ill and disabled older adults and the development of technology-based home care.

Currently, managed-care principles and plans dominate publicly funded home health care. The primary sources of publicly funded home care for older adults are Medicare and Medicaid. Additional sources of public funding, the Older Americans Act and the Family Caregiver Support Program, contribute smaller amounts to federal funding of home care. The Veterans Administration administers a separate home health care program. Privately funded care includes long-term-care insurance, and out-of-pocket spending accounted for at least one-third of home care spending in 1999. Consumer-directed care, funded primarily through Medicaid home and community-based waivers, is a recent innovation.

Issues for social work include a lack of fit between an acute-care, medical model of home care shaped by managed-care principles and a population of frail older adults who require costly medical and custodial care. Ultimately, program design and funding rather than client need determine the available publicly funded services, placing more responsibility for care on informal supports and older, chronically ill adults. A compounding factor is the minority status of home care social workers in "host agencies" dominated by medical disciplines and a medical mission. Social workers must acquire an understanding of the agency, program, and policy environment, as these factors exert as strong an influence on home health care social work practice with older clients as the needs of clients themselves.

2

THE SOCIAL WORK ROLE IN HOME HEALTH CARE

THIS CHAPTER provides an understanding of the role of social work practice in home health care. It discusses the following:

- public reimbursement policy and its influence on the social work role
- history of social work in home health care
- contemporary challenges to home health care social workers
- interdisciplinary teamwork
- social work advocacy
- ethical conflicts under managed care
- ethical conflicts related to patient autonomy and boundary issues

The history of social work practice, as well as contemporary social work roles, generally reflect the profession's holistic emphasis on the person-in-environment perspective and the biopsychosocial framework in addressing client problems. This chapter traces the historical development of social work practice and describes the influence of the managed-care environment under PPS on current practice. Challenges to social work in an environment dominated by managed-care reimbursement policies are also discussed, among them interdisciplinary teamwork and the unique ethical concerns of workers in a managed-care environment, as well as two generic ethical issues that are fundamental to social work practice in home care.

PUBLIC REIMBURSEMENT POLICY: INFLUENCE ON THE SOCIAL WORK ROLE

MEDICAL PRIORITIES

The primary factor shaping social work practice is the priority accorded medical health over social health by government policies, as reflected in reimbursement practices. Under Medicare Part A, social work is not a primary provider. Social workers are dependent on disciplines that are granted primary provider status (e.g., nurses, speech and physical therapists) for referrals to open cases. Once a case is opened, social work cannot be an independent provider. If a primary medical provider terminates medical care, Medicare reimbursement policies require termination of social work services whether or not the patient has a continuing need for social care. Further, social work is limited to addressing social and emotional problems that are expected to become impediments to the effective treatment of the patient's medical condition. A patient with a general problem that does not influence a medical condition is not eligible to become a social work client.

MEDICAID REIMBURSEMENT

Medicaid eligibility requirements vary from state to state, but only a small number of states cover social work services. The intent, as noted, of the legislation creating the prospective payment system (PPS) was to refocus home care on the provision of skilled medical care. Social work practice, as defined by several exploratory-descriptive studies, reflects this emphasis in a focus on efficiency and demonstration of effective outcomes (e.g., cost savings and a higher quality of patient care).

HISTORY OF SOCIAL WORK IN HOME HEALTH CARE

EARLY HISTORY: THE LATE NINETEENTH CENTURY TO 1965

Social work in home health care began in the late nineteenth century with the inception of the public health movement. During that time, high incidence and mortality rates of communicable diseases (e.g., tuberculosis, diphtheria, and typhoid fever) were aggravated by living conditions arising from urbanization and immigration (Harris 1997). Growing government concerns about public health led to an expanding number of both government-supported and voluntary public health agencies. The primary duty of early visiting nurses in the public health movement was twofold: care of the acutely ill and health education—"bringing the message of prevention and hygiene to the masses" (Reverby 1987:109).

At the same time, settlement house social workers (social reformers who lived and worked among the poor), such as Lillian Wald at New York's Henry Street Nurses' Settlement (later the Visiting Nursing Service) and Jane Addams at Chicago's Hull House, also worked to prevent and control epidemics and diseases. They used community action to reduce or eliminate substandard housing, poor sanitation, inadequate nutrition, poverty, and other conditions that contributed to unhealthy families and communities (Poole 1995). At this time, the differences between social work and public health nursing were not clear. Many of the early social workers were initially public health nurses who developed an appreciation for the relationship between social factors and disease in visits to their patients' homes (Poole 1995). In fact, training as a nurse was accepted as a background to prepare an individual for a career in social work; one-sixth of the hospital social work departments listed by the American Hospital Association in 1924 were directed by nurses (Jarrett 1933).

In the late nineteenth century, medical care shifted away from the home and into the hospital as a result of the development and acceptance of "scientific medicine" (for example, the discovery of antiseptic technique and the development of a new "germ theory" of disease that traced the cause of infectious disease to bacteria) and the transformation of hospitals from homes for the sick, dependent, and poor into scientific centers providing services to paying patients (Benjamin 1993; Popple and Leighninger 1993; Reverby 1987). A number of social workers continued to work in public health positions in the community, but the majority of them followed physicians into the hospitals and assumed positions as hospital social workers (Stark 1997). While home visiting was initially part of the hospital social workers' function in the early 1900s, when social work in the hospital setting was initiated, social workers largely relinquished the home visiting role and focused on working with hospital inpatients, as acceptance of the hospital social work role increased during the following two decades (Stark 1997).

Social workers were infrequently employed in public health visiting nurse agencies during this period (Jarrett 1933). While some social workers advocated for a social work role in public health, overlap between the functions of social work and public health nurses complicated the development of a social work presence in public health (Byington 1932). Until 1965 social work services continued to be provided infrequently in community-based agencies, such as public health settings (Stark 1997).

The continuing question of how to address the needs of the chronically ill led to the formation of the Commission on Chronic Illness in 1946. The commission's report issued in 1956 recommended the "organized home care program" as a way to address the needs of the chronically ill in the community. Organized home care programs were hospital-based and physician-directed, used a team approach to care, and provided physician services, nursing, social services, homemaker services, and physical and occupational therapies (National Commission on Chronic Illness 1956). Montefiore Hospital in New York City operated an organized home care program in the mid-1950s that was considered a model for these programs (Benjamin 1993). In 1955 the U.S. Public Health Service endorsed the use of social workers in organized home care programs (Auerbach et al. 1984).

While there were few organized home care programs in the country in the late 1950s and early 1960s (Follman 1963), the inclusion of social work services as part of a comprehensive approach to home care for the chronically ill is noteworthy. However, as indicated in chapter 1, while the federal government was aware of the benefits of comprehensive care for the community-dwelling chronically ill, apprehension about the cost of such a program led to the implementation of a model of government funding that emphasized only limited post-acute home health care under the Medicare program.

THE MEDICARE HOME HEALTH CARE BENEFIT

Though social workers did participate in public health and comprehensive home health care programs before the passage of the legislation creating the Medicare home health care benefit in 1965, this legislation officially formalized the role of social work in home health care by including social work as one of the covered home care disciplines (Stark 1997).

According to the current *Medicare Benefits Policy Manual*, medical social work services that are provided by a qualified social worker or a social work assistant under the supervision of a qualified medical social worker are covered when

- the beneficiary is qualified to receive home health care services;
- the services of social work professionals are necessary to resolve social or emotional problems that are or are expected to be an impediment to the effective treatment of the patient's medical condition or rate of recovery;
- the plan of care indicates how the services that are required necessitate the skills of a qualified social worker or social work assistant under the supervision of a qualified medical social worker in order to be performed safely and effectively (U.S. Department of Health and Human Services, Centers for Medicare and Medicaid Services 2005b).

The focus of Medicare's definition of the social work function in home health care is therefore on medical adaptation, stabilization, and recovery. Medicare Conditions of Participation for social work services circumscribe the social work role, allowing practice activities that solely address patient medical issues (U.S. Department of Health and Human Services, Centers for Medicare and Medicaid Services 2005b).

Medicare's definition of the social work role drives reimbursement regulations not only for the federal government but also for other third-party payers who apply Medicare's requirements as a standard for making decisions about the scope of covered social work services (Abel-Vacula and Phillips 2004).

It is consistent with the exclusively medical focus of home care that social work is not considered a "primary service" in home care under Medicare Part A and cannot be the sole discipline providing treatment for a patient. Social work depends on other primary services under Part A, such as skilled nursing, speech therapy, or occupational therapy, to provide treatment to a patient (U.S. Department of Health and Human Services, Centers for Medicare and Medicaid Services 2006).

PSYCHIATRIC HOME CARE UNDER MEDICARE

The parameters of home health social work assessment and intervention in the older adult's mental and emotional problems under Medicare restrict reimbursable services to assessment and intervention that is related to obtaining resources, intervening in family/patient adjustment to illness, management of illness, family conflict, and planning for long-term care. Social work assessment and intervention related to mental and emotional problems are reimbursed under Medicare only if they are necessary to address the patient's medical condition. Clinical social work treatment for a psychiatric illness that can be assigned a *DSM-IV* diagnosis is generally not reimbursed by Medicare, even if the social worker has the credentials to provide such treatment (Byrne 1999).

State regulations regarding credentials of home health psychiatric nurses and social workers to provide psychotherapy, local Medicare review policies interpreted by Medicare intermediaries, and reimbursement policies of other third-party payers may result in exceptions to the generalizations discussed above (Abel-Vacula and Phillips 2004).

It is important for social workers to be familiar with all regulations regarding the roles of professionals in their states, the consistency between these regulations, and regulations with respect to third-party payers (Abel-Vacula and Phillips 2004).

CONSTRAINTS ON SOCIAL WORK SERVICE IMPOSED BY REGULATION: MEDICARE REIMBURSEMENT AND MEDICAID POLICY

The designation of social work as a secondary service with no independent authority to open cases and the Medicare policy that social work services can be provided only if patients are also receiving skilled medical services have, both in the past and at present, resulted in a fragmented service delivery system and delayed or obstructed client access to services. Social workers must discontinue their services to beneficiaries when a skilled medical service discharges the client from care. The inability to open a case without a referral from a qualifying discipline and the resulting lag time before clients have access to social work services also fragment service delivery, especially when social workers lack sufficient time to develop an individualized plan of care (Blanchard, Gill, and Williams 1991).

An additional constraint on the use of home health social work services from the 1960s until the implementation of the prospective payment system in 2000 was the decisions about reimbursement made by private insurance companies that acted as intermediaries between the home health care agency and the Medicare home health care benefit program (Stark 1997). Inconsistent interpretation by these intermediaries regarding the scope of reimbursable social work services led to increases in rates of denial for social work visits and a tendency among home health care agencies to reduce the number of social work home visits. Fearing retrospective denials for social work home visits, some agencies assigned social work functions to nurses and also reduced the number of social work referrals and staff (Blanchard, Gill, and Williams 1991; Stark 1997).

A final constraint on the use and integration of home health care social work was a lack of federally mandated coverage for social work services under Medicaid. While states have the option of covering social work services under their state Medicaid plans, the majority of state plans do not reimburse for such services (Abel-Vacula and Phillips 2004). Home health care staff have identified lack of Medicaid reimbursement as a barrier to referring patients to social work (Goode 2000).

DEVELOPING A PROFESSIONAL IDENTITY FOR HOME HEALTH CARE SOCIAL WORK: THE 1970S THROUGH THE 1990S

During the 1970s and 1980s social work struggled to establish a professional role in home health care. The legislation authorizing the Medicare home care benefit promoted the use of interdisciplinary teams for the services of social workers, nurses, speech and occupational therapists, and home health aides. The introduction of an interdisciplinary home care team into the home care setting was a challenge for nurses, who were accustomed to being the sole primary providers (Stark 1997). For several decades before the passage of Medicare, home health agency nurses had been providing both skilled nursing and what they regarded as "social services" to their patients. Health care agencies were often unable to identify a role for social work, and despite the availability of Medicare reimbursement, many chose not to provide social work services (Axelrod 1978).

In 1974 only 26 percent of the 2,329 Medicare-certified home health agencies provided social services (Oktay and Sheppard 1978).

The number of social workers employed in home care increased during the 1980s, possibly because of an increase in the referrals received by agencies as a result of both shortened hospital stays under the DRG (Diagnostic Related Groups) system and an increasing number of for-profit home care agencies employing social workers. By 1984, 53 percent of the existing 4,271 home care agencies offered medical social services as part of their Medicare home care benefit (Kane and Kane 1987).

A focus of social work practice literature during the 1970s and 1980s was an effort to define the role of the professional social worker on the interdisciplinary team (Auerbach et al. 1984; Axelrod 1978; Levande, Bowden, and Mollema 1988; Oktay and Sheppard 1978). These articles argue that because home health care requires a psychosocial as well as a medical focus, social workers are essential members of the care team. The social work role was defined as primarily focused on providing direct/indirect services to patients/families, including psychosocial assessment, therapeutic and supportive counseling focused on adjustment to illness and treatment plans, discharge planning, and referrals (Auerbach et. al. 1984). Staff consultation, program planning, interdisciplinary teamwork, and administration are identified as components of the social work role in the literature but are discussed less extensively than direct client services.

The literature also reflects the concerns of home care social workers regarding the impact on practice of the host setting of home care, dominated and administered by nurses (Jacobs and Lurie 1984). The lack of consensus between nurses and social workers regarding their respective professional domains is discussed (Lotz 1997; Vincent and Davis 1987). Several other articles dating from the 1980s document a lack of consensus between the two disciplines with respect to professional roles. Nurses regarded both medical and psychosocial problems as within the nursing practice domain, while social workers viewed psychosocial issues as their exclusive responsibility (Fessler and Adams 1985; Kethley, Herriott, and Pesznecker 1982).

During the 1980s as their numbers grew, home care social workers began to organize professionally on the national level. The National Association of Social Workers Home Health Care Task Force was formed in 1985. This task force was instrumental in developing a 1991 NASW policy statement regarding guidelines for social work practice in home health care. Among the recommendations of the policy statement were that skilled status be granted to social work as a qualifying service under Medicare and that Medicaid cover social work services in home health care (Blanchard, Gill, and Williams 1991).

Neither of these recommendations has been implemented to date, and these issues continue to influence contemporary home health social work practice. In

1989 the task force and NASW were successful in getting Medicare regulations changed to allow social work reimbursement for family counseling when related to improvement of the patient's medical condition. Before this time, Medicare reimbursement for social work services was allowed for only the Medicare beneficiary (Stark 1997).

In the 1990s, the social work practice literature began to document a change in the locus of health care delivery from the hospital to the community. Third-party payers' efforts to avoid costly hospitalizations, the development of medical technology that could be used in the home, declining hospital admissions, and an increase in the number of chronically ill older adults requiring long-term community support contributed to an emphasis on community-based care (Rosenberg 1994; Simmons 1994). The literature called for the development of community-based social work practice to meet this challenge through the application of skills in care coordination, assessment, interdisciplinary collaboration, and support/education of patients and families so that older adults could maintain independent community living (Rosenberg 1994; Simmons 1994).

A survey of home health care social workers during this time provided empirically based data suggesting that the home care social worker role was complex and varied (Egan and Kadushin 2000). Home care social workers were characterized as advanced generalist practitioners, intervening at multiple system levels to alleviate client problems (Egan and Kadushin 2000).

In 1995 home health care social work began to display indications of increasing professionalism, with the foundation of the American Network of Home Health Care Social Workers (Stark 1997) and the NASW's publication of clinical indicators for home health social work practice (National Association of Social Workers 1995).

These developments coincided with the increasing numbers of patients using home care in the late 1980s and 1990s and the expansion of opportunities for social work practice.

THE CONTEMPORARY SOCIAL WORK ROLE
IN HOME HEALTH CARE

In the early 1990s the *Outcome and Assessment Information Set* (OASIS) began to be required for administration as an assessment instrument for all adult patients at admission and also at discharge to measure outcomes (U.S. Department of Health and Human Services, Health Care Financing Administration. 1999). The baseline administration of the OASIS is completed during intake by one of the primary medical providers (e.g., nurse, speech therapist, or physical therapist) (Abel-Vacula and Phillips 2004; Sienkiewicz 2001). The OASIS codes are intended to be the "triggers" for referral to social work. However, accurate interpretation of these codes so as to recognize appropriate clients for social work referral by medical disciplines is problematic (Abel-Vacula and Phillips 2004).

In 2000 the implementation of the Medicare prospective payment system (PPS), combined with the dominance of managed care in providing services to Medicaid clients and to the privately insured, led to new demands on home health care social workers. It should be noted, however, that although the payment methods for Medicare home care patients changed with the implementation of PPS, the conditions of coverage for social work services under Medicare remained the same as previously outlined.

The most recent research on home health care social work practice was completed within the context of the Medicare PPS. In the aggregate, this research documents core social work activities as follows:

- in-person psychosocial assessment
- documentation/paperwork
- education of clients about community resources
- discharge planning
- interdisciplinary collaboration
- care coordination (Kadushin and Egan 2004; Lee 2002; Malinowski 2002)

Overall, these activities suggest that agencies align social work practice with capitated payment limits and with the mandates of managed care for cost-effective, efficient practice (Balinsky and Blumengold 1995; Novick 2001; Sienkiewicz 2001). Cost-efficient and effective social work practice that expedites the transfer of patients/families from home care to family and community-based care without compromising quality of care is valued in the managed-care context.

CONTEMPORARY CHALLENGES TO SOCIAL WORK IN HOME CARE

INTERDISCIPLINARY TEAMWORK

Interdisciplinary teamwork in home care is a priority for social workers under managed care. In a capitated system the "value" of social work may be closely scrutinized by referring medical disciplines to determine the best mix of services for a patient. Nurses and other "skilled" providers will need an accurate understanding of the social work role if they are to use social work effectively (Lee 2002). Barriers to referrals, particularly between nurses and social workers, may reflect role conflict or "turf issues," as discussed above. Informational barriers, in the form of different referral criteria applied by home care nurses and social workers to identify appropriate social work referrals, may also reflect a lack of consensus regarding the social work role and reduce the type and number of social work referrals (Egan and Kadushin 2005; Lee 2002; Malinowski 2002).

Another factor contributing to the emphasis on interdisciplinary teamwork under PPS is preliminary evidence that social work home visits have decreased and that at the same time telephone contact for follow-up and routine referrals has increased (Kadushin and Egan 2004; Malinowski 2002). Social workers rely on consultation with providers from other disciplines, who already have knowledge of the client, to make decisions about whether a home visit is required (Malinowski 2002). In the absence of face-to-face contact with clients, case conferences, consultation with colleagues and supervisors, and ethics committees are useful resources to assist social workers in making these practice decisions.

Important indirect practice activities, such as care coordination, interdisciplinary collaboration, and discharge planning under PPS (Kadushin and Egan 2004; Malinowski 2002), also depend on interdisciplinary teamwork.

Finally, research has documented an association between social work advocacy and informal social work influence in the agency and a reduction in the frequency with which patients with unmet needs are discharged from home care (Egan and Kadushin 2002; Kadushin and Egan 2006). The research suggests that social workers with more informal influence may be more effective advocates.

Social workers with informal influence in the agency may have access to a network of colleagues and pivotal decision makers, such as supervisors and administrators, who control resource allocation or who can simplify bureaucratic barriers to resource provision. These informal allies may enable workers to reduce discharge with unmet need by obtaining services that the patient needs (Egan and Kadushin 2002).

A perception of social work's professional credibility has also been found to increase social work intra-agency influence. Effective advocacy is dependent on a network of informal allies and a perception by other disciplines of social work expertise, suggesting that interdisciplinary teamwork is pivotal to social work advocacy under PPS.

Social work faces three major challenges to effective interdisciplinary teamwork in home health care under PPS (Lee and Rock 2005):

- development of effective strategies to educate other members of the home health care team about the social work role, since social work relies on other disciplines for referrals

- documentation of outcomes that contribute to efficient and effective service delivery
- achievement of full integration as equal members of the home care team

With regard to the first challenge, strategies to educate home health care disciplines about the social work role may include development by the social work departments of a "marketing tool," perhaps a pamphlet or a more formal document, that highlights how social workers can reduce unnecessary home visits by providers from other disciplines and help them perform their jobs more efficiently. Discussion of the information in a continuing education session may open a dialogue regarding the recognition of psychosocial factors in improving risk management and quality assurance (Lee and Rock 2005). For example, research has found a positive relationship between psychosocial factors such as patient cognitive impairment or inability of the family caregiver(s) to provide care and patient discharge with unmet need (Kadushin and Egan 2006). Early referral of clients with these characteristics to social workers has the potential to reduce adverse outcomes, improve agency risk management, and contain home care costs.

Another strategy to improve communication is to develop a screening instrument to identify patients who need social work services (Lee and Rock 2005). Early identification of patients who are at high risk for hospital admission is a priority in home health care because of the high rate of hospitalization of home care patients under PPS (more than 25 percent) (Sevast 2007). Shorter hospital stays are rewarded in the capitated system of home care, particularly for patients who are older, sicker, and have more-complex care needs (Anderson et al. 2005). Social work demonstration of effective, efficient discharge of "high-risk" patients may assist other disciplines in understanding and valuing social work expertise.

The second challenge, the necessity for documentation of outcomes, results from changes in Medicare reimbursement policies. Under the previous fee-for-service system, reimbursement was based on the number of social work visits. Outcome measures applied in this context reflected the process of providing services (i.e., simply the number of visits). Under Medicare PPS, agencies are motivated by the profit incentive to avoid exceeding the capitated payment. A capitated system requires social work and other home health care disciplines to demonstrate and document their skills in generating revenue without compromising the quality of service. Referrals to social work by providers in medical disciplines may be influenced by their perception of social work's contribution to these agency objectives (Lee and Rock 2005).

One opportunity to document social work outcomes is to measure whether social work advocacy and social work financial planning with patients reduces the number of patients who are discharged with unmet needs (Kadushin and

Egan 2006). Documentation of other measurable outcomes of social work intervention, such as reduced length of patient stay, improved patient medication adherence, reduced rates of hospitalization, and improved depressive symptoms, also contribute to a record of social work's contribution to quality, cost-effective patient care (Lee and Rock 2005; Sevast 2007).

Success in meeting the third challenge, achievement of full integration of home care professionals as members of the interdisciplinary team, has the greatest likelihood of improving quality and cost-effective care under a capitated system (Lee and Rock 2005; Sevast 2007). Historically, social work has struggled for professional recognition in home health care, but effective teamwork is possible only if home health care disciplines share a mutual understanding of each other's professional expertise and competence; without such an understanding, role conflicts are likely to be exacerbated (Lee and Rock 2005).

THE SOCIAL WORK ROLE AS ADVOCATE

As noted in chapter 1, demographic trends suggest that the number of adults aged 65 and over, and particularly the oldest-old (those aged 85 and older), will increase dramatically during the early twenty-first century. These individuals and their families will require psychosocial care if they are to remain in the community. The Bureau of Labor Statistics expects the need for social workers, especially in gerontology and home health care, to grow twice as fast as that for workers in any other occupation (U.S. Department of Labor, Bureau of Labor Statistics 2006-07). Also noted were the lack of adequate reimbursement for social work services under Medicare and the absence of funding for social work by federal Medicaid policies. This increasing need for psychosocial care coupled with restricted reimbursement for home care social work is likely to result in professional and ethical conflicts for workers and unmet needs among older clients and their families. One suggestion for addressing the dilemma, which is consistent with the *Code of Ethics* and with the mission of the profession, is advocacy by home care social workers to change both federal and state legislation that restricts coverage of social work services.

ADVOCACY FOR CHANGES IN MEDICARE POLICY

A number of home health advocacy strategies addressed to Medicare can be implemented through participation in the Society of Social Work Leadership in Healthcare, the Council on Social Work Education, and/or the National Association of Social Workers. A national panel of experts and discussants who participated in a roundtable sponsored by the Fordham University Graduate School of Social Services in New York City and published in *Health and Social Work* (Lee and Rock 2005) recommended a number of action steps:

▪ The Centers for Medicare and Medicaid Services (CMS) should modify the home health care PPS case mix methodology to recognize and integrate caregiver and natural helping networks' needs for education and social and family support. This step is essential to the provision of quality care. The absence of these factors is related to the overall lack of acknowledgment of psychosocial factors in calculating the PPS home health care patient case-mix formula (Lee and Rock 2005).

▪ The CMS should also create a waiver program to evaluate outcomes under alternative case-mix models. Such waiver programs should include models incorporating social care and family caregivers. The outcomes of these demonstration projects could be applied to document the impact of social and psychological factors on cost containment and quality of care. Such data could provide facts to counteract the current Medicare emphasis on a biomedical view of health care that ignores psychosocial factors. This recommendation is not a radical break with previous CMS policies; waivers have been granted to test models of managed Medicare and Medicaid. This action step would be consistent with previous policies by creating a waiver program for Medicare PPS (Lee and Rock 2005).

▪ Currently, CMS is focused on biomedical quality assurance outcomes in home care (Sevast 2007). This is an opportunity for social workers to advocate for the recognition of psychosocial factors in influencing the health status of older adults, particularly frail older adults with chronic illness and/or disabilities. Home care administrators concerned with improving quality assurance outcomes and with cost containment may respond positively to social workers' ability to identify vulnerable clients who may require "expensive" care. If social workers are successful in contributing to agency quality assurance outcomes and reduced costs, this success can be documented and cited to advocate for the integration of client psychosocial characteristics and situations in all quality assurance protocols and procedures (Lee and Rock 2005).

▪ Advocate for the establishment by regulation of independent case finding by social workers (Lee and Rock 2005). As indicated, Medicare has historically not recognized social work as a skilled discipline with the authority to open cases independently, an omission that limits client access to psychosocial services and relegates social work to a secondary status in the medical hierarchy of home care disciplines. A National Association of Social Workers Policy Statement in 1991, cited by Blanchard, Gill, and Williams (1991), recommended that Medicare grant skilled status to home care social work. Sixteen years later, this recommendation has yet not been implemented. A more realistic goal might be to allow independent case finding. This recommendation could improve clients' access to social work services early in their trajectory of care. It could also facilitate the integration of social work on the interdisciplinary team.

ADDITIONAL ADVOCACY STEPS ADDRESSED TO MEDICARE

Another advocacy action, which was not part of the Fordham panel recommendations, suggests that social workers advocate for a uniform redefinition of home care social work services under Medicare to include provision of psychosocial care to clients admitted with a psychiatric diagnosis. By restricting home care social work interventions to situations that affect the patient's medical condition, current Medicare reimbursement policy prohibits qualified social workers from providing care to psychiatric clients who could benefit from these services (Byrne 1999).

MENTAL HEALTH PARITY: ADVOCACY STEPS

In the United States coverage for mental health care is more limited than coverage for physical illness. Mental health coverage is available through private insurance, Medicare, Medicaid, or private out-of-pocket payment. Under insurance plans, coverage of mental health care is less adequate than coverage of care for physical health. In the private sector, a 1996 law requires businesses with fifty or more employees to place an annual lifetime limit on spending regardless of type of illness. This law, however, has some loopholes: it does not prevent charging higher copayments or deductibles for mental health benefits or not providing mental health coverage at all. The law also permits restrictions on outpatient therapist visits and inpatient days of hospitalization (Barry 2006; Lee 2006). A General Accounting Office report in 2000 indicated that after the law was enacted, two-thirds of the compliant employers restricted mental health coverage, resulting in a 51 percent reduction in covered annual outpatient office visits and a 36 percent reduction in inpatient hospital days for mental health services (U.S. General Accounting Office 2000b). Business and the insurance industry oppose mental health parity because of cost concerns (Barry 2006).

The vulnerability of older adults to dementia, depression, suicide, and schizophrenia increases with age (Lee 2006; National Institute of Mental Health 2003). For example, in 2000 the 65 and older population was less than 13 percent of the total population but contributed to 18 percent of all deaths by suicide. The suicide rate for the oldest-old white men was more than five times the national average (National Institute of Mental Health 2003). Depression is one of the most frequent underlying causes of suicide. Subsyndromal depression (depressive symptoms that do not meet full diagnostic criteria for clinical depression) occurs in an estimated 5 million elderly. Subsyndromal depression is associated with an increased risk of developing major depression (National Institute of Mental Health 2003). Medicare has a limit of 190 lifetime days for inpatient psychiatric care under Part A and a 50 percent copayment for outpatient mental health services under Part B. This coverage is more restrictive than coverage for medical illnesses, which requires only a 20 percent copay of the Medicare-approved amount for outpatient doctor visits and sets no lifetime limit on inpatient hospital care (U.S. Department of Health and Human Services, Centers for Medicare and Medicaid Services 2007).

In the context of the growing number of older adults in the population who could become vulnerable to mental health problems, the advances in the treatment of disorders such as schizophrenia and depression, and the critical role of health insurance coverage in accessing health care (Cohen et al. 1997; Landerman et al. 1998), social work advocacy for mental health parity under Medicare and in the private insurance industry is an important issue.

EVIDENCE-BASED PRACTICE

Another focus for advocacy is to demonstrate the contribution of home care social work to improving patient and agency cost-effectiveness. To establish credibility in home care, practitioners and academics should collaborate in conducting evidence-based research on the effectiveness of social work services in home health care. Because all home care disciplines must demonstrate efficiency and effectiveness in the current environment, advocacy to fully establish the presence of social work in home health care will require evidence of social work's contribution to improved patient care and agency cost savings.

ETHICAL CONFLICTS UNDER MANAGED CARE

An ethical conflict can be defined as a conflict between competing professional ethical duties in which the worker must decide which duties should take precedence (Reamer 1998). Conflicts over access to services result from the simultaneous duty of fidelity the social worker owes to the client and to the agency (Galambos 1999; National Association of Social Workers 2000). The social worker has both a duty to the best interests or well-being of the client and an obligation to practice within agency policies and guidelines, including budget limits.

As noted, the implementation of PPS was intended to refocus home care on acute medical services and reduce social care. Because the flat-rate PPS payment does not cover emotional or social care, agencies may lack resources to fund services to meet the needs of chronically ill older adults with comorbid medical and social or emotional conditions. Given these cost constraints, ethical conflicts over access to services can occur (Kadushin and Egan 2004).

The NASW *Code of Ethics* gives priority to the duty to protect client well-being over the duty to adhere to agency policy when these principles conflict. The code also stipulates that when agency policy interferes with the ethical practice of social work, social workers have a duty to take "reasonable steps" to ensure that the agency policies are consistent with the code (National Association of Social Workers 2000). Practitioners can fulfill this duty by advocating for clients with administrators who control budget allocations. Administrators who are part of a worker's network of allies may be more responsive to advocacy and more willing to circumvent formal bureaucratic channels to access additional client resources (Kadushin and Egan 2004). Workers can also advocate for system change through the revision of agency policy. An example might be the development of an agency fund to cover cases requiring complex social and emotional care. Funds could be distributed by applying criteria developed by practitioners and administrators. Another mechanism might be the establishment of administrative teams of supervisors, administrators, and practitioners who meet periodically to review service delivery, quality care, and consumer feedback. These teams could review and revise procedures as needed (Galambos 1999).

ETHICAL CONFLICTS RELATED TO PATIENT AUTONOMY AND BOUNDARY ISSUES

While not as directly related to managed care, ethical conflict over patient autonomy or self-determination and beneficence warrants attention because this problem in one of the most frequently documented ethical concerns in home care (Arras and Dubler 1994; Davitt and Kaye 1996; Egan and Kadushin 2000; Healy 1998, 1999, 2003; Kadushin and Egan 2001; Kane and Caplan 1993).

The terms *patient autonomy* and *self-determination* are used interchangeably in the literature. A consistent element in both definitions is "control over decision-making" by the client (Healy 1998). Patient autonomy may present an ethical challenge in home health care when patients' decisions place them in situations that pose potential risks to their safety and/or when conflict between family and patient autonomy results in an unsafe situation. When these issues arise, the social workers' obligation to support patient autonomy may conflict with their commitment to protect the welfare of clients or the principle of beneficence, thus creating an ethical dilemma (Healy 1998).

The ethical principles of self-determination and patient autonomy are based on the requirement that the client has the cognitive capacity to make the choice in question (Kane and Caplan 1993). Health care providers use evaluation of the client's decision-making capacity to determine his or her ability to make health care decisions.

Decision-making capacity is distinguished from the client's global mental competence, which is generally decided in a court of law and answers the question of whether an individual is capable of self-care and of independently managing his or her affairs. A declaration of incompetence results in the delegation of authority by the court for specific decisions to a guardian or surrogate care provider (Levenson 1990; Tauer 1993). Decision-making capacity is also differentiated from mental status, which refers to psychological and cognitive aspects of mental life (Gallo et al. 2003). Cognitive aspects of mental status may refer to functions such as remembering, recalling, and paying attention. Psychological aspects of mental status include psychiatric diagnoses such as anxiety disorders, depression, dementia, Alzheimer's disease, substance abuse disorders, schizophrenia, and bipolar disorder.

By contrast, decision-making capacity is concerned with the ability of the individual to make a specific health care decision (Levenson 1990). Assessment of decision-making capacity is an evaluation of the client's capacity to understand the facts related to a situation or decision, to rationally consider options and consequences, and to make and communicate a reasoned choice (Tauer 1993).

Social workers have identified client decision-making capacity as the most significant factor influencing their support of patient self-determination when clients choose to remain in unsafe situations (e.g., clients in abusive relationships or those who repeatedly fall or burn themselves) (Healy 1998). However, social workers also experience difficulty in evaluating decision-making capacity, possibly because they do not distinguish assessment of mental status or global competence from assessment of decision-making capacity (Healy 1998, 1999, 2003).

Evaluation of decision-making capacity is influenced by the following considerations (Levenson 1990):

- Actual performance must be separated from the potential capacity for performance. A person who is delusional and/or depressed may not have the capacity for rational decision making, but with the use of psychotropic medication, he or she may have the potential for higher performance.
- There are degrees of capacity, and not all health care decisions require the same level of decision-making capacity. Minor decisions (for example, what personal items to take to a nursing home) require a lower level of capacity than health care decisions that have long-range or significant implications, such as relocation to a more-structured environment (for example, from home to assisted living or a nursing home), which require a higher level of capacity.
- Older adults do not require the same degree of skill to make adequate decisions. For example, a stroke patient may understand a decision but have difficulty communicating how the decision was reached.
- Decision-making capacity may fluctuate over time. The individual should be involved in decision making when performance is likely to be optimal (Levenson 1990).

Decision-making capacity can be evaluated at four levels, which build upon each other cumulatively:

1. assessment of whether the person is capable of giving informed consent to participate in decision making: can he or she respond appropriately either verbally or symbolically to pertinent questions or gestures?
2. assessment of the person's factual appreciation of the situation, determined by asking the individual to explain in his or her own words the problem and its implications
3. assessment of the client's reasoning ability, which he or she evidences by connecting the facts with personal opinions and values to come to a conclusion.
4. assessment of whether the client recognizes the consequences of giving and withholding consent and whether he or she has the capacity to recognize the need for additional information, to distinguish relevant from irrelevant information, and to apply additional information to make a decision

In general, the more long-lasting and irreversible the consequences of a decision are, the higher the standard for judging capacity is (Levenson 1990).

Because knowledge of whether a patient's performance can be improved or reversed is an aspect of assessment of decision capacity, social workers in home care require familiarity with cognitive and mental conditions that influence cognitive status and are treatable with medications or other medical intervention. Social workers who are consistently unsure of their clinical assessments of clients need to advocate for clinical supervision within the agency to help them develop this knowledge (Healy 2003). For best practice, the establishment of an agency protocol to assess client decision-making capacity that requires a final assessment, incorporating the contributions of a team of nurses, physicians, psychiatrists, psychologists, and social workers, is recommended.

Even if a client is evaluated as having the decisional capacity to make a specific choice, however, the duty to the principle of beneficence is given priority over the duty to the principle of autonomy if the client's choice is not voluntary (e.g., if the client is a drug addict or is coerced into making a choice by another individual) or if the client is unable or unwilling to address serious threats to personal well-being, such as physical or sexual abuse by others or failure/inability to accept care for basic needs such as essential health care, nutrition, hygiene, and warmth. In order to warrant beneficent intervention, however, these threats must be presently observable and not possible future threats (Tauer 1993).

ETHICAL CONFLICTS OVER BOUNDARY ISSUES

The following discussion of boundary issues addresses only the worker and the client. Boundary issues arise when social workers are in situations that pose a potential conflict of interest in the form of dual or multiple relationships (Reamer 2003). Dual or multiple relationships can be recognized when the worker engages with clients in more than one kind of relationship, such as professional and sexual, professional and business, or professional and social (Reamer 2003).

Boundary violations should be distinguished from boundary crossings. Boundary violations occur when a worker is involved in a dual relationship with a client that has the effect of exploiting, manipulating, deceiving, or co-ercing the client. Boundary violations involve a conflict of interest that harms the client. For example, a socially isolated worker who develops a friendship with a client is in a situation in which personal interests clash with professional duties. Boundary violations may also involve "undue influence," which occurs when the worker uses his or her authority to exploit or take advantage of the client. All of these issues—conflicts of interests, dual relationships, and undue influence—are prohibited by the *Code of Ethics* (National Association of Social Workers 2000; Reamer 2003).

Boundary crossings are defined as situations in which the worker is involved in a dual relationship with a client that is not intentionally exploitive, manipula-tive, deceptive, or coercive. For example, a home health social worker who is restrained in the use of self-disclosure or a home care worker who is a member of the same health club as a client's daughter is generally not harming a client and may in fact be helping the client by encouraging exploration of a difficult topic in the first example and by "normalizing" the relationship in the second example (Reamer 1998, 2003).

"Gray areas" can also be identified in defining a situation as a boundary vio-lation or a boundary crossing (Reamer 1998). Clients who come to see a worker in an agency are likely to regard the worker as an employee of that organization. The waiting area and the office itself convey to the client that the worker is a professional working for an agency. When social workers visit clients at home, their professional role may be less obvious. The informality of the home setting and the potential of the client and worker to assume complementary roles as "host(ess)" and "guest" may blur the boundaries between friendship and profes-sionalism. For example, the client as host(ess) may offer the worker something to eat or drink. On one hand, the social worker's acceptance of the invitation may help the client feel more "connected" and is therefore not harmful; on the other hand, such acceptance can be interpreted as extending the professional into a personal relationship (Naleppa and Hash 2001). Another example of a "gray area" in home health is gift giving. Gift giving has been reported to be more frequent in home-based than in agency-based practice, possibly because of the greater potential for blurred professional boundaries in home visiting (Naleppa and Hash 2001). Whether the worker who accepts a gift from a client is involved in a boundary violation or a boundary crossing depends on the situation, the type of gift, and how the worker manages the situation (Naleppa and Hash 2001; Reamer 2003).

Some situations in home health visiting, however, clearly represent potential boundary violations. For example, situations in which a client who asks the worker to stop by the store to buy a gallon of milk on the way over or to stay until the client's best friend comes over present the potential for a blurring of the professional and personal relationship, and by definition set up a dual relationship (Naleppa and Hash 2001; Reamer 2003). Another area in which there is clear potential for boundary violations in home visiting is sexual advances. Respondents in home-based practice perceived these problems to occur more frequently in the home than in the agency. For example, some clients were reported as exhibiting sexually provocative or inappropriate gestures (Naleppa and Hash 2001). In such situations the worker faces the potential for a professional relationship to become an intimate relationship, which is obviously unethical given the criteria for boundary violations discussed above.

How does the worker decide how to manage situations in which boundary violations, boundary crossings, or "gray areas" that do not clearly fall into either category arise? Reamer (2001, 2003) recommends that social workers develop a clear definition of what constitutes ethical and unethical relationships. A dual relationship is unethical if it meets the following criteria:

- interferes with the worker's professional discretion
- interferes with the worker's impartial judgment
- exploits clients for the worker's personal gain
- harms clients

Cultural issues are also a consideration in deciding whether a relationship is a dual relationship in home visiting. In some cultures, great significance is attached to "breaking bread" with the practitioner, and a client may be reluctant to trust a practitioner who refuses an invitation to dine with him or her (Reamer 2001). The response of the worker is constrained by the requirement to draw clear professional boundaries, while at the same time not transgressing cultural norms (Naleppa and Hash 2001; Reamer 2003; Wasik and Bryant 2001). Accepting an offer of crackers and a non-alcoholic beverage may maintain clear professional boundaries without violating cultural beliefs (Reamer 2003). The *Code of Ethics* does address these issues in stating that when "dual or multiple relationships are unavoidable, social workers should take steps to protect clients and are responsible for setting clear, appropriate and culturally sensitive boundaries" (Standard 1.06c) (National Association of Social Workers 2000; Reamer 2003).

A risk management protocol proposed to manage boundary issues would require workers to be alert to potential or actual conflicts of interest in their relationship with clients and to indicators of situations that may signal a boundary problem. For example, home health social workers should be aware of situations in which they treat a client as "special," self-disclose intimate details of their lives, or do favors for the client.

When a worker recognizes that boundaries have been violated, he or she should consult appropriate agency personnel such as supervisors and administrators and also discuss the situation with the client. The worker should then design a plan to remedy the boundary violation and to protect the client to the greatest extent possible. Documentation of all discussions, consultations, supervision, and any other steps taken to address the problem is essential for risk management. The worker should monitor the implementation of the plan, possibly by phone, to evaluate whether the remedy was successful in minimizing or reducing the boundary violation (Reamer 2003).

◈ ◈ ◈

This chapter provides a context for understanding of the role of the social worker in home health care, tracing the emergence of social work as a profession in home care and highlighting some of the constraints on social work practice, such as third-party-payment policies and the influence of the host setting of the home care agency. The role of the home health care social worker in the managed-care environment focuses on the delivery of efficient, cost-effective services and the documentation and evaluation of interventions and intervention outcomes. Home health care social workers today confront two primary challenges: (1) the need for a more solid understanding and integration of social work as a profession within the home health care team and (2) the importance of advocacy in bridging the gap between home care social work practice and home care policies.

Three ethical conflicts in home health social work practice were addressed. The first, the conflict between the duty to protect client well-being and the duty to adhere to agency policies and procedures, may occur in practice when third-party-payment limits under managed care (most prominently the Medicare prospective payment system) fail to provide sufficient resources to meet the needs of frail, chronically ill older adult clients for care. Social workers can address these conflicts through advocacy at both the interpersonal and the system levels. The second ethical issue, the conflict between patient autonomy or self-determination and beneficence, is less directly related to managed care but is a central ethical concern in home care. Social workers encounter this problem when older adult clients make decisions that endanger their safety and welfare. Because ethically the principle of self-determination is dependent on client decision-making capacity, workers must acquire knowledge and skill to accurately assess decision-making capacity in collaboration with providers from other involved disciplines. Finally, the presence of situations in home care that present the potential for boundary violations, boundary crossings, and gray areas that do not fall into either category requires familiarity with guidelines for distinguishing ethical from unethical relationships and development of a risk management protocol to resolve such issues.

MR. AND MRS. KASINKSY

Mr. Tom Kasinsky is an 88-year-old home health care patient with cardiovascular problems, including high blood pressure and heart failure. As a result of several small strokes, he also exhibits cognitive impairment that interferes with his ability to sequence tasks and with his memory. He is dependent in ADLs such as bathing and dressing. He uses a walker to compensate for limitations in his mobility.

His wife, Ethel Kasinsky, age 90, was his primary caregiver until two months ago when she suffered a mild stroke and was hospitalized. She is currently slightly cognitively impaired and has limited mobility as a result of the stroke. She can no longer provide adequate care to her husband without the introduction of more formal and informal resources.

The original referral from the hospital was for Mrs. Kasinsky to receive physical therapy at home. The couple was referred to the home health care social worker after a month and a half by the home health care nurse for information and referral for community resources and counseling for long-term planning and decision making.

The social worker's assessment is that the couple does not qualify for any publicly funded community services because their income and assets are too high. The Kasinskys have no children or relatives in the immediate area. The social worker has discussed the available options with the couple, including limited home health aide services covered by Medicare, private pay for fee-for-service home care for longer-term care, or a Medicaid spend-down to allow relocation to a nursing home. Both Mr. and Mrs. Kasinksy have difficulty communicating with the worker, and their decision-making capacity fluctuates. Mr. Kasinsky sometimes exhibits bad judgment and memory loss, for example leaving the stove on, which has resulted in blackened pots. Mrs. Kasinsky cannot consistently supervise his behavior. Both, however, say that they are willing to accept the aide but do not want to pay for services, and they refuse the option of a nursing home.

The nursing supervisor tells the social worker that the couple represent a risk management problem to the agency because their situation is unsafe; the supervisor says that the worker should try to pressure them to accept the nursing home placement. The social worker is concerned about whether she should accept the supervisor's directive to pressure the Kaminskys to accept a nursing home placement or whether she should accept their decision to remain at home with limited services. She keeps worrying that Mr. Kasinsky will start a fire in the house.

Questions:

1. What ethical principles are in conflict in this case?
2. What principles and aspects of the situation should the social worker consider in order to make a decision that is consistent with the NASW *Code of Ethics*?

3

CULTURALLY COMPETENT SOCIAL WORK PRACTICE IN HOME HEALTH CARE

CULTURAL COMPETENCE is receiving increasing attention in the professions, as evidenced by recent standards set for culturally competent practice in social work, medical and nursing fields, and research. Culturally competent social work practice in home health care necessitates acquisition of knowledge in several areas and subsequent application of that knowledge. Specifically, two current trends in the aging population—increasing longevity and diversity (Dhooper 2003; Pinquart and Sörensen 2005; Sudha and Multran 2001; Wan et al. 2005)—combine with the long-standing relationship between cultural background and health disparities to inform home health practice. These trends form a backdrop for understanding three components of cultural background that are germane to home health practice:

- spiritual orientation
- health care beliefs and practices
- family structure, roles, authority, and social values

These components of culture are pertinent to home health practice because that practice occurs in the client's home, in the context of caregivers who are most often family members, and with clients who are most often chronically ill and/or incapacitated older adults. Consequently, social work in home health inherently happens in the context of a client and his or her family's cultural background. It is probably the most intimate of settings for practice (Campinha-Bacote and Narayan 2000; McNeal 1998). This chapter discusses:

- culturally competent practice
- culture and cultural background
- Western biomedical model
- health disparities and cultural background
- spiritual orientation
- health beliefs
- family structures, roles, authority, and values

Before exploring these areas of knowledge, however, an overview of what constitutes cultural competence and a clarification of terms will be helpful.

WHAT IS CULTURALLY COMPETENT PRACTICE IN SOCIAL WORK AND IN HEALTH CARE?

Recent revisions to the NASW *Code of Ethics* reflect the importance of cultural competence to the profession (National Association of Social Workers
2001). Additionally, the federal government–established standards of cultural
competence for health care are a major national goal in the *Healthy People
2010* plan (U.S. Department of Health and Human Services, Office of Minority Health 2001; U.S. Department of Health and Human Services 2002). This
chapter employs the terms *culturally competent* and *culturally responsive* and
their derivatives interchangeably.

The National Association of Social Workers (2001) identifies the ethical obligation to provide culturally competent practice that recognizes and affirms
the valuè of cultural background in all areas by specifying, for example, the
following:

- specialized professional knowledge of the traditional values, family systems,
  and practices of major diverse groups
- transfer and integration of cultural knowledge into standards, policies, and
  practices
- skills, methods, and techniques that reflect the role of the culture in the
  helping process and in empowerment

The U.S. Department of Health and Human Services Culturally Appropriate Service Standards (CLAS) for all health care practice are similar (Thobaben 2002; U.S. Department of Health and Human Services, Office of Minority
Health 2001). These standards include ensuring that

- patients/clients receive effective, understandable, and respectful care from
  all organizational staff members
- care provided is compatible with patients'/clients' cultural health beliefs,
  practices, and preferred languages

In sum, culturally competent practice is a set of behaviors, attitudes, knowledge, skills, and policies that enable the work of agencies, organizations, programs, and professionals to be effective in cross-cultural interactions between
providers and health care consumers (Campinha-Bacote 2002; Chin 2000;

Leininger and McFarland 2002; Panos and Panos 2000). Becoming culturally competent is a process of lifelong learning, beginning with practitioners' understanding of their own cultural background and, specifically for workers in health care, their own culturally related health beliefs. This process is predicated on the commitment of the practitioner (1) to learn from health care clients and (2) to understand culturally related norms, family roles, and social values and beliefs.

Understanding that there are a variety of worldviews, social structures, beliefs, and values among cultural backgrounds and that all groups or populations are heterogeneous rather than homogeneous is a first step in becoming a culturally responsive practitioner (Campinha-Bacote 2002; Congress 2004; Núñez 2000; Omi and Winant 2001). That is, there is more variation within a cultural group than between cultural groups. For instance, suppose that each of two home health clients would be officially classified as African American. However, one was born in Haiti, while the other's identity centers on a family history of slavery in the United States. The differences in these two cultural backgrounds will influence each client and family's understanding of illness and of receiving home health care from Western health care providers and caregiving in differing ways.

WHAT IS CULTURE AND CULTURAL BACKGROUND?

In this chapter the terms *culture* and *cultural background* are used interchangeably. These two terms are defined conceptually as the means by which persons and groups understand the world around them—the lens that guides our perceptions, thinking, and interactions with others—and provides coherence in making sense of life events (Applewhite 1998; Green 1999; Lum 2003; McEvoy 2003). Culture is dynamic and shaped by interactions with other cultures, particularly those that are dominant (Imes and Landry 2002; Kemper and Barnes 2003). In illustration of the pervasiveness of culture in human life, the concept "family" organizes daily life of individuals and families and interactions with the social environment across cultures, but family structure and patterns also vary across cultural backgrounds. A spiritual orientation—a general way of understanding life—is part of human existence across cultures. The meaning of health, illness, methods of treatment, and cures also varies both across and within cultural backgrounds. Cultural groups have values, emphasize some values over others, and have social rules governing social interactions. In brief, culture is

- shared, learned, and passed on across generations
- a reservoir of beliefs, social norms, roles, institutions, and values

- fluid, changing over time in response to interactions with other cultures, particularly dominant cultures

More specifically, those in a cultural group share one or more of the following: a history and/or country or region of origin; a language, dialect, or system for communicating; spiritual orientation and beliefs; values; social, family, and/or health care values, patterns, and practices; an economic and/or social class (Pinquart and Sörensen 2005; Weaver 2005). Of particular relevance to health care practice, in response to increased stress or stressful situations, such as chronic illnesses or receiving health care in one's home, individuals and families may rely more heavily on culturally familiar traditions, values, and health practices as coping resources (Boyd-Franklin 2003; Kemper and Barnes 2003; McEvoy 2003).

It seems obvious, given the above discussion, that the dominant group in the United States is *itself* a culture (Anderson and Collins 2004; Kemper and Barnes 2003; Weaver 2005). Western medicine is also known as allopathic, biomedical, or curative health care. It is important for practitioners in home health to realize that the dominant culture's values and norms are embedded in Western health care and providers, including home health, which is clearly an allopathic model of medical care (Imes and Landry 2002).

THE VALUES AND NORMS OF THE WESTERN BIOMEDICAL MODEL

The biomedical health care model's beliefs and standards of acceptable behavior reflect the values and norms of the dominant culture of the United States (Imes and Landry 2002). These include:

- cause-and-effect thinking
- positively valuing individual autonomy
- positively valuing technology and efficiency

In order to understand how home health clients from various cultural backgrounds may respond to Western medical care, social workers can benefit from understanding its values and premises.

The biomedical model is based on the "germ theory" of disease: illness and disease are caused by bacteria, fungus, virus, trauma, injury, aging, stress, and/ or environmental factors (Imes and Landry 2002). Diagnosis follows accordingly, in linear fashion, by identifying the cause of the illness and the preferred treatment (e.g., antibiotics, chemotherapy, surgery). Those who are accepted as healers are highly trained in the curative model of medicine. Because allopathic medicine mirrors Western values and ideology, individual client autonomy in decision making and participation in health care is the norm and is expected (Aranda and Knight 1997; Imes and Landry 2002). However, clients and families of non-dominant cultures are likely to value collectivism, rather than individualism, in health decisions and may distrust biomedical treatment and providers (Al-Krenawi and Graham 2000a; Applewhite 1998; Boyd-Franklin 2003; Choi 2001; Crist 2002; Dhooper 2003; Weaver 2003).

Given that brief overview of the biomedical model of health care, and before a discussion of population trends and cultural background, a caveat is warranted with respect to the categorical labels that currently (though inconsistently) appear in the literature. This chapter accepts the view, also noted by others, that official census data labels (such as African American, non-Hispanic white, Hispanic) and others (such as Arab American or Southeast Asian) are socially constructed and obscure the heterogeneity within a cultural group (Green 1999; Omi and Winant 2001). For instance, though Asian/Pacific Islander is an official racial category in the census and in research, within that official category one finds Chinese—with high levels of internal heterogeneity—and Filipinos, who are culturally very different from Chinese (Choi 2001).

Reliance on such labels deters understanding cultural backgrounds and interpreting research findings, and can lead to generalizing and stereotyping (Anderson and Collins 2004; La Viest 1994; Omi and Winant 2001; Weaver 2005). Generalizations about cultural groups or their members are not productive in establishing effective social worker/consumer relationships or in understanding clients and families (Congress 2004). Accordingly, these categorical labels appear in this chapter when the research findings or data discussed utilized them. In other discussions, the terms employed respectfully draw upon the preferences of the cultural groups themselves. Preferences include, for example, First Nations People rather than American Indian, Latino rather than non-black Hispanic, Puerto Rican (when appropriate) rather than Hispanic or Latino, and black or African rather than African American (Boyd-Franklin 2003; Comas-Diaz 2001; Weaver 2005).

HEALTH DISPARITIES AND CULTURAL BACKGROUND

Any discussion of cultural background and cultural competence must begin with an overview of the relationship of health disparities and cultural background. The concept "health disparities" refers to the gaps between majority and minority populations in health status, access to health care, and health care outcomes (Institute of Medicine 2002). The term *health status* refers to the presence or absence of current illness.

Empirical research documents that health disparities exist among all minorities. Minorities are more likely to receive lower-quality health care and have higher mortality rates than non-Hispanic whites even when health coverage/insurance, income, age, and severity of health conditions are controlled (Centers for Disease Control and Prevention, Office of Minority Health 2002; Institute of Medicine 2002), including older adults (Lum, Chang, and Ozawa 1999; Sudha and Multran 2001; Thobaben 2002). For example, the percentage of people who are limited in their daily activities—often referred to as "instrumental activities," such as work, shopping, or household tasks—due to chronic conditions is higher in all minority populations than in majority populations, and in women compared to men across all cultures. Further, a higher proportion of African (14.3 percent) than non-Hispanic white Americans (11.5 percent) report that they are limited in daily activities due to chronic health conditions (Centers for Disease Control and Prevention, Office of Minority Health 2002).

As an example of a specific, and growing chronic illness, African Americans, Alaskan Natives, and American Indians have higher prevalence rates of diabetes than do non-Hispanic whites (U.S. Department of Health and Human Services 2001). Racial category and gender interact in health disparities as well. For example, the prevalence rate for diabetes for adult black women (25 percent) is nearly twice as high, and the mortality rate from diabetes 40 percent higher, than the rates for adult non-Hispanic white women (Auslander et al. 2002).

HOME HEALTH USE AND CULTURAL BACKGROUND

Recent empirical findings suggest that cultural factors may be related more to use than to health status or access. Crist (2002) reported that Mexican American elders use formal home health care only half as often as non-Hispanic elders even though Mexican American older adults have higher levels of functional impairment. In a study of Taiwanese elders, Kuo and Torres-Gil (2001) found that the use of home health care is related to cultural factors, such as the use of ethno-cultural health care, as much as to functional need.

Of import to home health social workers are findings indicating that differing cultural understandings, expectations, and beliefs about health, illness, and medical treatment between providers and clients led to frustration for all participants, complications in medications and diagnosis, and treatment avoidance and/or dropping out of care (Murguia, Peterson, and Zea 2003; Murguia et al. 2000; Núñez 2000). The empirical literature suggests, in addition, that health disparities may be linked to institutional bias, stereotyping by providers, and health clients' lack of trust in health care providers. These factors may cumulatively interact with clients' socioeconomic status and cultural background (Appel, Harrell, and Deng 2002; Brach and Fraser 2000; Chin 2000).

MINORITY POPULATION STATUS AND HOME HEALTH CARE

In fact, the implications of research findings on minority elders and caregivers support this possibility. For instance, minority home health care recipients have more severe medical conditions and greater numbers of impairments in daily activities, and minority caregivers are less stressed and perceive greater rewards from caregiving than their counterparts in the majority population (Aranda and Knight 1997; Cuellar 2002; White, Townsend, and Stephens 2000; Williams and Wilson 2001). Pinquart and Sörensen (2005), in a meta-analysis of 116 empirical studies on family caregivers of older adults and their care recipients, affirmed that:

- African American and Asian caregivers had significantly more caregiving tasks than white caregivers
- minority caregivers were more physically impaired, and care recipients more physically and cognitively impaired, than their white counterparts
- minority caregivers were also younger, more often adult children, particularly daughters, less educated, of lower economic status, and more likely to be employed in addition to being a caregiver, than their non-Hispanic white peers

Empirical research findings, then, indicate that culturally diverse home health clients are likely to be more prevalent than in the past, to be in poorer health and have multiple more-severe conditions than majority clients, and to have fewer financial resources than majority clients. In addition, their family caregivers are likely to have multiple additional non-caregiving responsibilities, be in poorer physical health, and experience greater rewards from caregiving than their majority counterparts.

Therefore it is imperative that social workers in home health understand relevant elements of cultural background to ensure culturally competent practice. An encyclopedic detailing of cultures here is impractical and unrealistic, and because of the continually expanding nature of cultural diversity in the United States (Imes and Landry 2002; Weaver 2005), it would almost instantly be out of date. While an in-depth discussion of all the dimensions of cultural background is well beyond the scope of this chapter, an understanding of those elements that relate to health, illness, and receiving health care treatment and services is essential for culturally competent practice in home health for two reasons. First, knowledge of culture is integral to effective practice because culture shapes a client and a family's experience of illness and health treatments and influences their interactions with Western, biomedically trained health providers. Second, research findings indicate that cultural differences between providers and health care clients and families are associated with negative health outcomes.

SPIRITUAL ORIENTATION

Spiritual orientation is often reflected in both health beliefs and family structure, authority, roles, and values. Here, spiritual orientation will be differentiated from religion and denomination, though several religions or denominations may have a similar spiritual orientation (Dhooper 2003; Murguia et al. 2000; Weaver 2005). By way of reference, the terms *denomination* and *religion* refer to very specific and organized sets of beliefs, rituals, and behaviors that generally include officially sanctioned roles for leaders, activities, and doctrine. In contrast, one's spiritual orientation refers to a general way of relating to others and making meaning of life—a worldview of external, sometimes called a transcendent or higher power, control, or influence in human life and a personal sense of connectedness to a higher power (Dosser et al. 2001; Hodge 2003; Van Hook, Hugen, and Aguilar 2001). The reader is again reminded not to overgeneralize particular spiritual orientations or religious affiliations with specific cultural groups in the following discussion.

In some instances, multiple cultural backgrounds may be similar in spiritual orientation (Dhooper 2003; Murguia et al. 2000; Weaver 2005). For instance, while the cultural backgrounds of First Nations People and Hispanics vary in many ways, they are somewhat similar with respect to spiritual orientation, since each emphasizes harmony with all of life and the primacy of an internal, personal path to and relationship with all of life. Among African Americans, spiritual orientation overall involves a belief in a higher power to heal and the role of prayer in healing (Van Hook, Hugen, and Aguilar 2001).

More specifically, the majority of black Americans are affiliated with conservative or fundamentalist Protestant denominations, most notably Baptist and American Methodist Episcopalian (Boyd-Franklin 2003; Van Hook, Hugen, and Aguilar 2001; Weaver 2005). For many Christian blacks prayer is an ongoing, conversational part of everyday life and an active coping strategy (Boyd-Franklin 2003; Brown 2000; Kane 2000). Empirical research findings suggest that prayer has positive health-related outcomes for blacks, particularly older adults and family caregivers (Brown 2000; DeCoster and Cummings 2004; Navaie-Waliser et al. 2001; Pinquart and Sörensen 2005; White, Townsend, and Stephens 2000) and that African American family caregivers deal with the stress of caregiving through faith and prayer more than their non-Hispanic white peers do, employing prayer to reduce levels of perceived stress in their family caregivers. Faith and church participation are central to the daily life of many black Americans and are related to positive health outcomes—factors that practitioners need to incorporate in engagement, assessment, and, when indicated, interventions (Boyd-Franklin 2003).

A spiritual orientation that is inclusive of nature, ancestors, and/or multiple higher powers is reflected in the cultures of several Asian, Middle Eastern, and First Nations Peoples. In this orientation spirit, mind, and body are integrated in a holistic framework with all of life and are inseparable from physical, emotional, and mental health and illness. Communal activities, such as collective prayer and sweat lodges, are traditional, along with individual activities, such as meditation or spiritual quests (Al-Krenawi and Graham 2000b; Voss et al. 1999; Weaver 2005). For example, First Nations People value the individual's spiritual life or path while also placing great importance on the collective experience of family, clan, and tribe. Similarly, the spiritual orientations of Middle Eastern and Asian cultures, though varied, as a whole reflect transcending values of being part of something greater than the individual, harmony with nature, and the importance of the family in a quest to achieve a higher state of being (Al-Krenawi and Graham 2000a, 2000b; Liu 2001; Van Hook, Hugen, and Aguilar 2001).

The spiritual orientation of Abrahamic religions involves belief in a higher power and in some instances other revered individuals (such as saints). In some denominations, communal prayer is a highly structured activity and may be specifically employed for healing of the ill. Hispanic populations are strongly influenced by the predominance of Roman Catholicism. Of relevance for home care practice is the tendency in some Hispanic cultures to infuse Roman Catholicism with culturally related fatalism and a consequent belief that control is beyond the individual's grasp. Some Hispanic cultural backgrounds (Cuban, Haitian, and Jamaican, for example) also incorporate elements of other spiritual orientations (e.g., African beliefs, voodoo, and Santeria) in their Roman Catholic faith (Applewhite 1998; Weaver 2005).

SPIRITUAL ORIENTATION AND SOCIAL WORK IN HOME HEALTH

It is important for home health practitioners to understand that an individual's or family's spiritual orientation and/or denominational affiliation can influence their views about their role in health care and interactions with providers. In some spiritual orientations, for example, illness is viewed as punishment for sins, victimization by an external force, or part of a divine plan. In each instance power resides in some external entity rather than in the individual (Al-Krenawi and Graham 2000b; Blackhall et al. 1999; Dhooper 2003; Ow and Katz 1999). In these circumstances, home care clients and families may not view themselves as having influence or control over health or illness, or they may not perceive the value of participating in health care decisions or treatments. Others, whose orientation includes partially individual and partially higher power control or influence in health and illness, may accept and participate in medical home care while also seeking help from higher power(s) (Van Hook, Hugen, and Aguilar 2001).

The challenge for practitioners is to understand and respect clients' and families' spiritual orientation and their self-determination while at the same time helping them to achieve positive health outcomes. Attending to the way that clients and families describe their spiritual life and its relationship to their illness and health is part of culturally competent practice (Al-Krenawi and Graham 2000b; Van Hook, Hugen, and Aguilar 2001; Voss et al. 1999). Several authors suggest that rather than making assumptions or generalizations about clients' spiritual orientation and affiliation (Boyd-Franklin 2003; Brown 2000; Hodge 2003, 2004; McEvoy 2003), practitioners can initiate a conversation along the following lines in order to assess all clients and client families:

- Do you consider yourself a religious person or a person of faith?
- If so, how is your faith/religion included in your life?
- How do you connect your faith/religion to your current illness? To getting better?

While a practitioner may find the spiritual orientations of some cultural groups personally challenging when they differ from his or her own views, ethically responsible and culturally competent practice requires an open and inquiring stance with respect to spiritual orientation and religious or denominational affiliation and practices. This knowledge can inform the ecological perspective, educate medically trained home care colleagues, and facilitate better client and family participation and relationships with providers other than the social worker. In addition, spiritual orientation and denominational beliefs are frequently bound up with health beliefs.

HEALTH BELIEFS

TERMS RELATED TO UNDERSTANDING HEALTH BELIEFS

Several terms appear in the literature in reference to health beliefs and practices of non-Western cultures, among them *traditional medicine, ethno-medicine, ethno-cultural medicine,* and *folk medicine.* These terms are used interchangeably here, and culturally specific names for ethno-cultural healers or physicians and treatments are used when appropriate.

In the present discussion, the term *health beliefs* is defined as beliefs about the meanings and causes of illnesses, appropriate treatments, and the designation of appropriate health care providers and help-seeking health behaviors. Understanding culturally related health beliefs is essential for culturally responsive social work practice in home health care, since minority elders and their caregivers are likely to enter home health in poorer health status, with resources that are more limited and greater reliance on family caregivers.

PATTERNS OF USE OF WESTERN AND/OR ETHNO-CULTURAL HEALTH CARE

A number of patterns emerge when the choices of health care among clients from non-Western cultural backgrounds are examined. Their practices range along a continuum that includes:

- exclusive use of ethno-cultural health care and traditional healers
- parallel use of folk medicine and indigenous healers with Western medicine and practitioners
- sequential use of one health care approach followed by another when the first fails
- use of traditional health practices for certain illnesses or health problems and Western health care for others

As an illustration of the last point, Applewhite (1995) reports that older Mexican Americans choose ethno-cultural health care or Western medicine for treatment of illness according to which kind of care is accessible and what seems appropriate to the health problem they are having; they see no conflict in using both types of health care simultaneously. Americans of an Arab cultural background tend to use biomedical health care for physical illnesses and ethno-cultural health care for emotional and mental problems (Weaver 2005). The following discussion provides an overview for understanding ethno-medical beliefs.

TRADITIONAL ETHNO-CULTURAL HEALTH BELIEFS

Three categories of ethno-cultural health beliefs are discussed in the literature (Imes and Landry 2002; McNeal 1998):

- the naturalistic belief set
- the supernatural/magico-religious belief set
- a combination of the naturalistic and supernatural/magico-religious belief sets

THE NATURALISTIC HEALTH BELIEF SET

Health in the naturalistic belief set is a balance or harmony of the body, spirit, and mind; illness is caused by an imbalance of certain elements, such as excessive heat (*caliente*) or excessive cold (*frio*) or yin and yang, in the body (Imes and Landry 2002; Ma 1999; Pachter, Cloutier, and Bernstein 1995). Excessive heat in the body may result in a "hot" disease, such as hypertension; excessive cold (which might be caused by eating too much cold food) may result in a "cold" illness, such as a gastrointestinal disorder. The purpose of care is to regain balance; treatment is directed at the imbalance rather than at the illness or its symptoms and employs herbal teas, tonics, massage, and/or acupuncture. The naturalistic health belief set is common in some Asian, Southeast Asian, Latino, and Native American cultures.

SUPERNATURAL/MAGICO-RELIGIOUS HEALTH BELIEF SET

The second health belief set in ethno-cultural medicine is referred to as the supernatural, personalistic, or magico-religious set (Imes and Landry 2002; Murguia et al. 2000). Illness is caused by the intentional acts of another (ancestors, gods, evil spirits, or God), who imposes the illness by stealing, casting a spell over, or possessing the person's soul or spirit; the ill person becomes essentially a "victim" of the evil spirit, as punishment for wayward behavior. Cure involves rendering the supernatural being innocuous through spell casting, meditation, or trance with the aid of a sanctioned healer, or the person who is afflicted; symptoms of an illness are of only secondary concern. Health and well-being are achieved by good personal and spiritual relationships.

COMBINATION OF NATURALISTIC AND SUPERNATURAL/ MAGICO-RELIGIOUS BELIEF SETS

Some cultures take this approach, understanding illness as having multiple causes, including an imbalance of yang and yin, a failure of harmony with the natural world, an obstruction of chi (life force), a curse by an offended spirit, or retribution for bad behavior. Folk medicine in some Latino cultures, referred to as *curanderismo*, is a combination of supernatural and naturalistic health beliefs. The goal of *curanderismo* is to cure psychological, spiritual, and physical problems, and it is centered on a belief in God's will (Applewhite 1995; Murguia, Peterson, and Zea 2003). Illness may be either natural or supernatural in origin, and healing occurs through those who have a divine gift and the use of herbs, candles, and prayer.

Native Americans' health beliefs are also often a combination of naturalistic health beliefs, a spiritual orientation, and specific spiritual practices. First Nations People generally believe that life expectably includes negative experiences and problems, including illnesses. Health care incorporates spiritual, physical, and emotional interventions such as herbs, vision quests, and sweat lodges. Indigenous healers, referred to as shamans or clan mothers, are highly revered and perform multifaceted roles including physical healing, psychological/emotional counseling, and spiritual guidance (Voss et al. 1999; Weaver 2005).

CHALLENGES FOR HOME HEALTH PRACTITIONERS

Unfortunately, empirical research reports that failure to assess culturally related health beliefs and the use of ethno-cultural health care may undermine client compliance with Western medical regimens and lead to adverse medication interactions, less than beneficial care, and clients' dropping out of care (Brach and Fraser 2000; Murguia et al. 2000; Pachter, Cloutier, and Bernstein 1995). Home health clients and families may be reluctant to disclose their use of folk medicine for fear of rebuke or ridicule (Boyd-Franklin 2003; Ma 1999; Murguia, Peterson, and Zea 2003). Consequently, culturally responsive engagement with home care clients and assessment of health care beliefs are pivotal to helping clients feel comfortable enough to disclose such use.

While an understanding of clients' culturally related health beliefs is very informative with respect to their attitudes toward the causes of illness, their use of ethno-cultural treatments and practitioners, and their views on biomedical care and treatment, it is not sufficient preparation for practice of culturally competent social work in home health. Social workers must also be knowledgeable regarding family patterns and dynamics related to cultural background.

FAMILY STRUCTURE, ROLES, AUTHORITY, AND VALUES

Perhaps more than any other practice setting, home health care positions the worker in the client's most intimate context—the family. For that reason and because care in home health is increasingly dependent upon family caregivers, social workers must be knowledgeable about the influence of cultural background on family structure, roles, authority, and values. It is also important to remember that, as in all other components of cultural background, families are heterogeneous: families from one cultural group are clearly different from those in another group, but also (and more significantly for home health care) families in the same cultural group differ from each other.

FAMILY STRUCTURE

Family structure provides a way of understanding just who is seen as being "in the family" by the family and its members. It might be said that family structure designates "who gets a T-shirt" at family reunions and answers the question "how does this family organize itself?" Understanding how a family is organized highlights what individuals in the family the social worker needs to engage, what family support systems are available and utilized, and where and how interventions will be most effective. Family structures vary, though some are more prevalent in certain cultures than others. The following section discusses three kinds of family structure: kinship or augmented, extended clan, and nuclear.

THE KINSHIP OR AUGMENTED FAMILY STRUCTURE

A family with a kinship or augmented structure includes members from multiple generations who are biologically related, legally related, formally adopted, and/or informally adopted through a decision of the family, and who may also share a common ancestry or geographical nativity. Research findings and several black scholars suggest that black families frequently evidence this kind of structure (Barnes 2001; Billingsley 1992, 1999; Boyd-Franklin 2003; Williams and Dilworth-Anderson 2002). Characteristics of African American families that illustrate this structure include the frequency with which such families "take kids in"—children who might or might not be biologically related—and the tradition of taking elders in when the need arises. The development of such a structure among families of this group is probably related to the exigencies of slavery and of economic disadvantage (Boyd-Franklin 2003). Barnes (2001) found that families with augmented structures were able to provide more care to members in need and suggested that they are more resilient in caregiving and stressful situations, since more adult caregivers are available. Other researchers remark that the extent of available members in augmented families may have become limited in recent years because economic challenges and welfare reforms have made employment and/or mobility necessary (Williams and Dilworth-Anderson 2002).

THE EXTENDED-FAMILY OR CLAN STRUCTURE

An extended-family structure includes biologically related persons from multiple generations. Families among First Nations Peoples, for instance, usually include all those who are linked by matrilineal descent; that is, all people related to the matriarch, known as a clan mother, are members of the family, or clan (Weaver 2003; Weaver and White 1997). One or more clans may constitute a specific tribe for some Natives, as well as for some Southeast Asian groups, such as the Hmong (Dhooper 2003; Weaver 2003). In general, families of Asian background are multigenerational both vertically and horizontally (Dhooper 2003). An extended-family structure, known as *hamula*, is traditional for Arab families, may also constitute a tribal affiliation, and includes those who are related biologically through patrilineal descent (Al-Krenawi and Graham 2000a). Daily life for Arab families is dominated by interactions with members of the *hamula*.

THE NUCLEAR FAMILY STRUCTURE

Though the nuclear family structure may be perceived as typical of the dominant non-Hispanic white culture in the United States, it may be more accurate to say that this particular structure in white families is a stereotype rather than a reality (Barnes 2001), since some culturally diverse families may be nuclear—particularly so with increasing geographic mobility. In its traditional form, a nuclear-structured family includes two or at most three generations of biologically related persons—parent(s) and child/children. With respect to home health care practice, nuclear families may not have large support systems to provide care or support in times of illness.

An understanding of the various kinds of family structure leads the home health practitioner to culturally salient approaches. In working with a home care client of a nuclear family, for example, involving only the parents and the adult children might be effective. However, culturally competent and effective practice with a patient and family that have a kinship/augmented structure might well require anticipating that family members who are not biologically related and/or are from multiple generations would need to be engaged and involved in assessment and intervention. Specifically, inclusion of "church family" members might be crucial in working with black clients and families (Boyd-Franklin 2003). Similarly, practice with Native American clients might best include the clan mother and/or tribal community members. And in practice with Arab American and Asian American home health clients and families, inclusion of members from multiple generations and incorporation of tribal and/or community leaders in assessment and care planning would be both appropriate and helpful.

ROLES AND AUTHORITY IN FAMILIES

In many non-Western cultures families are hierarchical, with clear lines of authority and prescribed roles in decision making. For instance, in Arab, Asian, and Latino families decision-making authority tends to be male-dominated, or patriarchal (Al-Krenawi and Graham 2000a; Dhooper 2003). Decision-making authority may move upward in the family system from one male to an older male, who is seen as having more authority. In considering clients from cultural backgrounds that adhere to matriarchal leadership patterns, such as several Native American tribes, the social worker should be aware that authority in the family often rests with the oldest female clan leader, even when the official chief of the tribe is male (Weaver 2003; Weaver and White 1997).

Familism, which shapes authority and caregiving, is conceptually defined as strong identification, attachment, solidarity, and loyalty to the family, and reciprocal supportive intra-family relationships, with deference to the collective force of the family in decision making (Luna et al. 1996). The importance of familism varies across cultures, but it is considerably more evident in non-Western cultures. Generally, familism and collective responsibility for the well-being of family members are highly valued in Southeast Asian and Hispanic cultural backgrounds. African American families view authority as collectively held in the family and include church leaders or ministers as consultants in decision making about family members.

Home health clients and family caregivers from cultures that value familism and collective responsibility and decision making differ from the norm of individual autonomy that is held as the standard in Western biomedicine. Research findings suggest, for example, that Mexican Americans and Japanese Americans believe that patients should not be told they are terminally ill, whereas both non-Hispanic whites and African Americans generally believe they should be informed (Blackhall et al. 1999). Gender roles are also related to authority in families, and they tend to be more clearly defined in non-Western cultures than in Eurocentric and dominant Western ones. Asian and Hispanic families, for example, tend to assign caregiving of older adults to daughters and daughters-in law.

An understanding of family structure, decision-making authority, and gender roles in the client's family enhances the likelihood of effective engagement, assessment, and intervention. Without this knowledge, social workers may falsely assume that a client's family patterns are the same as their own or they may overgeneralize. Either of these errors can lead to an over- or under-assessment of the family's strengths, stresses, social support resources and needs, and readiness to comply with recommended interventions (Campinha-Bacote 2002).

SOCIAL VALUES AND RULES IN FAMILIES

Social values and rules, transmitted through the family from one generation to the next, provide guidelines for human interactions and a sense of security during challenging, stressful events or crises. In times of stress or physical incapacitation these values assist in coping. Allopathic Western medicine reflects dominant U.S. culture, which values meeting one's own needs, the rights of the individual, and efficiency both attitudinally and behaviorally (Imes and Landry 2002; Panos and Panos 2000). Conflicts having to do with individualism, collectivism, and familism can disrupt or sabotage the achievement of positive patient outcomes in home health. For example, rules of social behavior among Chinese Americans emphasize saving face, maintaining group harmony and mutual protection—especially within the family group—adhering to hierarchical roles, and respecting authority figures, such as physicians and family elders (Ma 1999; Ow and Katz 1999). Protecting the family and respecting older adults may preclude disclosing difficulties in caregiving, sharing family secrets, and asking questions of medical providers, thus potentially undermining home health care planning. Consumer hesitancy arising from these values and social rules can interfere with establishing the trust necessary for effective provider-consumer relationship building. Understandably, consumers of cultural backgrounds with a history of oppression may not trust health care providers or professionals of the dominant culture. African American clients, for example, may seem reserved or even aloof. In such situations, the social worker's ability to demonstrate respect may be crucial in establishing a working alliance. It is best practice to use formal titles (Mrs., Mr., Miss) in addressing clients until given permission to do otherwise (Boyd-Franklin 2003).

Social rules about nonverbal behavior also reflect cultural norms, and social workers attempting to engage home health clients must be cognizant of such rules. For instance, crossing one's leg and letting one's foot point at another person is an insulting gesture in some Southeast Asian and Middle Eastern cultures, and silence and avoiding direct eye contact evidences respect among First Nations Peoples (Weaver 2005). Behaviors that show stoicism are highly valued in several Asian cultures. Consequently, Asian American home health clients and families may be reluctant to acknowledge discomfort and pain even to their medical providers, and they may accept as normal higher levels of pain than non-Hispanic whites do (Dhooper and Tran 1998; Ow and Katz 1999).

Values concerning older adults and the process of aging itself also vary across cultural backgrounds and are highly pertinent to home health practice. For instance, among Chinese or Japanese cultures older adults are seen as becoming increasingly venerable as they age, and they are revered as guides for the family and the community. Some cultures specify social values and behaviors concerning elders and the role of younger family members regarding them. One example is *hyodo*, or filial piety, a social value strongly held in the Korean culture that obligates the family to do whatever is necessary to delay the death of older adults (Blackhall et al. 1999). The implications for home care social workers with severely or terminally ill clients and families who hold the value of *hyodo* are obvious. Home care consumers and families who hold the dominant culture's values of individual autonomy and meeting one's own needs may have less difficulty in adapting to the norms and values of biomedicine than those whose cultural values are centered on collectivism and familism.

FAMILIES, ELDERS, AND DIVERSE SEXUAL ORIENTATIONS

It is beyond the scope of this chapter to discuss the full range of knowledge concerning sexual orientation. The present discussion seeks to explicate some of the potential issues encountered in home health practice with gay, lesbian, bisexual, and transgender (GLBT) elders. Information available in the literature is scant, of only recent origin, methodologically limited, and in some instances inconsistent (Cahill, South, and Spade 2000; National Gay and Lesbian Task

Force Policy Institute 1999). Though research on GLBT home health clients is not currently available, applicable research findings on GLBT elders in general are extrapolated for home health practice in the following discussion.

Current estimates are that one to three million, or 3 to 8 percent, of Americans over the age of 65 are gay, lesbian, bisexual, or transgender. The Gay and Lesbian Task Force and others posit that this figure is likely an undercount, resulting from persistent societal homophobic attitudes and associated stigma (Barranti and Cohen 2000; Cahill, South, and Spade 2000; McFarland and Sanders 2003; National Gay and Lesbian Task Force Policy Institute 1999). Cahill and colleagues (2000) estimated that the number of GLBT elders over 65 years of age will increase to between two and six million by 2030. Clearly, the number of GLBT elders needing and receiving home care will also increase.

Family attitudes and beliefs about sexual orientation derive from many interacting dynamics, including spiritual orientation, cultural background traditions, and influences of the larger society. Religious and denominational beliefs shape and interact with familial values, expectations about gender roles, and views about sexual orientation both within and across cultures. For some cultural, racial, and ethnic groups, such as those associated with fundamental or conservative faith traditions and doctrines, heterosexuality and heterosexual gender roles are viewed as a faith-based mandate (Weaver 2005). For example, Green (1999) proposes that African American cultural identity is a combination of race, gender identity, and sexual orientation, suggesting that GLBT African Americans experience multiple layers of oppression and stigma. Conversely, in some groups, such as the Native American culture, sexuality in all its forms is viewed as natural and sacred, and all sexual orientations are accepted (Weaver 2005). An understanding of the cultural backgrounds and spiritual orientations or faith affiliation(s) of home health clients has great import in engagement and assessment, particularly with GLBT elders.

STRENGTHS AND CHALLENGES

Several issues are particularly relevant with respect to home health care practice with elder GLBT clients, among them the strength of existing coping strategies, affiliation with a created family, the need for privacy in light of social stigma, isolation, social support systems, legal and psychosocial issues for themselves and/or intimate partners, and responsive, gay-friendly services and providers.

For the current population of GLBT people over 65 years of age, who grew up before Stonewall and the gay liberation movement, disclosure of sexual orientation may still be perceived as threatening and may prompt intense protection of privacy (Butler 2004; Cahill, South, and Spade 2000; McFarland and Sanders 2003). An elder's need for privacy may be challenged when home-based health care is indicated. Clearly it is necessary for practitioners to skillfully engage with the elder and her/his significant other, as well as members of the created family and the family of origin.

Some research findings and conceptual literature (Barranti and Cohen 2000; Butler and Hope 1999; Gabbay and Wahler 2002; Grossman, D'Augelli, and Hershberger 2000; Healy 2002; Orel 2004; Rosenfeld 1999; Van Wormer, Wells, and Boes 2000) suggest that GLBT elders might have significant advantages in aging, among them learned coping skills and well-developed social support systems.

In the process of accepting their own sexual orientation and managing associated familial or social reactions and perceptions throughout their lives, GLBT elders often have developed signficant coping skills (Barranti and Cohen 2000; Butler and Hope 1999; Gabbay and Wahler 2002; Grossman, D'Augelli, and Hershberger 2000). Orel's small study (2004) with focus groups of self-identified elder GLBT individuals reflected both those earlier findings and conceptualizations about this possibility. Ageism in the United States may have an unintended positive consequence for gay elders, as sexual activity is not often seen as part of an elder's lifestyle. Repressive societal attitudes contribute to making sexuality an avoided if not feared topic in practice with elders (Altman 1999; Butler 2004). In terms of coping, however, the societal stigma of being gay may be less severe in elder years because sexuality is "irrelevant"—and thus is disregarded—or created families of affiliation provide extensive support, thus alleviating the stress of social stigma and preserving privacy (McFarland and Sanders 2003).

Findings on living arrangements among GLBT elders are mixed. Some report that elder GLBT people are more likely than their heterosexual counterparts to live alone (Cahill, South, and Spade 2000), while others report that more live with other GLBT people and/or with intimate partners (Orel 2004) than do their heterosexual counterparts. Contrary to the stereotype, recent findings report that two-fifths to more than three-quarters of elder GLBT people are in a long-term, committed relationship (Butler 2004; Cahill, South, and Spade 2000) and thus have access to social support.

Legal barriers and lack of recognition of GLBT partners and created-family members by providers include the absence of spousal eligibility for Social Security benefits and employee/pension health benefits, as well as the exclusion of partners from care planning and health care provision. At present in the United States, GLBT partners have no legal status whatsoever (Cahill, South, and Spade 2000); the findings of McFarland and Sanders (2003) reiterated this fact and explored its ramifications, including financial, housing, and inheritance catastrophes.

Though some segments of American society in the twenty-first century are more accepting of GLBT people than previously, heterosexism is still pervasive, and coupled with ageism, it may well deter GLBT elders from seeking needed services (Cahill, South, and Spade 2000; Orel 2004). These factors may specifically act as deterrents to their engagement with home care services and practitioners. No empirical evidence is available concerning GLBT elders' experience with health care providers, but researchers have documented negative experiences of non-elder GLBT adults with health providers and the consequent deleterious effect on the patient's health and receptivity to providers (Schilder et al. 2001). Directly noteworthy for home health practice, Brotman, Ryan, and Cormier (2003) and Orel (2004) suggest that heterosexist attitudes are prevalent in organizations that provide services to the elderly, and that these attitudes have gone largely uncontested. McFarland and Sanders (2003) report that one-third of their sample had concerns about discrimination in the health care system and thought that a lack of understanding from providers would be a barrier to seeking services. The need for gay-friendly resources, supportive systems, and groups for GLBT elders indicates that agency, organizational, and community education and advocacy is an important area of social work practice.

PRACTICE WITH GLBT HOME CARE CONSUMERS

In line with general recommendations for culturally competent practice with GLBT elders, Healy (2002), Butler (2004), and Orel (2004) highlight the need for home health practitioners to increase self-awareness and question their assumptions about sexual orientation, gender identity, and gay lifestyles. It is imperative that social workers ask about significant others and friends in assessment without assuming or specifying gender. For example, the worker might ask the following: "Is there anyone who has been or is important in your life?" "Is there anyone who has been a confidant?" Because home care occurs in the home, respect and engagement with a GLBT's partner and affiliated family are pivotal. Protecting the privacy of the client and/or partner should be a consistent part of assessment and reinforced frequently, as should exploration of the existence and quality of relationships with the client's and/or partner's biological family. These last two issues relate specifically to social isolation. Knowledge gained can inform the practitioner as to whether locating or developing a support system or group would be a needed intervention.

The culturally competent practitioner in home health will also have at the ready knowledge of organizations, services, and resources that are recognized as GLBT-friendly. Knowledge of relevant policies and legalities concerning an intimate partner's role, responsibilities, and rights with respect to living wills, advance directives, durable powers of attorney, insurance, and Social Security benefits allows social workers to serve GLBT clients more effectively. Social workers are well equipped to advocate for policies and programs that are culturally affirming for GLBT elders in home care and associated services and resources (Butler 2004).

❖ ❖ ❖

This chapter has discussed culturally competent social work practice in home health in light of the expanding and increasingly diverse patient population. Social workers in home health care are encouraged to practice in culturally responsive ways with clients and families, as directed by the NASW *Code of Ethics* and the federal standards for health care practice. They will necessarily develop an array of skills that promote good practice in today's diverse environment, among them awareness of the heterogeneity of cultural groups, ability to listen to and learn from culturally diverse clients and their families, the use of culturally salient knowledge and skills as appropriate to engage the client and family, attention to the client's spiritual orientation and faith activities, and the ability to assess family configurations, roles and values, and support.

4

ENGAGEMENT OF THE CLIENT IN HOME HEALTH CARE

THE INITIAL PHASE of home health care is engagement of the client (Compton, Galaway, and Cournoyer 2005), which may be part of the social worker's interview visit with the client. Under the provisions of Medicare's prospective payment system (PPS), workers may visit the client only once; any necessary follow-up is completed over the telephone. During the engagement phase, the social worker seeks to:

- clarify a preliminary purpose for the meeting
- orient the client to the helping context and provide written and verbal information regarding the home care agency's policies, mission, and services (including social work)
- explore the client's view of the help needed
- collaborate with the client to formulate and prioritize preliminary goals
- clarify any unrealistic client expectations regarding the help that is available (Compton, Galaway, and Cournoyer 2005; Ell and Northern 1990; Weaver, Perloff, and Waters 1998)

Three tasks are essential to the successful engagement of the client:

- communication with older adults
- development of a helping alliance with the individual client and the family
- recognition of the challenges of engagement in home care

Communication is an exchange between individuals in which information is mutually understood (Giordano 2000). The ability of the worker and the client to connect is essential to their interaction and has implications for how they define their relationship (Naleppa and Reid 2003; Nussbaum et al. 2000). The helping alliance is a relational bond and an agreement to work on specific tasks and goals (Horvath 2000; Muran and Safran 1998). The bond emerges from the exploration of the client's needs and the identification of the tasks and goals to be addressed (Bachelor and Horvath 1999; Ell and Northern 1990).

The first part of the chapter discusses communication with older adults who are not impaired and with those who require accommodations in speech because of a physical or mental impairment. Communication with the caregiving family is also addressed. The chapter next focuses on developing a helping alliance or relationship between the social worker and the home health care client And finally the text describes the challenges of the engagement phase in home health social work, including the advantages and disadvantages of home visits for forming a helping alliance and cultural variations in communication and relationship.

The "best available" research, cited in this chapter, provides strong empirical support, based upon sound methodology on the topics of communication with the older adult, the helping alliance, home-based visiting, and cultural factors influencing the alliance. The evidence for the transition from the hospital to home care is limited to one empirical study, of weak methodological quality. In general, the research cited is the most recent available and was conducted in the United States.

COMMUNICATION WITH OLDER ADULTS AND FAMILIES

COMMUNICATION WITH OLDER ADULTS WITH AGE-RELATED DEVELOPMENTAL CHANGES

Older adults are heterogeneous in their communication skills, and many exhibit no impairments in language reception and expression or in cognitive or physical abilities (Hummert, Wiemann, and Nussbaum 1994). However, in a few areas the developmental processes of aging may result in unique age-specific communication characteristics. The discussion here identifies several of these changes and describes age-sensitive communication and counseling methods appropriate for older adult clients. Two issues require consideration at the outset. First, there is wide variation among older adults with respect to these behaviors and characteristics (Giordano 2000; Nussbaum et al. 2000). In general, the communication of older people does not differ substantially from that of younger individuals (Nussbaum et al. 1998; Nussbaum et al. 2000). Second, the impact of the processes of aging on elderly communication is not entirely negative. It is more accurate to characterize them as "changes" that require adaptation by older adults and their communication partners (Giordano 2000). For example, research has indicated that compared to younger adults, older adults have more vocabulary, better storytelling ability, and more warmth and sincerity (Giordano 2000; Nussbaum et al. 1998).

Age-related developmental changes influence communication among some, but not all, older adults. Imprecise articulation of consonants and a slowed rate of articulation, changes in voice pitch (higher in men and lower in women), and a tremor in the voice that obscures voice clarity can be attributed to physical changes in the larynx and the muscles of the tongue and lips. A slightly decreased rate of speech, word repetitions, interjections, and fillers, similar to a "stuttering effect," are evidence of the increased length of time required to process a message and retrieve and associate words. Some older adults therefore experience difficulty in producing speech that is loud enough, clear enough, and evenly spaced enough to be understood. Thus the listener is required to invest more energy in careful listening so as to communicate effectively with an older adult speaker (Dreher 2001).

In addition to changes in the quality of vocal production, other age-related changes include decreased sensory perception (vision, hearing, touch, and smell), which is associated with uncertainty in response resulting from loss of detail in the original communication, and problems in cognitive processing that may arise in the presence of excess or irrelevant information in messages and extraneous environmental noise. Some older adults need extra time to retrieve information and respond. Learning is facilitated when the older adult can set the pace of the conversation, since rapid speech may impede his or her processing of information (Giordano 2000).

EXPECTATIONS OF THE OLDER ADULT'S COMMUNICATION COMPETENCE

Another consideration is the effect on interaction of negative age-related expectations of conversations with older adults. At a time when some older adults experience changes that threaten conversational skill, and are in need of supportive and affirming interpersonal exchanges, these expectations can add more strain to interpersonal encounters, potentially obstructing communication and effective helping. Negative age-related expectations result in a cycle labeled "the communication predicament of elderly people" (Ryan et al. 1995). The cycle begins when negative expectations of older adults' conversational skills are activated in an encounter by the presence of such characteristics as white hair, a certain vocal quality typically associated with elderly people, and apparently decreased speed of cognitive processing. These characteristics confirm the assumption of the older adult's impaired conversational competence. The communication partner may seek to accommodate the assumed declining skills of the older adult by adopting speech patterns such as exaggerated high pitch, increased volume, repetition, simplified sentence structure, or baby talk. The older individual, however, frequently perceives such behavior as patronizing and disrespectful (Baltes and Wahl 1996; Brown and Draper 2003; Hummert, Wiemann, and Nussbaum 1994; Hummert et al. 2004). If the older adult does feel that she or he is declining and "old," the accommodation behaviors described above act to reinforce such feelings, thus eliciting dependent behavior and social withdrawal to avoid future unpleasant experiences. The negative expectations of the conversational partner are thus confirmed, creating the conditions for repetition of the cycle (Ryan et al. 1995).

AGE-SENSITIVE COMMUNICATION WITH OLDER ADULTS WHO HAVE EXPERIENCED AGE-RELATED DEVELOPMENTAL CHANGES

Age-sensitive practice requires workers to recognize the positive attributes that older adults bring to conversation, while at the same time adapting communication to account for age-related changes and individual differences (Giordano 2000).

One such adaptation is attentive listening, which requires concentration on understanding client perceptions. It is unbiased and empathic. Access to a space free of noise and other distractions is necessary to facilitate this process. In home care the worker lacks control over the everyday commotion of the home setting—phone calls, interruptions by children and other family members, sounds from television and stereos—which can interfere with quiet and privacy (Wasik and Bryant 2001). The worker who is limited to only one visit can try to anticipate the situation by consulting the nurse case manager ahead of time. If children are present, enlisting supportive family members to keep them occupied is one strategy. Holding the interview in an unoccupied room, explaining that quiet and private are necessary to complete the work of the visit, and asking for the client/family member's cooperation might also be helpful.

Attentive listening adapted to older adult communication employs several techniques, such as:

- volunteering frequent feedback to verify the essence of the client's message
- using feedback to check accurate understanding of message
- seeking to clarify information by specifying what is clear and unclear
- repeating the essence of the clarified statement to check for accuracy
- refocusing digressions or rambling
- staying focused by repeating the last focused exchange or summarizing.
- adjusting the interview pace to the client's pace
- slowing the pace by using silence, pauses, summaries, and thorough exploration of topics

- keeping questions to a minimum to diminish the client's efforts to please by giving the "right information"
- using feedback to gain clarification
- noticing patterns of conversational dominance and submission when a third party is present
- focusing the interview on the older adult
- encouraging third parties to speak for themselves, not for the client (Dreher 2001; Giordano 2000)

These techniques are intended to discourage the older adult from seeking responses that will "please" the interviewer and to minimize distrust arising from what the client views as patronizing exchanges. They incorporate the essential elements of feedback, empathy, and listening to support client self-determination, and they convey respect and acceptance.

COMMUNICATION WITH OLDER ADULTS WITH ILLNESS/DISABILITY

While the communication skills of the majority of older adults are slightly modified by age-related developmental changes, older adults who experience chronic illnesses and disabilities may have characteristics that present more intrusive barriers to communication.

PROBLEMS WITH VISION AND COMMUNICATION

The prevalence of vision problems increases with age (Nussbaum et al. 2000; Giordano 2000). In 2002, the prevalence of any vision trouble (even with glasses or contact lenses) among community-dwelling elders was 18 percent. Among adults age 85 and older, 33 percent reported trouble seeing. In 2002, among people age 65 and older who reported vision problems, 16 percent reported ever having had glaucoma, 16 percent also reported ever having had macular degeneration, and 44 percent reported ever having had cataracts in the last twelve months (Federal Interagency Forum on Aging-Related Statistics 2004). The most prevalent eye disease, cataracts, is a condition in which the lens of the eye becomes opaque or cloudy, reducing the range of vision; the treatment for cataracts is surgery (Beers and Berkow 2005). Less common diseases of the eye include glaucoma, which is caused by high pressure in the fluid of the eyeball that results in damage to the optic nerve, and macular degeneration, which involves a progressive loss of central vision, resulting in difficulty in distinguishing objects and colors. Glaucoma is responsive to medical treatment; in some cases surgery is necessary. Laser treatment may postpone but not prevent loss of vision due to macular degeneration (Beers and Berkow 2005). Among adults age 65 or older who were home care users in 2000 and for whom vision impairment could be determined, 17 percent had some level of impairment (Centers for Disease Control and Prevention 2000).

Strategies for communicating with visually impaired older adults include:

- asking the client what accommodations are most helpful
- sitting close enough to the person so that he or she can clearly see your facial expression
- conveying messages without incorporating additional visual information, since the person cannot see such clues as facial expressions
- announcing when you are entering and leaving a room and whether someone is with you
- using the client's name when addressing him or her
- using printed material that has large enough type for the client to see (usually at least 14 points) (Naleppa and Reid 2003; Nussbaum et al. 2000; Schneider, Kropf, and Kisor 2000)

PROBLEMS WITH HEARING AND COMMUNICATION

The prevalence of hearing loss also increases with age (Dreher 2001; Nussbaum et al. 2000). In 2002, a little less than one-half of older men and nearly one-third of older women reported trouble hearing (i.e., any trouble, including deafness without a hearing aid). This percentage was higher for those who were 85 and older (60 percent) than for those who were 65–74 (30 percent) (Federal Interagency Forum on Aging-Related Statistics 2004). Among home care users over age 65 in 2000 for whom hearing impairment could be determined, a little less than one-fifth (24 percent) had some degree of impairment (Centers for Disease Control and Prevention 2000).

Hearing loss associated with aging can be characterized by decreased sensitivity to sound, meaning that speech has to be louder to be clearly heard. A second symptom is difficulty in discriminating between consonants, particularly the higher-frequency consonants such as *f*, *t*, *s*, or *th*. The inability to discriminate between these higher-pitched sounds may make it difficult for older adults to understand the content of speech by detecting the difference between words, phrases, and sentences. The older adult with hearing loss describes speech as "fuzzy," with words blending into each other even when speech is loud enough to hear. The effects of hearing loss on older adults are exacerbated when individuals speak fast, when there is external interference from the social environment (e.g., background noise), reverberations, or distortions, and when the older adult is under stress.

Hearing losses compounded by reduced confidence in conversational skill may make it less likely that an individual will initiate conversation or ask for clarification. Talking may become frustrating and exhausting, contributing to social withdrawal. Some elders compensate by lipreading and using inference to fill in words they do not understand. Individuals of all ages are embarrassed by hearing loss and as a consequence may not let the worker know about their difficulty. It is wise to ask new clients about possible hearing impairments if you observe that they have problems understanding what you are saying, evidenced by signs of strain (leaning forward, cocked ear), asking for frequent clarification, constant scanning of the worker's face, or complaints of dizziness or tinnitus (buzzing or ringing noises in the head) (Dreher 2001; Naleppa and Reid 2003; Nussbaum et al. 2000; Villaume, Brown, and Darling 1994).

Recommended strategies for communicating with individuals who experience hearing loss include:

- facing the person directly
- standing or sitting close (a distance of about three to six feet) and engaging the client's attention before beginning to speak
- keeping hands away from the face while talking
- using facial expressions and gestures
- speaking at a relaxed pace (not too slow or fast)
- speaking slightly louder than normal (but not shouting)
- positioning the client facing away from the sun
- paraphrasing rather than repeating statements
- reducing background noise from televisions, radios, or street traffic
- asking the client whether he or she is wearing a hearing aid and whether it is turned on (Naleppa and Reid 2003; Schneider, Kropf, and Kisor 2000)

DEMENTIA AND COMMUNICATION DIFFICULTIES

SIGNIFICANCE OF ALZHEIMER'S DISEASE FOR
HOME CARE SOCIAL WORKERS

The major cause of dementia among older people, Alzheimer's disease (AD), is a progressive and incurable illness characterized by the death of brain cells. Over time—the disease's life span can range from eight to twenty years—memory, cognition, and the ability to perform simple tasks of daily living are destroyed (National Institute on Aging 2000). The risk and severity of Alzheimer's disease increases with age. For every five years beyond age 65, the percentage of people with the disease doubles (National Institute on Aging 2000). Because people are living longer, and because the risk of the disease increases with age, the number of older adults with Alzheimer's is projected to almost triple by 2050, jumping from 4.5 million to 14 million (He et al. 2005; National Institute on Aging 2000).

Those who are 85 and older, whose risk and severity of Alzheimer's disease are highest, are also the most rapidly growing group in the population (National Institutes of Health 2003).

The majority of Alzheimer's patients, approximately three-fourths, are cared for at home exclusively by family and friends (Alzheimer's Disease and Related Disorders Association 2006). The number of caregivers and patients with needs for both formal and informal care will grow as the population ages and the number of older adults with Alzheimer's disease increases (National Institute on Aging 2002). Home care services are part of the long-term-care continuum that can provide respite, linkage to resources, assistance with daily functioning, education, and counseling to patients and families (He et al. 2005; Ledoux 2003; Munson 1999; Willen, Harman, and Alexander-Israel 1997).

However, caregivers—spouses in particular—are unlikely to use community services (Robinson, Buckwalter, and Reed 2005). When caregivers do use community services, the client is often too frail to benefit. Services are likely to be terminated because of client illness, which may be followed by nursing home placement (Zarit et al. 1999). Caregivers are more likely to use services as client symptoms increase in severity, but the services used are those that provide medical care rather than more socially oriented services (e.g., respite care, homemaker services, case management and personal care) (Dorfman, Berlin, and Holmes 1998).

This section focuses only on the implications of the early stage of Alzheimer's disease for language, speech, and communication, as well as on skills to enhance communication. These strategies facilitate client engagement and model positive interaction for the family (Ledoux 2003). If the care recipient objects to services, the consequently guilty spousal caregiver may terminate them when service benefits are not perceived to be balancing service costs (Robinson, Buckwalter, and Reed 2005). Skilled client communication by the worker can reduce negative client reactions to formal services and possibly avoid discontinuation.

COMMUNICATION TECHNIQUES FOR CLIENTS WITH ALZHEIMER'S DISEASE

In early-stage Alzheimer's with mild dementia the older adult experiences impairment in recent memory. Problems with finding words or naming objects, people, or places (i.e., anomia) are characteristic of communication during this stage. Other symptoms are requests for repetition of words and temporary digression from the main topic. Generally, individuals at this stage comprehend most spoken and written language unless it contains complex grammar, syntax, figurative language (such as metaphors and analogies), or complicated story structure (Naleppa and Reid 2003; Orange 2001).

Communicating with clients with early/mild stage dementia requires such adjustments as the following:

- allowing the client time to retrieve a word independent of your help, thus helping to preserve memory and vocabulary
- supplying the word only if the client cannot recall it after reflection
- avoiding figurative language, which the client may interpret literally
- structuring communication by introducing a new topic followed by general information and details
- summarizing, rephrasing, and repeating to reinforce comprehension
- monitoring attention span and focus
- allowing "short breaks" for off-topic conversation, but also limiting such digressions
- using written information to reinforce verbal discussion (Naleppa and Reid 2003; Orange 2001; Small, Kemper, and Lyons 1997; Tappen et al. 1997)

In general the worker should speak in simple, direct, active sentences. Simplify grammar, syntax, and vocabulary. A message stated in active voice ("The doctor will fill out the form") is easier to understand than a message stated in passive voice ("The form will be filled out by the doctor"). Several shorter sentences are more likely to be understood than one long, complex sentence. Avoid professional jargon, since the client is unlikely to understand it. If the worker cannot understand what the client is saying, she or he should tell the individual what is misunderstood ("I don't understand what_____means") or provide a possible understanding ("Do you mean_____ ?") (Naleppa and Reid 2003; Orange 2001).

COMMUNICATION WITH FAMILIES

A caregiver who is a spouse or sibling and therefore also an older adult may experience the same sensory losses already discussed as characteristic of most older adults. The worker may apply similar communication accommodations with the caregiver as with the care receiver.

THE WORKER-CLIENT ALLIANCE IN HOME HEALTH CARE

As indicated in chapter 2, social workers in home health care practice are functioning in an environment shaped by government and third-party-payment policies based on managed-care principles. Given the emphasis of these payment policies on producing measurable outcomes and on the efficient and effective targeting of resources, social workers in home health care are adapting their practice to fit brief treatment models. Under PPS, all health care providers need to accomplish more with fewer visits (Malinowski 2002). Employing strategies to engage clients quickly, in particular establishing a working relationship or alliance, during the first visit can help the worker use time more efficiently and effectively (Wendt 1996).

The alliance (also referred to as *the therapeutic alliance, the working alliance,* and *the helping alliance*), a concept based in psychotherapy research and practice, comprises three interrelated components: a bond or interpersonal attachment (e.g., liking, trust, and other positive relationship qualities), agreement on tasks (what is to be done), and agreement on goals (outcomes) to resolve the client's problem. The strength of the alliance is determined by the degree of agreement between client and worker about tasks and goals and by the quality of the bond between them (Horvath 2000; Muran and Safran 1998). The alliance has been the subject of extensive research in psychotherapy because of the strong association across a variety of therapies and diagnoses between the alliance and positive treatment outcomes in traditional therapist/client dyads (Bachelor and Horvath 1999; Horvath 2000; Martin, Garske, and Davis 2000) and in case management programs for the chronically mentally ill (Howgego et al. 2003).

The concept of the alliance as used in this discussion is generic to all helping processes. It is a necessary but not sufficient condition for helping the client (Bachelor and Horvath 1999; Horvath 2000; Howgego et al. 2003). Different types of helping interactions focus on different types of tasks and goals and therefore require different types of bonds (Chrits-Christoph and Connolly 1999; Howgego et al. 2003; Muran and Safran 1998). While home health care practice is not therapy, the alliance concept is applicable since the worker and client must establish an atmosphere conducive to trust and understanding and come to agreement on tasks and goals for work (Trojan and Yonge 1993; Wills 1996).

The alliance is created with the contributions of both participants. The worker establishes a climate of safety through the communication of empathy, respect, trust, warmth, genuineness, and responsiveness. The client's contribution is a commitment to participate in the helping process by working on tasks and goals in collaboration with the worker (Bachelor and Horvath 1999; Kadushin and Kadushin 1997). Because the alliance is a necessary condition for achieving positive outcomes in any helping encounter, social workers develop alliances with individual patients and with the family. Unless the patient has no family, the development of an alliance with the family and with the patient is deemed necessary because the family system is affected by illness and the patient cannot be considered separately from the family (Christ, Sormanti, and Francoeur 2001). The health care literature applies the concept of alliance or relationship in home care and/or health care to individual clients (Heineken 1998; Kaakinen, Shapiro, and Gayle 2001; Trojan and Yonge 1993; Wasik and Bryant 2001) and to families (Raudonis and Kirschling 1996; Robinson 1996; Rolland 1999), suggesting that the concept is generalizable across systems.

There are, however, some subtle differences between developing an alliance with a family or a family member and developing one with an individual client in health care. For example, the social worker "joins" the family by empathizing with their thoughts and feelings (Rolland 1999). An impartial perspective that includes the perspectives of all family members is also a quality of the alliance between the worker and the family (Robinson 1996).

The elements of the alliance are described below. The term *client* refers to both individual patients and family members or families.

EMPATHY

Empathy is defined as the ability of the worker to respond to feelings and experiences from the client's perspective, and to accurately communicate that understanding to the client (Wasik and Bryant 2001). Dehumanizing health care settings that objectify clients as "cases," coupled with the isolation, uncertainty, and anxiety associated with illness/disability, increase the need for empathy and communication of understanding (Heineken 1998; Kaakinen, Shapiro, and Gayle 2001; Raudonis and Kirschling 1996; Robinson 1996; Wasik and Bryant 2001). Caregivers of patients at home who have been discharged from hospitalization for an acute episode may benefit from empathic responses to feelings of anger/frustration, lifestyle restrictions, and growing distance in the relationship with the care receiver (Kane et al. 1999). If clients feel understood they are better able to cope with these experiences (Northouse and Northouse 1998). Techniques for conveying empathy include:

- listening intently
- using silence to assimilate the message before responding (Wasik and Bryant 2001)
- being sure that verbal and nonverbal behaviors are consistent, since contradictory behaviors make messages confusing and reduce the level of disclosure (Dreher 2001)
- paraphrasing concisely, using language similar to the client's (Wasik and Bryant 2001)
- asking for clarification and checking perceptions (Dreher 2001)

RESPECT

Respect, another relationship quality, can be defined as recognition of the client's intrinsic dignity and value (Kadushin and Kadushin 1997). Respect implies that we regard clients as worthy of esteem and courtesy. Older clients are more likely to self-disclose to workers who treat them respectfully (Dreher 2001). Techniques for conveying respect in home care include:

- reserving time for the client and arriving punctually for home visits (Kadushin and Kadushin 1997; Stulginsky 1993)
- being flexible in scheduling visits to accommodate the client's lifestyle and privacy needs (Barton and Brown 1995; Wasik and Bryant 2001; Wendt 1996)
- observing boundaries of the client's "space" and asking where in the house the client prefers to talk, where you should sit, and whether to take your shoes off at the door (Trojan and Yonge 1993; Wendt 1996)
- addressing clients courteously and formally, for instance by using "Mr." or "Mrs." during the initial stage of the interview
- using a more informal style of address later in the interview, if the client permits
- avoiding patronizing language that clients perceive negatively (Baltes and Wahl 1996; Brown and Draper 2003; Hummert et al. 2004)

TRUST

Trust, a third relationship quality, develops when clients experience workers as protective of client well-being, competent, reliable, and predictable (Heineken 1998; Lynn-McHale and Deatrick 2000; Robinson 1996). Trust provides support to clients who have felt vulnerable and depersonalized as a consequence of their experience with illness or the health care delivery system. Clients who trust their workers are more likely to feel secure and are consequently more likely to self-disclose (McNaughton 2000; Northouse and Northouse 1998). The social worker may develop trust quickly with older clients by:

- demonstrating competence through attentive listening and asking questions that elicit the client's view of the problem and preferences for solutions (Bachelor and Horvath 1999; Carlat 2005)
- identifying and addressing an urgent client problem in the first interview (Barton and Brown 1995; Wendt 1996)
- conveying information about confidentiality in the initial interview (Wasik and Bryant 2001; Wendt 1996)

WARMTH, GENUINENESS, AND RESPONSIVENESS

Warmth is conveyed through eye contact, a relaxed, forward-leaning posture, smiling, verbal responses that are short and encouraging, and positive statements about the client. Speech should be calm, soothing, and delivered in a friendly tone (Kadushin and Kadushin 1997). Workers communicate presence and support for the client with these behaviors (Vivian 1996; Vivian and Wilcox 2000; Wendt 1996).

Genuineness is the ability to assume the professional role as yourself, without pretense or a facade (Wasik and Bryant 2001). Workers who are perceived as genuine talk to clients about "everyday" happenings (Vivian 1996). The genuine worker can use small talk at the beginning of the interview to allow time for the worker and client to become more familiar with each other and thus ease the transition to the formal interview (Northouse and Northouse 1998; Wasik and Bryant 2001).

Responsiveness has to do with giving careful attention to and monitoring the quality of the interaction (Bachelor and Horvath 1999). Research suggests that the client's perceptions of relationship qualities are variable. For example, some clients respond positively to expressions of empathy that focus on cognitive experience, while others prefer expressions of empathy that emphasize affective experience (Bachelor and Horvath 1999). Workers may therefore need to individualize their responses to meet client need by seeking confirmation of the helpfulness of goals, tasks, and efforts to establish a bond.

Attention to client-expressed reactions enables the worker to adjust responses appropriately (Bachelor and Horvath 1999). Older clients may require encouragement to respond honestly to professionals (Heineken 1998). The worker can increase client self-disclosure by giving the client permission to share his or her reactions ("I want to be helpful to you, so please tell me when I am off track in understanding something you say or want").

CLIENT COLLABORATION

A final aspect of the alliance is client collaboration. Research indicates that the client commitment to the alliance or relationship is a stronger predictor of positive outcomes than worker behaviors such as empathy, respect, and trust (Bachelor and Horvath 1999; Robinson 1996). To increase the client's participation and involvement, the worker explores the problem from the client's perspective and contracts to work toward client-determined goals (Wills 1996). Workers can facilitate client collaboration by listening carefully for what the client wants to gain from the home care contact (Hubble, Duncan, and Miller 1999). The following questions can also help to clarify client goals:

- What did you (think/wish/hope) would be different because of our meeting together?
- What do you want to change about your situation? (Hubble, Duncan, and Miller 1999)

If the client's goals are potentially self-destructive (e.g., a client living alone who cannot perform daily tasks wants to remain independent), the worker can provide information, resources, and assistance with decision making to help clients make informed choices.

Ultimately (unless the client does not have the capacity to make this decision or all decisions), the client's motivation to work toward a goal is decisive in determining collaboration (Vivian 1996; Vivian and Wilcox 2000; Wasik and Bryant 2001). Client receptivity to information, resources, or assistance with decision making is influenced by the degree to which the client experiences a bond with the worker based on the relationship qualities described above (Kadushin and Kadushin 1997; Vivian and Wilcox 2000).

ROLE UNCERTAINTY

Client collaboration and participation in the home care alliance may also be influenced by role uncertainty (Northouse and Northouse 1998). Older adults not be clear about what is expected of them and what to expect from the worker. It is unlikely that older clients have had previous contact with a home health social worker. A recent national survey found that only 8 percent of respondents had ever used a home care social worker, though 20 percent had used nurses and 12 percent had used therapists (Neal 2001). Uncertainty may be compounded by the fact that the older home care client may simultaneously be interacting with several other providers (e.g., social workers, aides, nurses, therapists).

The trend away from professional uniforms (such as a cap with a black ribbon for a nurse and a lab coat for a therapist) and toward street clothes and name tags with small identifying print (Northouse and Northouse 1998) may lead to confusion in differentiating providers from each other (Kadushin 1996). The need to respond to different demands from providers whose roles are blurred may increase the client's uncertainty about how to behave and what to expect (Northouse and Northouse 1998). The following techniques are useful in reducing role uncertainty:

- providing your name, your title, and agency affiliation at the beginning of the first visit (Stulginsky 1993)
- being aware that clients may hold inaccurate stereotypes or lack knowledge about the social work role (Kadushin 1996; LeCroy and Stinson 2004)
- correcting stereotypes or knowledge deficits by asking the client to describe his or her expectations of what home health social workers do to help clients
- clarifying what the client expects from the helping process (Bachelor and Horvath 1999)

CHALLENGING ISSUES

THE PHYSICAL ENVIRONMENT OF THE HOME VISIT:
AN OPPORTUNITY AND OBSTACLE TO THE RELATIONSHIP
AND THE ALLIANCE

In their own home, clients may feel more in control and less anxious than they feel in an unfamiliar agency setting. For example, in the home, the client decides where the worker sits during the interview. A higher level of client comfort may facilitate self-disclosure and the development of the alliance (Clark 1999; Naleppa and Hash 2001). The neighborhood that the worker observes in traveling to the home and the physical appearance of the home itself can help the worker identify the client's strengths, which can be called upon in building an alliance (Wasik and Bryant 2001).

On the other hand, the home visit may also create barriers to the formation of an alliance. The worker's comfort level may be challenged by the cleanliness and condition of the client's home. Cigarette smoke, infestation of rodents or bugs, bad smells, or dirt can result in tension and anxiety for the worker. Similarly, worker concern about personal safety if she or he is exposed to hazardous neighborhoods, aggressive animals, or dangerous activities (e.g., guns in the house or evidence of drug use) may result in tension (Clark 1999; Naleppa and Hash 2001). And if, during the first visit, the worker requests that the client alter the environment to improve the worker's comfort level, the client may perceive the request negatively, and thus the process of developing rapport could be slowed down (Naleppa and Hash 2001).

Some clients may not initially permit workers to enter their homes, viewing them as untrustworthy strangers (Naleppa and Hash 2001). In such a situation, "getting in the door" may the first indication of the possibility of an alliance (Flowers 2000).

THE FAMILY DURING THE TRANSITION FROM HOSPITAL
TO HOME CARE

It has been reported that the majority of family caregivers described a need for more ongoing communication with home care staff regarding medical information (such as information about the client's abilities and restrictions) and addressing the psychological needs of the care recipient. Caregivers also stated that they needed more information about agency services in general, the "strangers" coming to their homes, and the specific services they would receive. Overall, caregivers experienced anxiety about what to expect and felt that there was a lack of preparation before hospital discharge and that the home care staff provided inadequate information (Weaver, Perloff, and Waters 1998).

During the transition from hospital to home care in the post-acute period, family caregivers most urgently need information about home care and about what to expect from the patient physically and psychologically. A pre-discharge visit scheduled by the home care social worker with the family will facilitate timely communication of this information (Weaver, Perloff, and Waters 1998), providing an opportunity to introduce the family to the agency, prepare the family for home care, give the family information about the care recipient's functioning at home, and potentially reduce family anxiety and uncertainty during the transition period. Such a visit also has the potential to accelerate the process of engagement, as the family will subsequently be less likely to think of a nurse or a social worker as a "stranger," with all the threatening connotations of that word. It also provides an opportunity for home care personnel to become familiar with the hospital discharge planner, thus improving collaboration and continuity of care. Finally, the worker can use the visit to do a prescreening of the patient and family so the home care agency can provide cost-effective, efficient care.

CULTURAL FACTORS INFLUENCING THE FORMATION OF AN ALLIANCE

In the following examination of cross-cultural issues/strategies for improving communication and enhancing an alliance with African Americans and Hispanic clients, the terms *African American* and *Hispanic* are used, assuming the inclusive connotations of other aspects of cultural identity and with no intention of referring only to "racial/ethnic categories."

The home health social worker who tries to form an alliance with an older African American client should be aware of the possibility that the client has experienced discrimination in the United States and should therefore show respectful behavior by using formal titles ("Mr.," "Mrs.," or "Ms.") to address the client unless invited to use more informal forms of address. Respect is also indicated through congruence between verbal and nonverbal behavior and by attentive listening behavior. An example of an inattentive worker would be one who listens to the client while shuffling through a pile of papers; an attentive worker would lean forward, establish eye contact, and use abbreviated verbal utterances to connect with the client (Schneider, Kropf, and Kisor 2000; University of Washington 2005). While all clients should be asked about their preferences regarding touch, this caution applies more stringently to African American clients (Northouse and Northouse 1998; University of Washington 2005).

To improve communication with African American clients, it is advisable that the worker acknowledge and respect the meaning of the illness for the client. The worker who takes into account the client's health care beliefs will be perceived as more trustworthy and thus will find it easier to establish communication with the client (University of Washington 2005). The worker can display respect by incorporating into the treatment plan beneficial or neutral remedies that are consistent with the client's health care beliefs. For example, the worker could suggest that a client who believes that "weakened nerves" lead to hypertension might study meditation or try to get more sleep (University of Washington 2005).

The African American client who is told that she or he has a right to a service for which she or he is eligible may respond more positively to the offer of service (Schneider, Kropf, and Kisor 2000). A small amount of research suggests that African American clients respond negatively to workers whom they associate with "welfare" and/or poverty programs (Bass, Noelker, and McCarthy 1999).

Hispanic clients value respect and personal relationships in interacting with health care professionals, including home health social workers (Beutter and Davidhizar 1999; Schneider, Kropf, and Kisor 2000). Respect is communicated by using formal titles to address the client ("Mr." or "Mrs.," "Señor" or "Señora"). The interaction can be personalized by greeting the client by name and asking about the general well-being or health of his or her family before beginning the formal interview (Schneider, Kropf, and Kisor 2000).

The client may avoid eye contact with health care providers as a sign of respect (Clark 1999; University of Washington 2005). For some clients, eye contact may be associated with evil spirits and a belief that illness can be caused by receiving the "evil eye" or "*mal ojo*" (University of Washington 2005).

Because of the cultural values of courtesy and respect, Hispanic clients may be silent when they disagree with or do not understand the worker's communication. To ensure understanding, it is advisable for the worker to ask open-ended questions and to encourage the client to ask questions (Beutter and Davidhizar 1999; University of Washington 2005).

Further information about communication and relationship norms in health care interactions for a variety of cultures is available at the "Culture Clues" tip sheets available from the University of Washington (http://depts.washington. edu/pfes/ cultureclues.html) and in chapter 3 of this book.

◈ ◈ ◈

In summary, older adults are heterogeneous in their communication skills. The communication skills of the majority of older adults may differ slightly from those of younger adults. A minority of older adults have problems in communication as a result of impairment in sensory perception, decreased information processing skills, and reduced reaction time. These older adults require accommodation in communication skills on the part of the worker to overcome potential barriers to worker-client understanding.

The helping alliance consists of a bond of a trust and liking, and agreement on tasks and goals between worker and client. The alliance is strongly associated with positive outcomes across a variety of therapies and diagnoses. It is regarded as generic to all helping interactions, including the interaction between the home health care worker and the individual client, a family member, or the entire family. Worker behaviors that communicate empathy, respect, trust, warmth, genuineness, and responsiveness help to establish the bond between worker and client. Client collaboration on tasks and goals, the strongest variable influencing the formation of an alliance, is fostered by incorporating the client's agenda.

Role uncertainty or client confusion about his or her own role and the role of the home health care provider may reduce the client's ability to participate in the helping alliance. Discussing the client's expectations at the beginning of the initial visit and using this as a basis for role clarification can reduce role uncertainty.

The home environment can function as both an obstacle and an opportunity for developing a working alliance. Clients may feel more comfortable at home and have more control over the environment than in a hospital or nursing home, enhancing client self-disclosure and contributing to the development of the alliance. However, the home environment may present challenges for the worker's comfort level, resulting in anxiety on his or her part. Workers must also be aware of boundary issues during home visits that can complicate the development of the alliance.

Communication behaviors and behaviors that build positive bonds vary across cultures and must be considered if efforts to communicate with clients and to develop the helping alliance with clients from diverse backgrounds are to be successful.

MR. HOWARD JENSEN

Mr. Jensen is a 90-year-old man who has been widowed for two years. He has been referred to home health care for his problems with medication adherence related to managing his type 2 diabetes and heart disease. He suffers from hearing loss and wears two hearing aids, but these are of limited value in improving his hearing. He neglects his hygiene, and he frequently experiences a buildup of wax in his ears that impairs the effectiveness of the hearing aids.

The home health care nurse has visited Mr. Jensen, but he has resisted her efforts to educate him about his medications and does not comply with her instructions, though he has private insurance coverage that pays for medication. The nurse has made a referral to the home health care social worker to evaluate Mr. Jensen for clinical assessment of social and emotional issues related to his need for care.

The social worker called ahead to schedule a visit, but Mr. Jensen had difficulty understanding her over the phone, so she is unsure about whether he is expecting her or knows the purpose of their meeting. On arriving at the home, the worker rings the doorbell, but Mr. Jensen does not answer the door. After she has made several attempts over a twenty-minute period, Mr. Jensen answers the door. When the worker introduces herself with her name, title, and the name of the agency, Mr. Jensen responds that he does "not need another one of those young girls" coming out to his home to tell him what to do. He has lived his life his way since he left home at fifteen. He does not need anyone to help him after making his own decisions all this time. These medical people assume he is an old man who is too senile to take care of himself.

Questions:

1. What are some of the problems that engaging and communicating with Mr. Jensen present for the home health social worker?
2. What skills of communication and engagement might be effective?

5

SOCIAL WORK ASSESSMENT OF THE INDIVIDUAL
IN HOME HEALTH CARE

SOCIAL WORKERS in home health care have been characterized as generalist practitioners who apply a person-in-environment framework, in which the patient, family, and community environments reciprocally influence medical outcomes for patients (Abel-Vacula and Phillips 2004; Egan and Kadushin 2000). However, as noted in chapter 2 on the social work role, Medicare Conditions of Participation require that all home health social work practice activities reflect a connection between social and emotional needs of patients and the medical condition or rate of recovery of the beneficiary. The following categories were approved in 1996 to further refine the parameters of social work home health practice (only those categories relevant to individual assessment are listed):

- assessment of social and emotional factors related to the patient's illness, need for care, response to treatment, and adjustment to care
- assessment of the relationship of the patient's medical and nursing requirements to his or her home situation, financial resources, and availability of community resources (U.S. Department of Health and Human Services, Centers for Medicare and Medicaid Services 2005b)

The following discussion of patient assessment is based on the literature regarding adaptation to illness for common chronic illnesses of older adult clients admitted to home health care (Munson 1999), as well as that regarding the assessment of patients and families who are home health care clients and the community-dwelling disabled population. A chronic illness is defined by the duration of the illness (longer than three months), by the impact on lifestyle (it interferes with physical, psychological, or social functioning), and by the fact that it is not curable (Sidell 1997). The most common diagnoses of older home health care users, according to the most recent published data from the Centers for Disease Control and Prevention and the National Home and Hospice Care Survey (Munson 1999), were:

- diseases of the circulatory system (hypertension, heart disease, and cerebro-vascular disease)
- disorders of the endocrine system, nutritional and metabolic diseases (disorders of the endocrine glands and nutritional deficiencies)
- diseases of the musculoskeletal system and connective tissue (arthritis, osteoporosis, and rheumatism)

The purpose of the home health social worker's assessment of the chronically ill older adult client is to identify social and emotional risks and strengths that influence the degree of client safety in continuing to live in the community. The following factors are associated with assessment of the individual client:

- characteristics of the client's disease or disorder that have psychosocial implications
- medication management ·
- execution of advance directives and the client's attitudes toward advance directives
- health beliefs
- self-efficacy
- depression
- suicide risk screening and assessment
- anxiety
- substance misuse

CHARACTERISTICS OF THE CLIENT'S DISEASE OR DISORDER THAT HAVE PSYCHOSOCIAL IMPLICATIONS

ILLNESS TRAJECTORY

Knowledge of the illness trajectory provides information about how the illness will change over time and about the psychosocial implications of those changes for the patient's ability to live safely in the community (Christ, Sormanti, and Francoeur 2001; Rolland 1999). The illness trajectory includes the type of onset (acute or gradual), the course of the illness (progressive, constant, relapsing), and the outcome (shortened or normal life span) (Christ, Sormanti, and Francoeur 2001; Rolland 1999). For example, adult-onset non-insulin-dependent diabetes has a gradual onset, but if the disease is not managed appropriately it can be progressive and fatal (Rolland 1999). To achieve the goal of keeping the adult diabetic patient living safely at home, the social worker will require knowledge of the illness trajectory during assessment so that appropriate inter-

ventions can be implemented to prevent hospitalization and institutionalization (DeCoster 2001).

TYPE AND SEVERITY OF IMPAIRMENT

Assessment of the type and severity of impairment, including ADL/IADL functioning and cognitive impairment, provides information to the home health
social worker regarding the need for environmental modification, support services, income supports, and durable medical equipment (Cowles 2003). In fact,
ADL status is the most significant factor in determining the use of home health
care services (Kadushin 2004). Nurse case managers admitting the elderly to
home health care complete the OASIS form during the initial intake interview.
The OASIS form collects data on patient cognitive status, sensory status (hear-
ing/sight), ADL/IADL functioning, and ability to take medication. The OASIS
information may be the basis for the referral to social work, and therefore the
social worker should be familiar with the nurse's OASIS assessment before the
initial assessment interview. Consultation with providers from the appropriate
disciplines (nurses, physical and occupational therapists) that have provided
services to the client subsequent to the OASIS interview but before the social
work contact may also provide up-to-date information about the client's functional and mental status.

While the OASIS thoroughly assesses ADL/IADL impairment, it collects
less-detailed information about cognitive impairment. *Cognitive impairment*
refers to a loss of ability in the storage, retrieval, or manipulation of information
(Morrison 1995). Dementia is a type of cognitive impairment characterized by
difficulty in learning and remembering information, lack of recognition of
familiar objects, disturbances in the use of language (difficulty remembering
words), difficulty with motor coordination (e.g., problems in copying designs
or figures), and loss of executive functioning or cognitive capacity to plan, organize, and carry out behavior (American Psychiatric Association 2000; Ferry
2001). Dementia-related illnesses impair the client's ability to perform instrumental activities of daily living (IADL) and activities of daily living (ADL),
affecting the client's capacity for self-care and continued community living
(Ferry 2001).

The Short Portable Mental Status Questionnaire is a ten-item test that
screens for the presence and degree of cognitive impairment. It requires about
two minutes to administer. The score is calculated according to the number
of items to which incorrect answers are given. Both omissions and incorrect
answers are counted as errors. Higher scores indicate higher levels of dementia. Scoring is adjusted for level of education and race (Hayslip et al. in press;
Pfeiffer 1975). It can be obtained by contacting Eric Pfeiffer, Director, Suncoast

Gerontology Center, 12901 Bruce B. Downs Blvd., MCD 50, Tampa, Florida 33612-4799. Voice: 813-974-4355, fax: 813-974-4251 (Hayslip et al. in press).

This screening test can be supplemented with observation of the patient's behavior during the interview. Some relevant aspects of the interaction for observation include the patient's ability to follow the conversation and respond to questions, knowledge of the date and names of family members, the ability to remember the worker's name a few minutes after introduction, and perceptions about problems with memory. It is also desirable, with the patient's permission, to obtain the impressions of family members regarding changes in the patient's memory (Raue et al. 2002).

TREATMENT REGIMEN

Familiarity with the treatment regimen required by the illness is an important aspect of formulating a social work assessment, since the complexity, frequency, time, and energy involved has implications for the coping strategies required of patients and their significant others (DeCoster 2001; Rolland 1999). Coping strategies are emotional, behavioral, and cognitive responses made to manage illness-related demands that exceed or tax the resources of the patient and significant others involved in care (Lazarus and Folkman 1984). Relevant questions for home health care assessment are these: What types of knowledge, skills, and lifestyle changes are required to care for the disease? What are the time demands of treatment? Is treatment on a fixed schedule or dictated by the occurrence of symptoms? What are emotional responses to treatment demands? What new or existing coping strategies do clients require in order to master the disease? (Rolland 1999; Sidell 1997). For example, newly diagnosed adult diabetics must master information about diabetic pathology and physiology and learn to recognize symptoms of hypoglycemic (low-glucose) and hyperglycemic (high-glucose) reactions. They also must develop skills and knowledge to monitor glucose levels, oral medications, and insulin; to interact with health care providers; and to maintain a diabetic diet and an appropriate exercise regimen. The requirements of diabetic disease management may make demands on time and energy and contribute to feelings of fear, anxiety, anger, and sadness (DeCoster 2001; Dittbrenner 1997). Individuals who are illiterate, who have limited intellectual capacity, who are unfamiliar with the roles, language, and norms of the health care delivery system, who lack economic resources to buy recommended foods or access to exercise facilities or a safe neighborhood for walking, or who respond with excessive emotion may experience difficulty in coping with treatment regimens. By contrast, the treatment plan for hypertension requires only oral medication and frequent checkups and may make fewer coping demands on the individual and significant others (DeCoster 2001; Rolland 1999).

MEDICATION MANAGEMENT

Medication management is an important component of the treatment regimen that is influenced by psychosocial as well as medication-related factors and therefore should be included in the social work assessment of the individual. It has been estimated that nearly one-third of older home health care patients experience medication errors or problems related to medication use (Meredith et al. 2001).

This discussion will refer to medication management problems using the term *patient adherence*. Patient adherence has been defined as the extent to which a person's behavior, in this instance taking medication, corresponds to agreed-upon recommendations from a health care provider (Heneghan, Glasziou, and Perera 2006). The substitution of the term *adherence* for *compliance* indicates a recognition that a patient-doctor partnership, rather than passive acceptance of the doctor's demands, is a prerequisite for engagement of the patient in treatment (Heneghan, Glasziou, and Perera 2006).

Older home health care patients may be at risk for non-adherence to medication regimens because they use both prescription and nonprescription medication more frequently than other populations, take a median of five different drugs (a little less than 20 percent take more than nine drugs), and are vulnerable, even if relatively cognitively intact, to memory loss severe enough to forget medication schedules (Dyeson, Murphy, and Stryker 1999; Meredith et al. 2001). The consequences of medication non-adherence are increased morbidity, mortality, more frequent contacts with medical providers, and rehospitalization (Flaherty et al. 2000; Happ, Naylor, and Roe-Prior 1997; Hughes 2004). The purpose of a social work assessment of medication management is to identify adherence problems and, in collaboration with the home health care team and the physician, prevent negative client health outcomes and greater consumption of health care resources.

To identify non-adherence the social worker should ask a question that is not confrontational: "I know it must be difficult to take all your medications regularly. How often do you miss taking them?" This approach facilitates honest responses from patients because adherence is framed as a difficult and challenging task (Osterberg and Blaschke 2005:490). The communication to the patient, that failure to achieve adherence is expected for many people, "normalizes" non-adherence.

Questions that can help to identify reasons for client non-adherence to medical regimens include the following (questions regarding medication management that focus on the client's interaction with social systems are addressed in chapter 6):

- Is the patient forgetting to take medications? Patients with memory problems may have difficulty remembering their medication schedules as the number of drugs increases (Meredith et al. 2001; Ryan 1999; Salzman 1995) and/or the dosing regimen becomes more complex (Ryan 1999; Salzman 1995).

- Does the patient communicate concerns, doubts, and misunderstandings about the medication regime to health care providers (e.g., nurses and physicians)? (Belcher et al. 2006; Hughes 2004; Osterberg and Blaschke 2005; Ryan 1999)
- Has the patient experienced adverse drug events and/or side effects that have led to missed doses? (Osterberg and Blaschke 2005; Ryan 1999)
- Do the patient's health beliefs and perceptions of the efficacy of the medication in treating the illness influence medication adherence? Health care beliefs that are culturally based may conflict with the medication recommendations of conventional medicine. This issue may be more relevant for indigenous people with different perspectives (Hughes 2004; Mitchell et al. 2001; Ryan 1999).
- Is the patient depressed? Depression (Carney et al. 1995; Gehi et al. 2005), depressive symptoms (Wang et al. 2002), and depressive symptom severity (Ciechanowski, Katon, and Russo 2000) have been associated with medication non-adherence. Several reasons have been suggested to explain this association. Depressed patients may lack the energy and focus required to implement treatment recommendations. They may have an outlook of hopelessness that negatively influences confidence in the benefits of therapy. Depressed patients may be more sensitive to adverse effects of medication and consequently more likely to discontinue medication. Depression may also compromise the cognitive functioning of patients, resulting in missed doses or failure to reorder medication. Finally, depressed patients may be non-adherent because they are engaging in intentional self-harm (Gehi et al. 2005; Wang et al. 2002). The association between depression and non-adherence suggests that social workers should screen non-adherent patients for depression using the GDS and the open-ended questions presented in this chapter.

PHASE OF THE PATIENT'S ILLNESS

Home health care social workers are most likely to have contact with patients and families during the chronic or terminal phase following the diagnostic period of the crisis phase, which is more likely to occur in a hospital setting.

During the chronic phase, the patient's and family's task in adapting to the illness is to come to terms with the requirements of living with the illness on a daily basis without unduly compromising the autonomy of the individual/significant others (Rolland 1999). Social work assessment at this time focuses on identifying barriers (e.g., lack of financial resources, illiteracy, emotional reactions) and strengths (active coping strategies) for completing the tasks of this phase (DeCoster 2001; Schillinger et al. 2002; Sidell 1997; Taylor and Armor 1996).

During the terminal phase, the task of the family and the patient is to begin to shift their perspective from attempting to control the illness to preparing for death and letting go (Rolland 1999). During this phase social work assessment focuses on the patient's and family's beliefs, values, abilities, and resources that are barriers or strengths in making end-of-life decisions (Ratner, Norlander, and McSteen 2001).

END-OF-LIFE DECISIONS: ADVANCE DIRECTIVES

The Patient Self-Determination Act mandated that hospitals, nursing homes, and home health care agencies receiving Medicare and Medicaid coverage for services develop written policies regarding advance directives. Such institutions are required to ask patients whether they have executed an advance directive and to provide information regarding their right to complete these documents (Naleppa and Reid 2003).

The purpose of an advance directive is to protect an individual's autonomy over medical decisions if the individual is deprived of decision-making capacity in the future (Soskis 1997). Common forms of advance directives are living wills and durable powers of attorney for health care. A living will outlines an individual's choices for specific treatments under certain clinical circumstances if the patient is not competent to make health care decisions. A durable power of attorney for health care provides a legal means for the patient to transfer authority for health care decision making to a specific person if the patient can no longer make decisions. This individual is referred to as a *surrogate decision maker* (Fischer, Arnold, and Tulsky 2000). Advance care planning is a process of planning for future medical care that helps patients identify and clarify their personal values and goals about health and medical treatment (Emanuel, von Gunten, and Ferris 2000; Norlander and McSteen 2000). Advance care planning may result in the completion of an advance directive, but that document is only one component of advance care planning (Ratner, Norlander, and McSteen 2001).

A complicating factor is that each state has individual laws and different advance directive forms (Hobart 2001). Therefore, it is important for the social worker to be familiar with the state statutes and ensure that the client's decisions are addressed within the framework of these statutes (Hobart 2001; Naleppa and Reid 2003; Soskis 1997).

While research suggests that individuals endorse the idea of advance directives, few individuals actually complete them (Dyeson, Murphy, and Stryker

1999; Fagerlin et al. 2002; Hobart 2001). Information on completion rates of directives among home health care patients is scarce. Dyeson, Murphy, and Stryker (1999), in a survey of older home health patients in one state, found that while approximately one-third of the patients had either a living will or a durable health care power of attorney, only 4 percent had completed both documents. Factors associated with non-completion of advance directives include:

- delegation of decision making to family
- a belief that physicians do not understand preferences for life-sustaining treatment
- a view of advance directives as "binding" (Beck et al. 2002)
- a belief that completion of an advance directive would mean deprivation of any treatment at the end of life, including pain control and symptom management (Norlander and McSteen 2000)
- a view that advance care planning is a social process in which they involve family members in a discussion of their wishes but that it is unnecessary to involve medical providers and that the outcome of advance care planning is not the completion of a written advance directive (Singer et al. 1998)

Cultural factors have been found to influence the completion of advance directives. African Americans are less likely to complete advance directives than non-Hispanic whites and Hispanics (Eleazer et al. 1996; Hopp 2000; Hopp and Duffy 2000). African Americans are also more likely to prefer prolonging life unconditionally and less likely to choose to limit care than non-Hispanic whites and Hispanics (Eleazer et al. 1996; Hopp and Duffy 2000). African Americans and Hispanics are also significantly less likely to appoint a health care agent than non-Hispanic whites (Morrison et al. 1998), presumably because of greater opportunities for exposure to education about health care agents among non-Hispanic whites than other ethnic groups (Morrison et al. 1998). However, the explanations for the majority of these findings regarding differences in end-of-life decision making between cultures are not well understood, and future research will be required to provide information for practice.

While it is important to consider variations among groups in beliefs and behaviors related to end-of-life decisions, providers also need to be aware of variations within groups with respect to these attitudes. Information about ethnic differences should not become the only factor that practitioners consider in assessing the preferences of patients for end-of-life care. Instead, such information should stimulate practitioners to attempt to clarify patient and family attitudes toward different care options (Hopp and Duffy 2000).

A significant problem with advance directives is that they have not been found to be effective in communicating the preferences of patients to surrogate decision makers. Patients may complete advance directives without informing their physicians, and therefore the directive may not be not available when it is required (Fischer, Arnold, and Tulsky 2000). There is also evidence that surrogates' (e.g., spouses' and children's) predictions regarding patients' preferences for different end-of-life treatments are no better than chance even when they have discussed and reviewed the advance directive with the patient (Ditto et al. 2001). Physicians also experience difficulty in accurately interpreting patient preferences expressed in advance directives (Covinsky et al. 2000; Fischer, Arnold, and Tulsky 2000).

 ˙ Hypotheses about these problems in implementing advance directives focus on several factors. Advance directives may be too vaguely worded to apply to a specific treatment situation. Research has found that patients' discussion with families about life-sustaining treatment may leave unanswered questions. Patients may indicate they do not want "life support," but patient preferences for specific life-sustaining treatments such as antibiotics, hydration, or dialysis are less likely to be clarified (McDonald et al. 2003). Surrogates who are family members may also have difficulty in identifying the underlying similarity between the treatment scenario in the advance directive and the current health care situation. Family and physician surrogates may unknowingly project their own preferences regarding a patient's decision onto the situation, assuming that the patient shares their opinion. Specifically, family surrogates tend to overestimate the frequency with which the patient would prefer invasive treatment near the end of life, possibly reflecting their own sense of guilt and/or unfinished personal business with the patient (Fagerlin et al. 2002; Haley et al. 2002).

It has been suggested that advance directives might be more successfully implemented by surrogates, and patients might be more willing to discuss these documents, if the completion of advance directives were incorporated as part of a process of advance care planning during which surrogates and patients could gain a deeper mutual understanding of how patient preferences for end-of-life care reflect the values and individuality of the patient (Covinsky et al. 2000; Fischer, Arnold, and Tulsky 2000). This process will be discussed in more detail in chapter 8.

HEALTH BELIEFS

Even when patients and health care providers share similar cultural backgrounds and socioeconomic statuses, their perceptions may differ with respect to the cause of illness, the patient's role in participating in self-care, the experience of the illness, and what should be done about the illness. Greater diversity in cultural and socioeconomic backgrounds between patients and practitioners may be associated with greater discrepancies regarding these perceptions.

Health beliefs constitute the patient's beliefs, concerns, and expectations about his or her illness and the encounter with the health care provider. This conceptualization of the experience of illness is referred to as the client's or patient's *explanatory model* (Carrillo, Green, and Betancourt 1999; Hall, Stone, and Fiset 1998). Patients' explanatory models are influenced to a great extent by culture, education, and socioeconomic status (Carrillo, Green, and Betancourt 1999). An example of an explanatory model influenced by cultural belief documented among Mexican Americans is the view that the cause of type 2 diabetes (and other diseases) is *susto*, or a specific traumatizing event that changes the body's condition, causing a vulnerable person to be more susceptible to disease (Poss and Jezewski 2002). Treatments include herbal remedies.

Health care providers may have their own explanatory model—the medical model, derived from Western science and Western medicine (Hall, Stone, and Fiset 1998). The provider who does not recognize that he or she brings an explanatory model to the encounter with the client or patient may display ethnocentric behavior by dismissing the patient's views as inferior and regarding his or her own views as correct (Hall, Stone, and Fiset 1998). When health care providers interact with patients in this way, patients/families may feel "misunderstood" (Rolland 1998:10), potentially leading to their withdrawal from collaboration with providers. Because of the power differential favoring providers, this reaction is often viewed as noncompliance on the part of the patient/family when in fact it may be a manifestation of a breakdown in communication (Rolland 1998).

It is therefore important to elicit the patient's explanatory model and compare that model to the health care beliefs of providers to ensure accurate, respectful communication and the formation of an alliance. Several questions that may be useful in assessing health beliefs of patients/significant others are:

- What do you think has caused the problem? What do you call it?
- Why do you think it started when it did?
- How does it affect your life?
- How severe is it? What worries you the most?
- What kind of treatment do you think will work?
- How can I be most helpful to you?
- What is most important for you? (Carrillo, Green, and Betancourt 1999)

Patients may initially be reluctant to discuss their health beliefs because they anticipate a negative reaction from the worker. The social worker can address this issue by taking the focus off the client through techniques such as posing a question as a hypothetical situation or by asking what others believe (Carrillo, Green, and Betancourt 1999). Communicating a respectful, nonjudgmental, and supportive stance is also likely to elicit information.

Different explanatory models may influence clients to adopt the treatments and practices of "complementary and alternative medicine" (CAM). The Institute of Medicine defines CAM as "a broad domain of resources that encompasses health systems, modalities and practices and their accompanying theories and beliefs, other than those intrinsic to the dominant health system of a particular society or culture in a given historical period" (Institute of Medicine 2005:19). The definition goes on to state that these resources are perceived by those who use them as being associated with positive health outcomes. However, the separation between CAM and the dominant health care system is not always clearly fixed. An example of this last point might be the use of vitamin supplements to promote health or reduce the risk of disease. Examples of complementary and alternative health care practices are the use of herbal products, minerals, specialized diets, chiropractic manipulation, massage therapy, meditation, prayer, and alternative medical systems based on theories and practices separate from conventional medicine (Institute of Medicine 2005).

Approximately one-third of adults in the United States use complementary and alternative medicine. Women use CAM more than men do, and educated individuals use CAM more than poorly educated individuals use it. At least one-third of people age 65 or older use CAM. The practices most commonly used by older adults are chiropractic, herbal and dietary supplements, relaxation and meditation techniques, and high-dose vitamins (Institute of Medicine 2005).

While CAM use is common among people in all ethnic groups, use patterns vary by ethnicity. For example, prayer is more prevalent among African Americans than among non-Hispanic white or Asian adults, while non-Hispanic white adults are more likely than other groups to use manipulative body-based therapies such as massage and chiropractic treatment. However, Asians are more likely to use CAM (excluding vitamin therapy and prayer) than non-Hispanic whites or African Americans (Institute of Medicine 2005).

It has been hypothesized that surveys of CAM practices are underestimated in minority cultures because these practices (for example, consumption of herbs and spices for medicinal purposes) are institutionalized in everyday routines so they are not regarded as unusual or worthy of reporting. A similar pattern may apply to religious-spiritual practices that may be everyday ways of coping with adversity and reported only in extraordinary situations. In other words, it is difficult to identify what members of minority cultures classify as CAM practices and what individuals who are not members of those cultures label as CAM practices. Inclusion of a greater number of culturally sensitive questions in larger surveys with representative samples may be more effective in determining the prevalence and pattern of CAM practices among minority populations (Institute of Medicine 2005).

The majority of adults, including older adults, who use CAM do not disclose their use of CAM to their medical providers (Institute of Medicine 2005). Reasons given for non-disclosure are that:

- it is not important for the doctor to know
- it is not the doctor's business
- the doctor would not understand (Institute of Medicine 2005:19)

However, patients generally combine CAM practices with conventional medicine. For problems like aches, pains, and headaches patients believe that CAM is more effective than conventional medicine, while they regard conventional medicine as more effective than CAM for the management of disease. The majority of CAM users therefore value both CAM and conventional medicine. They avoid disclosure not only because they anticipate that their physician would disapprove but also because they do not believe the physician will integrate CAM practices with conventional medicine (Institute of Medicine 2005).

The problem of lack of disclosure raises safety issues, since there is the possibility of an interaction between medications and some of the herbs or vitamins used as part of CAM practices. There is also little empirical evidence of the safety or effectiveness of these treatments.

From a social work perspective, it is important to elicit information about clients' use of CAM in order to understand their ideas about effective treatment and how these ideas influence adherence to the medical plan. The social worker may also wish to determine whether the patient has disclosed use of CAM practices to medical providers and if not, why not. It is important to obtain and share this information (with the patient's consent) with other members of the health care team, given the fact that patients are unlikely to discuss these practices with medical providers (Institute of Medicine 2005).

Suggested questions for obtaining information about CAM practices are:

- Have you seen anyone else for this problem besides a physician?
- Have you used remedies or treatments for your problem other than those suggested by your physician/nurse?
- Who advises you about your health?
- Have you told your physician/nurse about your use of these remedies? (Carrillo, Green, and Betancourt 1999)

SELF-EFFICACY

The concept *perceived self-efficacy* refers to "beliefs in one's capabilities to organize and execute the courses of action required to produce given attainments" (Bandura 1997:3). Self-efficacy contributes to enhanced motivation, perseverance, and better decision making in the management of chronic illness (Bandura 1997; Lorig and Holman 2003). Beliefs in personal efficacy influence the challenges that individuals will undertake, how much effort they put into a task, and how long they persevere despite obstacles. Self-efficacy motivates people to try to attain their goals. When they are faced with failure, belief in their own capability spurs them to redouble their efforts and to persist. Such strong perseverance usually results in accomplishment of goals and objectives. Bandura (1997) suggested that self-efficacy mediates health behavior because individuals require a belief that they can master and persevere with healthy habits to devote the necessary energy to succeed.

Consistent with these assumptions, interventions that enhance self-efficacy have been related to improved health status among individuals with chronic disease (Bandura 1997; Lev et al. 2001; Lorig and Holman 2003). Improved self-efficacy in several randomized controlled trials of a chronic disease self-management program that sampled older adults with comorbid chronic disease was also associated with reduced health care use and costs (Leveille, Wagner, and Davis 1998; Lorig, Ritter, and Gonzalez 2003; Lorig et al. 2001). In the one study implemented in home health care, a significant improvement in patient diabetes management self-efficacy was found after at least two nursing visits for patients with low to moderate levels of diabetes self-efficacy at baseline (Corbett 1999).

The six-item Self-Efficacy Scale (Stanford Patient Education Research Center 2005), which has a reliability of .91, measures self-efficacy related to management of fatigue, pain, emotional distress, disease-related tasks, everyday activities, and other health problems. A higher score indicates a higher level of self-efficacy. This instrument, available in the public domain, can be obtained by going to the Stanford Education Research Center Web site, www.patient-education.stanford.edu.

DEPRESSION

MAJOR DEPRESSION, DYSTHYMIA, AND SUBSYNDROMAL DEPRESSION

Major depression is a syndrome that evidences symptoms of depressed mood, loss of interest or pleasure in almost all activities, changes in appetite or weight, disturbed sleep, slowed or restless movements, fatigue, loss of energy, feelings of worthlessness or excessive guilt, trouble in thinking, concentrating, or making decisions, and recurrent thoughts of death or suicide. A diagnosis of major depression requires at least five symptoms to be present most days for at least two weeks, with at least one of the first two symptoms listed above (American Psychiatric Association 2000).

Dysthymia is characterized by a chronically depressed mood that occurs most of the day most days for at least two years. During periods of depressed mood at least two of the following additional symptoms are present: disturbances in appetite, disturbances in sleep, low energy, low self-esteem, poor concentration, difficulty making decisions, and feelings of hopelessness. The symptoms must cause clinically significant distress or impairment in social roles (American Psychiatric Association 2000).

Subsyndromal depression is characterized by depressive symptoms that are identical to those of major depression but involve fewer symptoms and less impairment. An episode involves a sad or "depressed mood" or loss of interest or pleasure in nearly all activities. Subsyndromal depression is defined as the presence of at least two but fewer than five depressive symptoms with sad or depressed mood for a period of at least two weeks. Symptoms cause clinically significant distress in the performance of social roles (American Psychiatric Association 2000). These individuals would be given a diagnosis of adjustment disorder with depressed mood if the depressive symptoms occur in response to psychosocial stressors such as acute or chronic illness. Otherwise the diagnosis would be depressive disorder not otherwise specified (American Psychiatric Association 2000).

PREVALENCE, SYMPTOM RECOGNITION, AND SCREENING

Clients admitted to home care may have a primary admitting diagnosis of major depression (only 2 percent of patients receiving Medicare-reimbursed home care in 1997 had a primary diagnosis of a psychiatric disability) or a primary admitting diagnosis of medical illness but also suffer from major depression (Bruce 2002). In the former case, the patient has been discharged to home care after inpatient psychiatric treatment, and the primary need is for psychiatric nursing care. In the latter case, the patient is referred to home care for skilled care (e.g., nursing, physical or occupational therapy) and is admitted without a psychiatric diagnosis, but subsequent behaviors suggest that an assessment for depression is indicated. Patients with a primary medical diagnosis and a secondary diagnosis of a psychiatric disorder are the most common types of psychiatric patients seen in home care (Byrne 1999).

A patient whose primary diagnosis is a psychiatric diagnosis and who is admitted to home care from an inpatient psychiatric facility without a medical diagnosis is defined by Health Care Financing Administration (HFCA) regulations as the primary responsibility of the psychiatric home care nurse (Abel-Vacula and Phillips 2004; Byrne 1999). The patient served by a psychiatric home care program must have a psychiatric diagnosis, be under the care of a physician who supervises the plan of care, require the skilled services of a psychiatric nurse, and be homebound. A patient with a primary medical diagnosis and a secondary diagnosis of subsyndromal depression would be automatically assigned to a social worker (Byrne 1999).

The following discussion primarily describes the social work role in assessment and screening of home health care patients with a primary admitting diagnosis of a medical illness and a subsequent diagnosis of major depression, dysthymia, or subsyndromal depression.

Little is known about the prevalence of depression in home health care populations. In one study based on a random sample of patients admitted from a medical setting to a home care agency, 13.5 percent were diagnosed with major depression (Bruce et al. 2002). A prevalence of major depression among 7 percent of elderly clients in a primary-care setting has been reported, suggesting that major depression may be more common among elderly home care clients (Lyness et al. 1999). There are no estimates of dysthymia or subsyndromal depression among elderly home care clients; among the community-based elderly, however, estimates of subsyndromal depression are between 13 percent and 27 percent (Lebowitz et al. 1997).

Chronic illnesses such as stroke, heart disease, cancer, and rheumatoid arthritis (common admitting diagnoses to home care) are frequently associated with depression (American Psychiatric Association 2000; Mulsant and Ganguli 1999). Depression among chronically ill patients has been shown to decrease adherence to treatment regimens and rehabilitation programs and to increase functional impairment, cognitive impairment, morbidity, mortality, and the use of health care resources (DiMatteo, Lepper, and Croghan 2000; Fifield et al. 1998; King 1997; Lebowitz et al. 1997; Lustman et al. 2000).

While depression can be successfully treated among older adults (Bartels et al. 2002; Unützer et al. 1999), patients admitted to home care with medical illnesses as their primary diagnosis may be under-diagnosed for depression by home care nurse case managers (Brown et al. 2003; Bruce et al. 2002). This underrecognition is a barrier to effective treatment for patients.

It may be, however, that the environment of home care presents challenges to identifying depression. Physicians are unlikely to have an opportunity to directly assess home care patients. Nurse case managers, who are responsible for the initial patient assessment, may not have the formal training needed to accurately identify depression (Brown et al. 2003; Brown et al. 2004). In particular, nurse case managers may fail to detect anhedonia, or the loss of the ability to express pleasure, which is a primary symptom of depression in the elderly (Brown et al. 2004). The nurse case manager who does not recognize depression will not make the appropriate referrals to psychiatric nurses, social workers, other mental health providers, and physicians, thus depriving patients of access to treatment and preventive services (Brown et al. 2003).

A potential solution to this dilemma might be for agency social workers to offer consultation/training to nurse case managers regarding accurate identification of psychological and somatic symptoms of patients whose depression is related to a medical condition. This training could be provided both formally in team meetings and informally on a case-by-case basis. Alternatively, social workers who receive a referral from a case manager to assess eligibility for and coordinate services can screen patients for depression when appropriate psychological and somatic symptoms are present and the patient has a medical condition.

In deciding whether to screen a patient admitted with a primary diagnosis of medical illness for depression, it is important to be aware of the difference in the presentation of symptoms of depression among older adults as compared with younger adults. Older adults may not describe themselves as experiencing a depressed mood or use the word *depression*. They may perceive the label as stigmatizing and may not want to "bother" health care providers with their emotions and "distract" them from the "real" physical problem (Gallo et al. 2003). Anxiety and somatic complaints (atypical pain, sleep disturbance, apathy, fatigue) without sadness have been observed in elderly depressed patients (Gallo et al. 2003; Kennedy, Polivka, and Steel 1997). Memory difficulties may also be a symptom of depression among the elderly. Once depression is successfully treated, memory problems resolve themselves. In some individuals, particularly the elderly, however, major depression may coexist with dementia (American Psychiatric Association 2000).

A tendency to acknowledge somatic complaints but not feelings of sadness may also be more typical of the presentation of depression in cultures in which somatic illness is more socially accepted than mental illness (Szanto et al. 2002).

While research on the specific situation of depressed home care patients is rare, Dyeson (2000) found that "burden self-image" (perception of self as a burden to the caregiver) was the largest contributor to the variance in depressive symptoms among older adult home care clients as assessed by the Geriatric Depression Rating Scale. A negative appraisal of the caregiver was identified as the largest contributing factor (Dyeson 2000), suggesting that the perception by the care recipient of a strained relationship with the caregiver may contribute indirectly to depressive symptoms.

A recommended approach to interviewing elderly home care clients who may be reluctant to acknowledge feelings of emotional distress is to begin the interview by making a statement that universalizes negative feelings. For example, "it is not unusual for people who use home health care services to go through a period of adjustment that is distressing" (Raue, Brown, and Bruce 2002:156). This may be followed by open-ended questions about specific symptoms and follow-up questions for clarification. If patients deny feeling distressed but display contradictory behavior, such as tear-filled eyes, the worker should gently share this observation to obtain clarification with the client: "I noticed you became somewhat upset when we spoke about being unable to do the things you used to do. How much has this been on your mind? Have you been feelings sad about that?" (Raue, Brown, and Bruce 2002:156).

In screening home care clients with a primary diagnosis of medical illness for depression, the worker can use a depression screening scale. The Geriatric Depression Scale is a self-report instrument that can be administered in ten to fifteen minutes (long form) or five to seven minutes (short form) and is recommended by the Institute of Medicine for clinical use with geriatric patients (Yesavage et al. 1983). To obtain a copy, contact Jerome A. Yesavage, Stanford University School of Medicine, Stanford, California 94305-5538. Voice: 650-852-3287, fax: 650-852-3297. Web site: www.stanford.edu/~yesavage/GDS.html (cost: none) (Hayslip et al. in press).

If the screen is positive for depression, some recommended follow-up questions (questions should be asked for a time frame within the last couple of weeks) are the following:

- Have you been feeling blue, sad, or down in the dumps?
- Have you lost interest in activities that you previously enjoyed?
- How well are you sleeping?
- How well are you eating?
- How is your energy level?
- Have you been critical of yourself, feeling you have let yourself or others down?
- Have you had trouble concentrating or making decisions?
- Do you feel hopeless or that things won't improve?
- Have you thought life was not worth living or you would be better off dead?
- Have you had thoughts of suicide?
- Have you done anything to hurt yourself?
- Are you using alcohol, sedatives, or tranquilizers?
- Do you feel your caregiver would be better off if he/she were not caring for you?
- Do you ask for help from your caregiver when you need it? (Dyeson 2000; Gallo et al. 2003; Raue, Brown, and Bruce 2002)

It may be advisable, with the client's consent, to also interview the caregiver/ family, since the reporting of symptoms by depressed clients can be compromised by problems in concentration, memory loss, and a tendency to discount, deny, or rationalize symptoms (American Psychiatric Association 2000). However, families should be regarded as more than simply resources for information.

The elderly person who is depressed needs familiar surroundings and care from those to whom the individual feels close. Family members in home health care may be involved in meeting the patient's emotional needs as well as managing medications and troublesome behavior. In providing this care, the family generally relies on help from the natural support system (family, friends, and neighbors) as well as from professional caregivers. Therefore, it is important to assess whether the home care client with possible medical and psychiatric comorbidities has access to adequate family support and whether the family, in turn, has access to informal and formal support (Farran et al. 1998).

To rule out physiological causes and/or medication reactions, and to initiate a full assessment of the client, the worker should refer the client to the primary-care physician and the psychiatric nurse. A psychiatric examination and a medical examination are required to make a differential diagnosis and to develop a treatment plan.

SUICIDE RISK SCREENING AND ASSESSMENT

Medical illnesses that are associated with pain, disfigurement, dependency on others, and restricted functioning can impair the will to live. A comprehensive review of the literature found that specific illnesses, including cancer, HIV/AIDS, Huntington's disease, multiple sclerosis, peptic ulcer, renal disease, spinal cord injury, and systemic lupus erythematosus increased the risk for completed suicide. The authors suggest that these illnesses are associated with mental disorders such as mood disorders, substance abuse, or both, and it may be these factors that explain the connection between the diseases and suicide (Harris and Barraclough 1994).

High-risk indicators of suicide in individuals with a physical illness are:

- a diagnosis of major depression
- past suicide attempts
- social isolation
- alcoholism
- psychosis
- life crises (e.g., financial stress, loss and grief)

- male gender (Kishi, Robinson, and Kosier 2001; Krach 1995; Salvatore 2000; Yeates et al. 2000)

Older adults in particular have a high suicide success rate. They are less likely than younger individuals to communicate their intent, more likely to take precautions against discovery, and more likely to use highly lethal methods. In addition to overt suicide attempts, the elderly may also engage in self-destructive behavior that leads to premature death, such as medical noncompliance, medication overdoses, self-starvation, dehydration, and accidents (Salvatore 2000; Szanto et al. 2002).

In interviewing clients for suicidal intent social workers should ask the following questions:

- In the past few weeks how have you been feeling about the future?
- Have you had any thoughts of hopelessness or feelings that things won't improve?
- In the past couple of weeks have things ever been so bad that you thought life was not worth living?
- In the past couple of weeks have you thought of committing suicide?
- Have you ever done anything in the past to hurt yourself? (Rauc, Brown, and Bruce 2002:158)

The social worker should then ask more-specific questions about plans and access to lethal methods. Any available firearms should be removed from the house, as they are associated with a high rate of successful suicides. If an elderly patient denies suicidal ideation but the social worker suspects suicide risk, the worker should interview family members or friends about whether the patient has given any warning or clues, such a making a will or giving away property (Szanto et al. 2002).

If a patient reports any degree of suicidality, it is important to empathize with the expression of feeling, communicate concern for his or her safety, and help to instill hope by conveying that effective treatment is available to help him or her to feel better (Raue, Brown, and Bruce 2002).

The assessment of suicide risk should also include an assessment of other risk factors, such as physical health diagnosis associated with suicidal completion (see above), psychosis, major depression, substance abuse, treatment noncompliance, past suicide attempts, lack of social support, and recent stressful life events (Szanto et al. 2002).

Elderly clients may require a more indirect approach to assessment, since they grew up in a period when suicide had criminal implications and was a highly stigmatized behavior. It may be helpful in assessing suicide risk among the elderly to depersonalize the subject by asking more philosophical questions, such as the following:

- Under what conditions do you think a person has a right to take his or her life?
- What are your opinions about the present interest in euthanasia?
- Do you think suicide is a sign or strength or weakness?
- Have you ever believed you would be better off dead? (Krach 1995:63)

ANXIETY

ANXIETY PREVALENCE AND SYMPTOM RECOGNITION

·Kennedy, Polivka, and Steel (1997) identified anxiety as the second most frequently reported psychiatric symptom in a sample of home health care patients. Anxiety is the most frequently reported psychiatric problem among older adults, affecting 20 percent of the community-residing population (Gellis 2006). Anxiety is frequently comorbid with depression in older adults, suggesting that symptoms of anxiety should also be assessed when patients display symptoms of depression. Among the home health care sample cited above, half of the patients with anxiety symptoms also had symptoms of depression (Kennedy, Polivka, and Steel 1997). The same HFCA regulations for case assignment of patients admitted to home care with a primary diagnosis of depression would be applied to patients admitted to home care with a primary admitting diagnosis of anxiety. Patients with a primary admitting diagnosis of anxiety would be assigned to a psychiatric nurse, while patients with a primary admitting diagnosis of a medical illness and a secondary diagnosis of anxiety would become social work clients (Byrne 1999).

Whether an anxious patient requires further screening and assessment can be determined by the amount of distress experienced as a result of anxiety and the extent to which anxiety interferes with the patient's life. Sleep deprivation resulting from constant worry, fears that are not based in reality that prevent the patient from leaving the house when he or she is physically able to do so, or restlessness and distractibility that interfere with learning self-care may be considered indicators of clinically significant anxiety.

Some preliminary questions to determine whether screening for anxiety is necessary are:

- Have you been feeling particularly nervous or anxious lately?
- Do you often worry about unimportant things? How often? (Raue et al. 2002)

Symptoms of anxiety in older home care clients may indicate several types of anxiety disorders, such as agoraphobia, panic disorder, or generalized anxiety disorder. Agoraphobia is diagnosed when there is anxiety about being in places and situations from which escape is difficult or in which help might not be available in the event of a panic attack. The anxiety leads to avoidance of situations such as being alone outside the home, being home alone, or being in a crowd of people. Panic disorder is a discrete event in which there is a sudden experience of intense apprehension, fearfulness, or terror, often associated with feelings of imminent doom. These attacks include symptoms such as shortness of breath, heart palpitations, chest pain, a choking sensation, or a fear of going crazy or dying. Individuals may become excessively apprehensive about the consequences of everyday activities and experiences, in particular those related to health (e.g., thinking a headache is a symptom of a brain tumor or a stroke). As attacks become more frequent and severe, concerns about the next attack may be associated with avoidant behavior that meets the criteria for agoraphobia. Generalized anxiety may be present when the individual experiences excessive anxiety and worry occurring more days than not for a period of at least six months. The anxiety and worry are combined with at least three additional symptoms such as restlessness, fatigue, difficulty concentrating, irritability, and muscle tension. Among older adults anxiety may be focused on health-related issues (e.g., worry that a headache is a symptom of a brain tumor). Sub-threshold anxiety disorders include disorders with severe anxiety or phobic avoidance that do not meet the criteria for any specific anxiety disorder, adjustment disorder with anxiety, or adjustment disorder with mixed anxiety and mood (American Psychological Association 2000).

Anxiety disorders may aggravate existing physical conditions by exaggerating the natural response of worry and concern experienced in relation to a chronic physical illness and by interfering with the individual's ability to perform daily activities and to learn self-care routines (Busch 1996; Raue et al. 2002). Individuals who are more anxious may also experience a more complicated physical course if they self-medicate by using drugs or alcohol (Busch 1996).

SCREENING FOR ANXIETY

Few instruments have been developed to screen anxiety among older people, and the instruments that are available are of limited value in practice (Carmin, Pollard, and Gillock 1999). Despite these limitations, these instruments do provide the home health social worker with some information on the severity, frequency, and type of anxiety a client experiences. When combined with a comprehensive physical and psychosocial evaluation completed by collaborating providers, this information can contribute to a thorough assessment of client anxiety.

The Beck Anxiety Inventory (Beck et al. 1988), which takes only five minutes to complete, is a 21-item self-report instrument that distinguishes common cognitive and somatic anxiety symptoms from depression. It has good psychometric properties with older adults (Carmin, Pollard, and Gillock 1999). No geriatric norms for the test are available, and it should be used cautiously until further normative data become available (Carmin, Pollard, and Gillock 1999). It is copyrighted and can be purchased for $1.42 per scaling sheet (Halverson and Chan 2004) from the Psychological Corporation at http://hartcourtassessment. com. If these screens are positive, the social worker should consult with the primary-care physician and the psychiatric nurse to complete a comprehensive assessment and develop a treatment plan.

SUBSTANCE MISUSE

ALCOHOL PROBLEMS

PREVALENCE AND SYMPTOM RECOGNITION

Prevalence estimates of problem drinking in older adults in the community range from one percent to 15 percent (Blow 1998). This wide variation results from differences in definitions of alcohol problems and the methodologies used to obtain samples. Estimates of the prevalence of alcohol problems are higher in health care settings. Between 6 percent and 20 percent of hospitalized patients have been classified as alcohol abusers (Council on Scientific Affairs, American Medical Association 1996). Higher rates of alcohol problems among health care clients reflect the adverse consequences of alcohol use, which include an increased risk of the onset of illness/disability and the exacerbation of already existing illness/disability. The prevalence of alcoholism among the home health care population is unknown. Though estimates may appear to be low, problems related to the interaction of alcohol with over-the-counter and prescription drugs are the most frequent substance abuse problems among older adults (Levin, Kruger, and Blow 2004).

The elderly are at risk for adverse consequences with even small amounts of alcohol because the physical effects of alcohol have a greater impact on older adults than on young adults. Age-related physiological changes, resulting in higher blood alcohol levels, increased nervous system sensitivity to alcohol, the interaction of alcohol with chronic medical conditions, and the interaction of alcohol with over-the-counter and prescription drugs are all potential contributing factors to intoxication in older adults even when only a small amount of alcohol is consumed (Levin, Kruger, and Blow 2004).

Some agreement about terminology is important in discussing alcohol problems in older adults. *DSM-IV* criteria were developed for younger adults and may not be as relevant to older adults (Hanson and Gutheil 2004). The majority of older adults who experience problem drinking do not meet *DSM-IV* criteria for alcohol abuse or dependence, but those criteria are less likely to apply to older adult alcohol users because consumption and frequency levels that apply to younger adults are not as appropriate to older adults, for whom less alcohol is likely to result in impairment (Blow 1998; Blow and Barry 2002; Hanson and Gutheil 2004).

These changes in how alcohol is processed in the bodies of older adults led the National Institute on Alcohol Abuse and Alcoholism to develop different drinking guidelines for older adults, as follows:

- one drink/day for older men (age 65 and older)
- less than one drink/day for older women (age 65 and older) (Barry, Oslin, and Blow 2001; Blow 1998)

To put this information in context, compare the guidelines for younger adult males (under age 65), which are two drinks a day, and for younger adult females, which are no more than one drink a day.

A standard drink is defined as:

- 12 ounces of beer or ale
- 1.5 ounces of spirits (whiskey, gin, vodka)
- 5 ounces of table wine
- 4 ounces of sherry
- 4 ounces of liqueur (Barry, Oslin, and Blow 2001; Blow 1998)

Older adult binge drinking is considered to be two to three drinks in one day (Blow 1998). Differences in how alcohol affects the elderly have also contributed to the development of a separate classification system of patterns of alcohol use for older adults. The following definitions are drinking guidelines for older adults:

- Abstinence: no alcohol use for past year. Approximately 60–70 percent of older adults are abstinent.
- Low-risk drinking: staying within drinking guidelines; setting reasonable limits on drinking, not driving and drinking, not mixing medication and alcohol. Estimates are that 20 percent of the older population are low-risk drinkers.
- At-risk drinking: drinking that exceeds drinking guidelines, drinking that creates hazardous situations (for example, drinking when driving or taking medications). This kind of drinking increases the chance that individuals will develop future social, psychological, and physical problems, though they do not currently manifest such problems.

- Problem drinking: exceeding the drinking guidelines and having problems such as exacerbation or triggering of chronic or acute medical conditions, financial difficulties, relationship conflicts, and depression or anxiety. Approximately 10 percent of the older population are at-risk or problem drinkers.
- Alcohol dependence: a medical disorder characterized by loss of control over drinking, preoccupation with alcohol, and continued use despite adverse consequences. Individuals who have developed alcohol dependence display symptoms of tolerance and withdrawal. Five percent of the older population are alcohol dependent (Barry and Blow 1999; Barry, Oslin, and Blow 2001; Begun 2005)

The majority of older adults are not problem drinkers. However, the consequences of even moderate alcohol consumption can put the older individual at risk for medical and psychological problems. At-risk and problem drinking can increase the likelihood of strokes from internal bleeding, breast cancer, impaired driving, sleep disturbance, adverse medication reactions, falls, and fractures. Excessive consumption (e.g., more than four drinks a day or alcohol dependence) is associated with COPD, liver disease, anxiety, depression, suicide, and cognitive impairment (Barry, Oslin, and Blow 2001; Levin, Kruger, and Blow 2004). Social workers should keep these comorbidities in mind when screening an older adult for alcohol problems, though the direction of causality is not clear (Begun 2005).

Several barriers interfere with recognition of alcohol problems among older adults. Ageism, or the tendency to stereotype older adults and attribute their problems to old age, can mask professional and family recognition of a problem. Lack of awareness of the symptoms of alcohol problems by older adults, their families, and the community, and the stigma associated with alcohol consumption among the elderly may also represent barriers. Because of a low index of suspicion and difficulty in applying the DSM-IV diagnostic criteria to older adults, health care providers may not identify alcohol problems in an older adult. Other chronic physical and mental health problems may obscure recognition of alcohol problems in older adults by health care providers and family.

Specific vulnerable populations such as women, minorities, and the homebound may experience barriers to identification and treatment. Women live longer than men and they live alone longer, contributing to barriers to detection of problems. Women are more susceptible to the effects of alcohol because of age-related changes in body composition. They are also more likely to receive prescriptions for psychoactive medications that interact with alcohol and to use these medications for a longer period of time than men. However, stereotypes of older women are that they do not drink. The vulnerability of women to alcohol problems because of the factors outlined above suggests that it would be desirable to screen women for alcohol problems (Blow and Barry 2002; Levin, Kruger, and Blow 2004).

Ethnic minorities who are new immigrants may confront language barriers and ignorance on the part of the health care provider regarding their belief systems that block effective communication and access to acceptable care. African Americans and Hispanics are also less likely than other groups to seek specialized alcohol treatment (Barry and Blow 1999; Levin, Kruger, and Blow 2004).

Though the homebound elderly may experience chronic health problems that interact with alcohol, they may also be isolated, thus blocking detection of their alcohol problems by professionals or neighbors (Levin, Kruger, and Blow 2004).

MEDICATION PROBLEMS

PREVALENCE AND SYMPTOM RECOGNITION

Adults age 65 and older consume a larger quantity of prescribed and over-the-counter medications than any other age group in the United States (Blow 1998). A substantial proportion of the medications prescribed for older adults are psychoactive (mood-changing) medications that have the potential for abuse, misuse, or dependency (Blow 1998). As is true with respect to alcohol, changes in the physiology of the elderly place them at risk for adverse drug reactions; elderly individuals are more sensitive than younger individuals to psychoactive drugs, even in lower doses (Monane and Avorn 1996). Estimates of the use of psychoactive medications suggest that approximately one-fourth of the community-dwelling elderly use psychoactive drugs on a regular basis (Finlayson 1997). Information about the prevalence of use of psychoactive medications in elderly home health care patients is limited. In a sample of patients in two urban home health care agencies, benzodiazepines (for treatment of insomnia and anxiety) were used by 10 percent of the respondents, antipsychotics (for management of problem behavior among dementia patients) by 5 percent, and tricyclic antidepressants (for management of mood disorders) by 4 percent (Meredith et al. 2001).

Adverse consequences related to the use of psychoactive medication may occur for a variety of reasons. While elderly individuals rarely use psychoactive drugs nontherapeutically, unintentional misuse may occur if the patient does not understand the directions for proper use, a problem that has more-serious consequences when multiple medications are prescribed (Blow 1998). For any prescription drug, increased medication monitoring may be needed for patients with impaired cognition (Gray, Mahoney, and Blough 2001). A contributing factor to the development of drug dependence is a pattern of physicians' prescribing psychoactive medication for an extended period of time without adequate monitoring (Gallo et al. 2003). For example, benzodiazepine use for longer than four months is a cause for concern (Blow 1998). Meredith and colleagues defined possible errors in prescribing psychotropic medications for older home health care patients as use of benzodiazepines or other psychotropic medications "with signs of confusion or a fall in the past three months" (2001:720). Benzodiazepines were the most frequently implicated class of psychotropic drugs in medication errors (Meredith et al. 2001). Tolerance and physical dependence on drugs such as benzodiazepines and opioids (used to treat pain) may develop rapidly even when these drugs are taken therapeutically (Blow 1998; Finlayson 1997). Unintentional misuse can progress into abuse if an older adult continues to take a medication for the "high" it produces, in the same way that abuse of any drug occurs (Blow 1998).

Confusion and falls are adverse effects of the use of psychoactive medications among the elderly. Patients using multiple psychotropic medications are at greatest risk for falls (Leipzig, Cumming, and Tinetti 1999; Weiner, Hanlon, and Studenski 1998). Because anxiety and insomnia are symptoms of depression, primary-care physicians might prescribe benzodiazepines to treat those symptoms when what is actually indicated would be an antidepressant, the appropriate medication for treating depression. Long-term use of benzodiazepines may produce or complicate the symptoms of depression (Fingerhood 2000; Finlayson 1997).

Use of more than one drug or use of a drug in combination with a psychoactive medication can have adverse consequences. Interaction between opiates and alcohol can enhance the sedative effects of each substance, leading to a risk of death from overdose. Use of alcohol in combination with tricyclic antidepressants can increase levels of depression. High doses of benzodiazepines used with alcohol can also be lethal (Blow 1998; National Institute on Alcohol Abuse and Alcoholism 1995).

SCREENING FOR SUBSTANCE MISUSE

Prevention and early intervention depend on effective screening (Barry and Blow 1999). The following discussion focuses primarily on screening for alcohol problems, since alcohol is the drug most frequently used by older adults and because prescription and over-the-counter medications are most dangerous to the health of older adults when they interact with alcohol. The goals of screening are to identify at-risk, problem, and dependent drinkers and to make a decision about further assessment and treatment (Blow and Barry 2002).

- Every individual over age 60 should be screened by a medical provider as part of the individual's regular physical examination.
- Rescreening by non-medical providers, including social workers, should be triggered if physical symptoms are present, such as frequent falls, injuries the individual does not remember, slurred speech, lack of coordination, tremors, sleep

complaints, cognitive impairment, incontinence, self-neglect, malnutrition, altered mood, depression, suicide, anxiety, agitation, liver function abnormalities, and/or gastrointestinal distress.

■ Older adults who are experiencing significant life transitions, such as being widowed, or assuming stressful roles, such as that of caregiver, may be particularly vulnerable to alcohol problems and/or misuse of prescription drugs (Blow, Brockman, and Barry 2004; Levin, Kruger, and Blow 2004).

In asking screening questions, the provider should communicate a nonjudgmental attitude because older adults are sensitive to the stigma of drug abuse and generally respond negatively to a psychological as opposed to a medical explanation for their problem. Introducing questions by linking alcohol with a medical condition is likely to elicit more cooperation from the respondent than framing it as a component of a psychological problem (e.g., "Your nutritional problems are not improving in response to the treatment. I wonder if your use of alcohol is hindering your recovery") (Blow 1998; Levin, Kruger, and Blow 2004). Workers should avoid the use of words like *alcoholic* or *drug abuser* during these discussions so that the client does not feel "labeled." Use of active-listening techniques to monitor patient reactions can be helpful in detecting underreporting. Patients may be concealing information if they display such nonverbal behavior as blushing, looking away, or looking at the floor (Blow 1998; Levin, Kruger, and Blow 2004).

Before the provider asks screening questions, she or he should ensure that the older adult understands both the concept of confidentiality and any limits to confidentiality. The purpose of the questions and the questions themselves should also be clear and understandable. The older adult should understand the definition of a standard drink. The phrasing of the questions should normalize drinking and medication use; for example, "I always ask people about their use of alcohol and prescription drugs because it is important to talk about all aspects of life. Alcohol and medication use are particularly important issues for someone with malnutrition such as yourself because misuse of these substances may influence how well you respond to treatment and whether you feel better" (Hanson and Gutheil 2004:369).

Alternatively, screening questions used by social workers can be embedded in a series of inquiries about the social aspects of health-related issues (e.g., "Do you have any problems with preparing meals or getting prescriptions filled?"). The worker may wish to introduce the question by saying, "Alcohol can affect many areas of health and even influence how your medications affect you. It is important for me to know whether you use alcohol so that you have a better chance of feeling better as soon as possible" (Blow 1998). The same questions can be asked of individuals who use medications.

Screening questions and instruments that are useful with older adults include frequency/quantity questions, the SMAST-G, and the CAGE (Blow et al. 1992; Ewing 1984).

Examples of screening/quantity questions are:

- Do you drink alcohol, including beer, wine, and distilled spirits?
- On average, how many days a week do you drink?
- On a typical day when you drink, how many drinks do you have?
- What is the maximum number of drinks you have had on any given day in the past month? (Barry and Blow 1999; Blow 1998)

An older adult who is drinking more than seven standard drinks a week is considered an at-risk drinker.

Before using the following standardized tests, the worker should ensure that the individual is currently drinking and that his or her answers reflect recent consumption of alcohol (Blow 1998). The SMAST-G is a standardized test for an alcohol screen developed for older adults. It consists of ten questions that can be answered "yes" or "no." Two positive responses constitute a positive screen. However, even one positive response indicates a need for further exploration. The test is available in the public domain and can be downloaded from the Internet (Blow et al. 1992). The CAGE (C-Have you ever felt you ought to cut down on your drinking? A-Have people annoyed you by criticizing your drinking? G-Have you ever felt bad or guilty about your drinking? E-Have you ever had an eye-opener drink first thing in the morning to get over a hangover?) is most effective in identifying individuals with patterns of heavy drinking who have developed alcohol dependence. It is less effective for identifying alcohol problems among women (Blow 1998; Ewing 1984). Because the CAGE is most useful with heavy drinkers, and because most older adults with alcohol problems are in the category of at-risk and problem drinkers, follow-up questions and quantity/frequency questions are needed to complete the screen when using the CAGE. One positive response on the CAGE suggests the need for further exploration (Blow 1998). The CAGE is available in the public domain and is not copyrighted. The worker should also examine all prescription bottles of medications that the client currently uses (Barry and Blow 1999; Ewing 1984; Fleming 2002).

If clients have difficulty answering questions because of impaired cognition, it may be necessary to enlist participation from collateral family or friends. In this situation the worker should respect the autonomy of the client by first asking permission to question others on his or her behalf (Levin, Kruger, and Blow 2004).

For older adults with a positive screen, a complete assessment is generally needed to confirm the results, identify the dimensions of the problem, and develop an individualized treatment plan. The recommendation is that the assessment follow the guidelines of the *DSM-IV* criteria in order to qualify for insurance reimbursement. Given the time constraints of home health social work, workers are most likely to be able to perform a screening and then refer the client to the primary-care physician, who can arrange a comprehensive assessment of the problem. The results of a positive screen should be communicated to the client, to the home health care team, and to the primary-care physician for follow-up.

❖ ❖ ❖

Social workers in home health care are generalist practitioners who apply a person-in-environment framework in which patient, family, and community reciprocally influence each other. Home health care social work assessment focuses on identifying social, economic, and emotional factors that affect patient and family adjustment to illness, home health care, and discharge from home health care.

With regard to physiological factors, the assessment of the home health social worker focuses on the psychosocial implications of the client's illness, including the illness trajectory, the type and severity of the illness, the treatment regimen, and the phase of the illness. Medication management is recognized as a significant aspect of the treatment regimen that involves psychosocial as well as drug-related factors. Inadequate medication adherence is associated with morbidity, mortality, and increased consumption of health care resources.

An aspect of the patient's physiological functioning that has psychosocial implications is whether a patient has an advance directive. The purpose of an advance directive is to protect patient autonomy over medical decisions if the individual is deprived of decision-making capacity in the future. Two common forms of advance directives are living wills and medical power of attorney. Advance care planning is a process of planning for future medical care that helps a patient identify and clarify personal values and goals about medical treatment. While many individuals endorse the idea of advance directives, few actually complete them. Cultural factors may influence completion of advance directives. A tool to help social workers engaged families in advance care planning is presented in chapter 7.

With respect to psychological factors, health care beliefs merit attention, since they reflect the patient's explanation for illness and what should be done about it. Health care beliefs are the patient's beliefs, concerns, and expectations about the illness and the encounter with the health care provider. Providers may have their own explanatory model for the illness—the medical model. If health care providers do not respect the patient's explanatory model, patient-provider interaction can be characterized by lack of communication and misunderstanding. It is therefore important to elicit the patient's explanatory model and compare it to the provider's model to modify treatment (if possible) to convey respect and acceptance to the patient/family.

Different health care beliefs may influence clients to adopt complementary and alternative forms of medicine (CAM) such as herbal products and specialized diets. While patients may combine CAM with conventional medicine, they frequently do not disclose their use of CAM to their providers. Safety concerns are raised by the possibilities of interaction between medication and CAM products and the lack of empirical evidence for some CAM treatments. Social workers can elicit information about use of CAM from clients and, with the client's permission, share this information with the health care team or encourage the patient to share it.

Perceived self-efficacy to manage chronic disease is a second aspect of psychological functioning that should be included in an assessment. In the context of chronic illness, an evaluation of self-efficacy informs the social worker and client about how confident the client is in accomplishing the activities necessary for managing the disease. Depression is another component of the social worker's psychological assessment of the client in home care. While depression can be successfully treated, it is underdiagnosed in home care populations. In assessing depression, social workers should be aware that the presentation of depression is different in older patients than in younger ones. A useful depression screening instrument is the Geriatric Depression Rating Scale. It is important to communicate a positive screen to the patient's primary-care physician so that a comprehensive assessment can be completed.

Social work assessment of the depressed older client should include a screening for suicidal ideation and plans. Home care clients who are depressed may also have an anxiety disorder. The Beck Anxiety Inventory can be used to screen for the presence of an anxiety disorder.

Screening patients in home health care for alcohol and prescription drug use and misuse is important in order to identify patients who are at risk for or who have developed alcohol problems, which characterize a small proportion of the elderly population. Home care clients over the age of 60 should be screened for alcohol and prescription drug abuse and then rescreened if they display specific physical symptoms and/or if they are undergoing a major life transition. Valid and reliable screening tools include frequency/quantity questions, the SMAST-G, and the CAGE in combination with frequency/quantity questions. Clients who screen positive for alcohol should also be asked about concurrent prescription drug use, and the results should be communicated to the patient's physician and to the home health care team.

6

SOCIAL WORK ASSESSMENT OF SOCIAL SYSTEMS IN HOME HEALTH CARE

THE SOCIAL context, including the patient's social network, social support, and family relations, influences recovery from illness, disease management, and rates of disability and mortality (Lubben and Gironda 2003; Trief et al. 2003). The illness/disability of the patient, in turn, influences the physical and psychological health of the family (Gaugler, Kane, and Langlois 2000; Kane et al. 1999). As has been discussed, while the social work role in home care is frequently misunderstood, assessment of the client's social resources and family relations are social work domains about which there is some consensus. Social workers who complete a thorough social assessment that results in a cost-effective, efficient plan and positive patient outcomes have an opportunity to enhance their reputation in the agency and more solidly establish their area of expertise on the home health care team.

This chapter discusses the home health care social worker's assessment of the following social factors:

- unmet service needs
- the social support system
- environmental resources
- the family system
- risk for nursing home placement

UNMET SERVICE NEEDS

The goal in completing an assessment of the support system and resources of the home health care client is to answer the question "Does the individual have enough support from formal and informal sources to remain in the community after an acute episode or to continue living in the community with a chronic condition?" While ideally the goal of a social assessment is to improve the psychological and social well-being of the patient and family, the bottom-line goal in home care is to determine if the client has any unmet service needs and to ensure that the client's needs can be met at some level of adequacy in the community (R. A. Kane 2000). As used in this discussion, the term *unmet service needs* refers to unavailable, insufficient, inadequate, or inappropriate assistance from formal and informal sources to compensate for impairments in activities of daily living and instrumental activities of daily living (Allen and Mor 1997; Desai, Lentzner, and Weeks 2001; Li, Morrow-Howell, and Proctor 2005; Lima and Allen 2001). Unmet service needs are estimated to affect between one-fifth and one-third of elderly people who have ADL or IADL impairments (Desai, Lentzner, and Weeks 2001; Kennedy 2001; Lima and Allen 2001).

In conceptualizing unmet service needs, a distinction can be made between needs resulting from inaccessible or unavailable services and needs related to insufficient and inadequate services (Li, Morrow-Howell, and Proctor 2005). It is possible for an older adult to access a service but continue to experience unmet service needs if the available services are inappropriate, inadequate, or insufficient. For example, poorly trained staff, inconvenient scheduling, and increase in caregiver stress related to the use of formal services are reasons for unmet service needs still to exist even when services are accessible (Kosloski, Montgomery, and Youngbauer 2001; Morgan et al. 2002).

Adverse consequences for older care recipients associated with unmet service needs include running out of food, dehydration, burns, falls, and rehospitalization (Desai, Lentzner, and Weeks 2001; LaPlante et al. 2004; Proctor et al. 2000). Caregivers who report unmet service needs are likely to experience higher levels of emotional strain than caregivers who do not report unmet service needs (Li, Chadiha, and Morrow-Howell 2005). These outcomes may not only impair patient health but also result in additional costs to the home health care agency because of longer patient lengths of stay. Rehospitalization and/or readmission to the agency of a patient within the sixty-day episode of care lowers the capitation fee under Medicare prospective payment policies and therefore reduces revenue (St. Pierre and Dombi 2000).

Unmet service needs are influenced by functional status, informal support networks, socioeconomic characteristics, culture, and the organization of formal services (e.g., lack of qualified service providers, availability of service, cost of service, and poor communication between service providers) (Branch 2000; Desai, Lentzner, and Weeks 2001; Egan and Kadushin 2000; Li 2006; Lima and Allen 2001; Thomas and Payne 1998). Self-reported poor health and high levels of ADL/IADL impairment are associated with unmet needs (Allen and Mor 1997; Desai, Lentzner, and Weeks 2001; Kennedy 2001). Because family and friends provide the majority of care received by disabled and chronically ill older individuals in the community (LaPlante, Harrington, and Kang 2002), living alone is a consistent predictor of unmet needs (Desai, Lentzner, and Weeks 2001; Kennedy 2001).

When individuals with unmet service needs who live with others are compared to individuals with unmet service needs who live alone, the latter experience twice the shortfall in hours of informal help received (LaPlante et al. 2004). The client's cultural expectations regarding IADL assistance can shape a perception of unmet service needs for formal and informal care (Branch 2000).

Inability to purchase social services and health care when insurance/financial resources are inadequate may leave an individual without any care. For example, Medicaid enrollment is associated with access to homemaker services among rural older adults with disabilities (Li 2006). Inadequate insurance/financial resources and inability to purchase care are particularly significant for older adults living alone, who are more likely to receive paid help than those who live with others (LaPlante et al. 2004).

A final factor influencing unmet need for services is inadequate discharge plans. Participation of home care social workers in discharge planning rounds at hospitals that refer a high volume of patients to the home care agency may improve communication regarding referrals between discharge planners and home care social workers and thus reduce unmet client needs (Egan and Kadushin 2000).

There are two approaches to measuring unmet service needs: function-specific measures, which focus on the functioning of older adults, and service-specific measures, which focus on specific home and community-based services (Li, Morrow-Howell, and Proctor 2005). A measure with high reliability and evidence of validity that provides information about ADL and IADL impairment, the source of assistance, informal or formal service providers, and the adequacy (quantity and quality) of assistance in relation to a "desired" level (Li, Chadiha, and Morrow-Howell 2005) has been developed by Morrow-Howell, Proctor, and Dore (1998). The instrument measures the older adult's functional ability in fourteen areas: taking medication, transfer, walking, toileting, bathing, grooming, dressing, eating, preparing meals, shopping, managing money, housekeeping, transportation, and administering medical treatment by asking whether the older adult can perform the activity without help, can perform it with some help, or is completely unable to perform it. The source of help is operationalized by asking who helps with a particular activity and whether the source of help is formal or informal. An individual can have help from both formal and informal sources, help from only formal sources, help from only informal sources, or no help from either source in an area. Level of service is determined from questions that ask about the amount of help provided by formal and/or informal sources in a particular time period (for example, per week or per day), depending on the task. The quality of help is operationalized by asking the respondent how good the help is that the (nurse, aide, family, friend, etc.) is able to give him or her (Morrow-Howell, Proctor, and Dore 1998:90).

These are rated on a scale from 1 = "poor" to 4 = "excellent." Sufficiency of quantity of help from formal and informal sources is measured by asking how often the individual is without help when it is needed. Response categories are 1 = "without help at most times" to 4 = "always enough help; no more help is needed" (Morrow-Howell, Proctor, and Dore 1998:91). The adequacy of services is calculated through a ratio score, with the numerator representing actual help quantity and quality ratings in each area and the denominator representing maximum quantity (always enough help) and quality (excellent quality). These calculations are made for formal and informal care in each area (Morrow-Howell, Proctor, and Dore 1998). This approach can be used by the social worker to target interventions more systematically by providing information about:

- the particular ADL/IADL needs that are unmet
- the quality of care for each area
- the quantity of care for each area
- whether the quality in each area is deficient
- whether the quantity of care in each area is deficient

This tool also answers the following questions to help the social worker view the care plan as a whole:

- In how many areas are the older adult's care needs unmet?
- What is quality of care in the entire care plan?
- In how many areas is the quality of care deficient?
- In how many areas is the quantity of care deficient?
- How sufficient is quantity of help in the whole care plan? (Morrow-Howell, Proctor, and Dore 1998:96–97)

The instrument and instructions for calculating scores are available from the authors (Nancy Morrow-Howell, George Warren Brown School of Social Work, Washington University, Campus Box 1196, St. Louis, Missouri 63130-4899).

Service-specific measures of unmet needs collect information on whether specific services meet older adults' needs for care (Li, Morrow-Howell, and Proctor 2005). For example, Thomas and Payne (1998) determined unmet service needs by asking nurses to assess whether the patient needed a specific service but was not receiving any or all of the service needed. Unmet needs were assessed for the following services: homemaker, home health aide, equipment, mental health services, social work, transportation, occupational therapy, speech therapy, and nutrition.

Additional function-specific and service-specific measures are reviewed and critiqued by Li, Morrow-Howell, and Proctor (2005).

These two approaches provide the social worker with different information about a client's unmet service needs. The function-specific measures provide information on whether the client's needs for care are met for specific ADL/IADL impairments. The service-specific approach provides information on the quality of care of specific services in targeting unmet service needs. However, service-specific measures do not provide information about the specific ADL/IADL impairment that is the target of service. Personal care, for example, can be provided as an intervention for any ADL impairment. Ideally, both function-specific and service-specific measures should be used to collect comprehensive information about a client's unmet service needs (Li, Morrow-Howell, and Proctor 2005).

However, this procedure may be unrealistic for home health care social workers because of the time required (it is recommended that testing be completed in two separate sessions) and the possible fatigue of older clients that may preclude completion of both assessments in one session. When it is necessary to choose one approach over another, the function-specific approach is recommended, as it is considered more appropriate for the purpose of social work assessment in home health since it provides information that the worker can apply to develop and monitor a care plan to target unmet client needs.

In selecting a function-specific measure, it is desirable to use a tool that collects information about both ADL and IADL impairment. It is also important to be conscious of unmet needs that are influenced by the social and cultural context. For example, because of traditional gender roles, men may report that they are dependent with IADLs when in fact they have the functional ability to perform these tasks (Branch 2000). In these situations, support of the client's maximum independence is desirable (Li, Morrow-Howell, and Proctor 2005).

Because assistive technology (canes, crutches, walkers, crutches, bath stools, hand bars or rails) can substitute for formal and informal care in specific groups of older disabled adults (Agree and Freedman 2003; Allen, Foster, and Berg 2001) and can reduce unmet service needs, social workers should collect information about clients' use of and access to such resources (Dyeson, Murphy, and Stryker 1999; Li, Morrow-Howell, and Proctor 2005).

The source of information is also a consideration in assessing unmet service needs. Ratings of unmet needs by care recipients, caregivers/proxies, and professionals differ because they reflect the perspectives of each stakeholder (Morrow-Howell, Proctor, and Rozario 2001; Walters et al. 2000). In general, the care receivers' views of unmet service needs should be given priority and reports by professionals and caregivers/proxies regarded as supplementing those of the care receiver (Li, Morrow-Howell, and Proctor 2005).

When unmet needs are identified, it is important to determine the reason for the deficiency (Li, Morrow-Howell, and Proctor 2005). For example, is a homemaker being provided to a client who has an unmet need for personal care, such as bathing, that would be more appropriately met by a home health aide? Are informal caregivers unable to provide the level of care required by the care recipient? The answers to these questions can move the worker beyond collecting information to formulating a care plan to address unmet service needs effectively. Social workers should share the evaluation of unmet needs with the client and caregivers and present a plan that links unmet needs with specific services or informal service providers and service outcomes for their feedback and the development of a final plan (Li, Chadiha, and Morrow-Howell 2005). Client preferences and expectations should be discussed and addressed by the final plan (Li, Chadiha, and Morrow-Howell 2005). Ideally, because client service needs vary over time, home health social workers should monitor care plans and adjust them to meet emerging needs for service (Li, Chadiha, and Morrow-Howell 2005).

Workers should be aware that measures of unmet needs do not yet have firmly established psychometric properties and have not been tested. Practitioners should therefore use such measures with caution (Li, Morrow-Howell, and Proctor 2005).

THE SOCIAL SUPPORT SYSTEM

COMPONENTS OF THE SOCIAL SUPPORT SYSTEM

The client's social support system influences levels of unmet needs (Desai, Lentzner, and Weeks 2001; Kennedy 2001; LaPlante et al. 2004). Longitudinal studies of elderly ill and disabled patients have found that perceived adequacy of social support and contact with a social network are associated with reduction in levels of ADL impairment (Mendes de Leon et al. 1999; Oxman and Hull 1997) and depression (Oxman and Hull 1997).

In assessing the client's social support system, the worker evaluates the client's social network and social support (Antonucci 2001; Gallo et al. 2003; Lubben and Gironda 2003). The social network refers to the objective details of an individual's social relationships, such as size (i.e., number of people in the network) and frequency of contact (Antonucci 2001; Lubben and Gironda 2003). Assessment provides information about the people with whom the client interacts but not about the quality, nature, or content of those relationships (Antonucci 2001). The social network is generally composed of informal, formal, and semiformal relationships. The informal network includes family, friends, and neighbors; the formal network includes paid professionals in social service agencies and social welfare programs; and the semiformal network includes members of religious groups (church or synagogue) and/or neighborhood organizations (Gallo et al. 2003).

Social support is the assistance provided by social networks (received support) and the perceptions of the helpfulness of that support (perceived support) (Levine 2000). Common forms of social support are emotional support (expressions of caring), instrumental or tangible support (help with chores, for example), and information and advice (Antonucci 2001; Levine 2000). Network size does not automatically translate into social support. For example, a son can be part of an elderly individual's social network but provide no social support (Gallo et al. 2003). The perceived quality of social support is sometimes more important in influencing positive health and mental health outcomes for older adults than the actual receipt of support.

ASSESSMENT OF THE CLIENT'S SOCIAL NETWORK AND SOCIAL SUPPORT

A standardized instrument that is useful for clinical purposes to collect data regarding social network composition and receipt of social support is the Lubben Social Network Scale, a ten-item scale. Three items focus on family networks, three items focus on friendship networks, and four items measure interdependent social support and living arrangements. Most of the items ask the respondent to recall a particular person (e.g., relative, friend) and answer a question about that person. For example, "Other than the people you live with, how many relatives do you see or hear from at least once a month?" and "Do you have any close friends? That is, do you have any friends with whom you feel at ease, can talk to about private matters, or can call on for help? If so, how many?" Response options range from 0 to 5, with anchors for each option (Lubben 1988). Total scores on the scale range from 0 to 50. A score below 20 is considered to be an indicator of older persons at risk because of a limited social network. The copyright to the scale is held by Aspen Publishers, Inc., 200 Orchard Ridge Drive, Suite 200, Gaithersburg, Maryland 20878. Voice: 301-417-7500, toll-free: 1-800-638-8437, fax: 301-417-7550. Web site: www.aspenpub.com. Sample items reprinted with permission. To receive a copy of the scale, contact James F. Lubben, Department of Social Welfare, University of California–Los Angeles, Box 951656, Los Angeles, California 90095-1656. Voice: 310-825-2041, fax: 310-206-7564, e-mail: lubben@ucla.edu (Hayslip et al., in press).

ENVIRONMENTAL RESOURCES

ASSESSMENT OF SOCIAL RESOURCES

Social resources include tangible resources such as income, insurance, assets, employment, adequacy of housing, availability of transportation, and access to medication (Dyeson, Murphy, and Stryker 1999; Levine 2000; Piette et al. 2006). Inadequacy of these resources can have deleterious effects upon clients' living situations. For example, low-income home care clients may have difficulty paying bills, and nonpayment may result in termination of electrical, water, or gas services, which can contribute to hypothermia, inability to prepare meals, dehydration, and lack of water to take medications. Adequacy of housing and affordability of medication are two issues that will be highlighted below as significant influences on continued community living. Assessment of economic resources is important to determine the client's eligibility for federal, state, and community social services and income support programs. General questions that the home health social worker can pursue to evaluate economic resources include:

- Does the older adult have enough money for regular living expenses?
- Has the individual restricted purchase of food or medications because of inadequate income?
- Is money available for emergencies?
- Is money available for small luxuries?
- Is the individual covered by any health insurance?
- Does the individual have long-term-care insurance?
- Is the individual receiving any money from income support programs?
- Is the individual receiving any in-kind assistance (e.g., energy subsidies, food stamps)? (Gallo et al. 2003; McInnis-Dittrich 2005)

Observation of the individual's appearance (i.e., condition of shoes, clothing) and the home environment (i.e., any repairs needed?) is another source of information in formulating an economic assessment.

Because clients may regard a discussion of financial issues as an invasion of privacy, the social worker should be prepared to confront client resistance. It may be helpful to remind the client that the purpose of gathering the information is to determine eligibility for programs and services, that all information obtained is confidential, and that without this information the worker's ability to make appropriate referrals is limited (Emlet 1996).

FALL HAZARD ASSESSMENT

A specific type of tangible resource is adequacy of housing. Housing can be regarded as inadequate when the home environment is not a good "fit" for the needs and capabilities of the older individual (Lawton 1999). The primary purpose of a home health social worker's home safety assessment is the evaluation of the client's living space to identify hazardous conditions that may contribute to falls. Approximately one-third of people over age 65 living in the community fall each year (Gillespie et al. 2003). While risk of falling is influenced by multiple factors and requires a multidisciplinary approach, the appropriate social work role is the assessment of home safety factors that can lead to falls (Gillespie et al. 2003; McInnis-Dittrich 2005; Tinetti 2003). Several home hazards may contribute to falls and should be evaluated to reduce the risk of falling. The most significant variable associated with falls that result in injury is the absence of grab bars in the bathtub or shower (Sattin et al. 1998). Answers to the following questions can provide information for a useful home safety assessment:

- Are loose rugs tacked down or do they have nonskid backing?
- Are bathtubs and showers equipped with non-skid mats?
- Are grab bars installed next to the toilet and in the tub or shower?
- Are there handrails on both sides of stairways?
- Is lighting installed throughout the home? (Gillespie et al. 2003)

While assessment of home safety is the primary role of the home health social worker in preventing and reducing falls, the worker should also be knowledgeable about additional intrinsic risk factors (or risk factors that are characteristics of the client) that should be evaluated through a referral to a nurse and/or the patient's primary-care physician:

- lower-body weakness
- problems with walking and balance
- taking four or more medications or any psychoactive medications (Gillespie et al. 2003)

Fall risk is four times higher in the first two weeks after discharge from the hospital than three months after discharge for older patients who have been hospitalized for an acute medical illness and are receiving home nursing services (Mahoney, Palta et al. 2000). These patients should be assessed for home hazards that can contribute to falls (American Geriatrics Society, British Geriatrics Society, and American Academy of Orthopaedic Surgeons Panel on Fall Prevention 2001).

MEDICATION ADHERENCE

An important area for social work assessment of obstacles to patient adherence to medication regimens is out-of-pocket prescription drug costs. Research has found that elderly patients, especially those with low incomes, who have out-of-pocket prescription costs, no prescription drug coverage, and multiple chronic conditions restrict their medication use because of financial concerns (Piette, Heisler, and Wagner 2004; Steinman, Sands, and Covinsky 2001). Medicare Part D, implemented in 2006, is a program intended to provide Medicare beneficiaries with prescription drug coverage. Individuals who previously received full drug coverage from Medicaid began to receive prescription drug coverage from Medicare rather than Medicaid in 2006. All home health care social workers need to have a thorough knowledge of Medicare Part D and how it could potentially affect different clients. (For a description of the basic facts about Medicare Part D, go to www.medicare.gov.)

The most basic question is whether the client is informed about Medicare Part D so that he or she can make good choices. Medicare Part D is a complex program to navigate, particularly for older adults without computer skills (Kolata 2006). The social worker may wish to assess what aspects of the program the client does not understand and/or whether the client is informed about the program at all. If the client is not enrolled in the program, the social worker may wish to assess the reasons for this decision.

A second basic question is whether the client can afford the necessary medications under Medicare Part D. Gaps in coverage and cost-sharing mechanisms under Medicare may result in out-of-pocket expenses that disproportionately affect the most vulnerable—those with multiple chronic conditions, African Americans, Hispanics, and low-income elderly people who are not eligible for any government assistance to offset some of these costs (Gellad et al. 2006; Stuart et al. 2005).

Clients who received Medicaid previously had comprehensive drug coverage. Former Medicaid clients will pay more for medication under Medicare Part D, which does not provide comprehensive coverage. Medicare Part D requires a small copayment from former Medicaid clients that varies according to whether a drug is generic or brand name and according to the income and assets of the client. For an individual on a limited income, with multiple chronic conditions and multiple prescriptions, these copayments can add up to a noticeable portion of income.

Individuals who received drug coverage under Medicaid were automatically enrolled by the government in a drug plan under Medicare Part D (different drug plans cover different drugs) and may now be in a plan that does not cover all of their drugs. The client may therefore need to choose another plan that will cover most or all of the necessary drugs and/or use another, similar drug prescribed by the primary-care physician that is covered under the plan's formulary. However, older adults with impaired physical and mental health, terminal illness, and/or dementia may not understand how to compare and choose drug plans or where to go for help, and they may not have the energy to engage in the process (Pear 2006). Research suggests that when individuals are faced with out-of-pocket drug costs that they cannot afford they may not fill prescriptions, may skip doses, and may take their medication only when severely ill (Stuart et al. 2005; Stuart, Simoni-Wastila, and Chauncey 2005; Tseng et al. 2004). As noted in chapter 5, medication non-adherence is associated with serious negative health outcomes for clients.

Low-income clients who do not qualify for Medicaid may be eligible for government subsidies to reduce out-of-pocket expenses under the Medicare program. However, it may be that clients do not apply for these benefits because they do not know about them or do not understand application procedures. Some may be reluctant to accept government help (Kaiser Family Foundation 2006). Social workers may wish to assess the eligibility of all low-income clients who did not receive Medicaid previously for this "extra help" and assess their attitudes toward receiving such help.

THE FAMILY SYSTEM

CAREGIVER BURDEN AND WELL-BEING

Research suggests that helping families cope with caregiving is an increasingly important role for home care social workers, as patients are being discharged more quickly from care (Lee 2002).

While there is no standard definition, in this discussion *caregiving* will be defined as informal or unpaid care activities that exceed the normative and customary care included as part of the routine obligations and social expectations between family members or friends (Ory et al. 2000). For example, a wife who provides care to a chronically ill husband by preparing meals or cleaning house might be regarded as engaging in normal obligations. However, assisting with complex medical routines reflects "extraordinary care" and is beyond the scope of what are regarded as the normal responsibilities of a wife; therefore that task would more clearly be regarded as caregiving (Ory et al. 2000, p. 7).

The impact of caregiving on the individual is referred to as *burden*. In general, burden includes the emotional, psychological, physical, and financial demands assumed by caregivers, as well as the individual's subjective perception of how the performance of these tasks affects his or her life (Gaugler, Kane, and Langlois 2000). The development of burden is explained through the application of stress-coping models of caregiving. These models suggest that if an environmental event is appraised as threatening, and there is a lack of resources to reduce the threat, the event will be perceived as a stressor. In this situation, there is an increased likelihood of negative outcomes such as caregiver burden, depression, and impaired physical and mental health. The stress-process model is based on the concept of stress "proliferation" or the spread of stress from care provision to other areas of life (e.g., work, family relations, finances), potentially resulting in such negative physical and mental health outcomes for the caregiver as depression, morbidity, and mortality (Gaugler, Kane, and Langlois 2000).

Recent research has suggested that caregiving events and/or the caregiving role may not only be appraised negatively, in terms of strain or stress, but can also be appraised positively, in terms of gain (e.g., satisfaction, rewards, benefits, uplifts) in the presence of specific caregiver characteristics, activities, and resources (Kramer 1997). Burden and subjective well-being are conceptualized as two distinct dimensions of caregiving that can be experienced simultaneously by caregivers (Chappell and Reid 2002; Kramer 1997; Pinquart and Sörensen 2004).

There is no empirical research on home health social work assessment of burden. The following discussion is grounded in empirical research from related disciplines and the practical implications of this research for home health care social work. The issue of burden among older adults is emphasized here because the majority of published research on the consequences of caregiving discusses this factor (Kramer 1997).

The home health social work assessment of caregiver burden is important because of the relationship between burden and negative outcomes of home health care, including poor caregiver mental health (Bookwala and Schulz 2000; Lawrence, Tennstedt, and Assmann 1998; Yates, Tennstedt, and Chang 1999) and physical health (Schulz and Beach 1999); elder mistreatment (Choi and Mayer 2000; Schumacher, Beck, and Marren 2006); nursing home placement (Chenier 1997; Gaugler et al. 2003; Tsuji, Whalen, and Finucane 1995); and hospital readmission (Proctor et al. 2000; Proctor, Morrow-Howell, and Kaplan 1996; Sevast 2007).

AREAS FOR ASSESSMENT: CONTEXTUAL OR BACKGROUND FACTORS

Contextual factors such as caregiver health, gender, and ethnicity affect the stress process that can result in burden and negative outcomes of care. Poorer caregiver health is associated with higher levels of burden, since illness and disability can make the performance of caregiving tasks more difficult (Bookwala and Schulz 1998; Bull, Maruyama, and Luo 1995; Mui 1995b). Among caregivers of older individuals with dementia, poorer self-rated health was related to expedited nursing home placement (Gaugler et al. 2003).

Specific subgroups may be considered at "high risk" for burden. Female caregivers report higher levels of care recipient behavior problems, more hours of care provided, higher number of caregiving tasks, and higher levels of burden than male caregivers (Pinquart and Sörensen 2006). Physical impairment, behavior problems, and longer duration of care are more strongly associated with caregiver burden in spousal caregivers than in adult children caregivers

(Pinquart and Sörensen 2003). Spouses are more vulnerable to age-associated chronic illness and may be less likely than adult children to have multiple roles and activities outside the home to buffer stress (Pinquart and Sörensen 2003).

With regard to ethnicity, while research has found that American Asian, Hispanic, and African American caregivers experience higher levels of stress (e.g., poorer health, fewer financial resources) than non-Hispanic white caregivers, African Americans report lower levels of burden than non-Hispanic white caregivers. It should be noted, however, that these differences are statistically small and should not be over-interpreted. Asian and Hispanic caregivers did not differ from non-Hispanic white caregivers in levels of burden (Pinquart and Sörensen 2005).

AREAS FOR ASSESSMENT: STRESSORS RELATED TO CAREGIVING ITSELF, OR PRIMARY STRESSORS

Primary stressors are those stressors that arise from the patient's illness itself and the objective demands for care dictated by the patient's condition, as well as the caregiver's subjective experience of these demands for care (Gaugler, Kane, and Langlois 2000; Pearlin et al. 1990). The literature suggests that home care social workers' assessment for caregiver burden should focus on characteristics of the care recipient, including behavior problems (e.g., wandering, emotional outbursts, inappropriate behavior) (Chappell and Reid 2002; Pinquart and Sörensen 2003), cognitive impairment, and ADL/IADL impairment (Pinquart and Sörensen 2003).

Primary stressors related to the caregiver that are important targets for assessment include the intensity of caregiving (e.g., hours and number of tasks) and the duration of caregiving (Pinquart and Sörensen 2003). Assessment of these stressors may differ by type of illness. While physical impairments in patients increase burden for caregivers of individuals without dementia, among dementia caregivers unmet needs for help with care responsibilities (e.g., tasks information, family support) may be more important (Sörensen et al. 2006).

AREAS FOR ASSESSMENT: APPRAISAL OF THE CAREGIVING EXPERIENCE

Different caregivers' interpretations of the same situation may be influenced by their personalities (Bookwala and Schulz 1998), their level of stress, a previously positive relationship with the care recipient (Spaid and Barusch 1994), and/or their own personal and social resources (Gaugler, Kane, and Langlois 2000). Social workers should assess the meaning of the caregiving experience for the caregiver because this perception of caregiving contributes to outcomes of either strain or well-being and negative or positive mental and physical health consequences.

Thus, a positive appraisal of the caregiving role or a caregiving event has been associated more strongly with positive indicators of caregiving outcomes such as subjective well-being or positive overall quality of life than with negative indicators of caregiving outcomes such as burden and depression. Similarly, caregiver stress or strain is more strongly associated with negative indicators of caregiving outcomes such as burden and depression than with positive indicators of outcomes such as subjective well-being (Pinquart and Sörensen 2003, 2004).

Ethnicity has been found to influence appraisal of the caregiving experience. African American and Hispanic caregivers experience more "uplifts" of caring than non-Hispanic white caregivers do, but there are no differences between Asian American caregivers and non-Hispanic white caregivers (Sörensen et al. 2006). In addition, studies find that the number of hours spent on caregiving does not influence well-being, suggesting that spending more time as a caregiver will not diminish social well-being if the caregiver protects opportunities to engage in positive social roles and activities (Pinquart and Sörensen 2004). This research suggests that caregivers experiencing burden or depression may wish to engage in positive experiences (getting enough rest, enjoying time with family and friends, maintaining a healthy diet) that are components of overall quality of life to protect their well-being (Chappell and Reid 2002; Pinquart and Sörensen 2004).

AREAS FOR ASSESSMENT: SECONDARY STRESSORS

The term *secondary stressors* refers to the spread of stress from the caregiving situation itself to other areas of the caregiver's life, potentially resulting in family conflict (discussed as a separate topic below), impaired relationship quality, work-role conflict, financial strain, decreased self-care activities, social isolation, and loss of leisure time (Gaugler, Kane, and Langlois 2000; Kane et al. 1999; Pearlin et al. 1990; Sörensen et al. 2006).

An important focus for social work assessment is the relationship between caregiver burden for chronically ill older adults with and without dementia and interference with work—missing work, forgoing promotions, passing up new job opportunities, and facing termination of work as a result of caregiving demands reduce retirement income and earning potential (Bull and McShane 2002; Sörensen et al. 2006; Starrels et al. 1997). A qualitative study of spousal caregivers for individuals with hip fracture and stroke found that financial and employment problems were the subjects of the most frequent negative comments in response to a question about the impact of caregiving (Kane et al. 1999).

Other secondary stressors that are important areas for assessment are poor caregiver self-care (e.g., disrupted sleep, lack of exercise, poor diet) and a perception of activity restriction because of caregiving responsibilities (e.g., little or no time for shopping, household chores, visiting friends, pursuing hobbies, or other forms of recreation) (Bookwala and Schulz 2000; Chenier 1997; Sörensen et al. 2006).

The quality of the caregiver/care recipient relationship in the presence of care recipient behavior problems influences levels of burden. The presence of behavior problems has been found to negatively affect the relationship, leading in turn to higher levels of subjective burden (Yates, Tennstedt, and Chang 1999). Among older caregiving wives, care recipient behavior problems are related to restriction of personal and leisure activities, negatively affecting the quality of the caregiver/care recipient relationship (Bookwala and Schulz 2000). Higher levels of relationship quality have also been directly related to lower levels of subjective burden (Lawrence, Tennstedt, and Assman 1998). A longer duration of caregiving among spouses caring for elders who experienced stroke or hip fracture influenced the frequency of negative feelings of anger, resentment, frustration, and growing distance from the care recipient (Kane et al. 1999). A poor relationship between care recipient and caregiver has also been related to negative effects for the care recipient, expressed in depressive symptoms and a self-perception as a "burden" on the caregiver (Dyeson 2000).

AREAS FOR ASSESSMENT: MEDIATORS OF CAREGIVING STRESS
Social workers should also examine adequacy of personal and social resources as mediators of caregiver burden. Social support and psychological resources (e.g., coping and mastery) are the most frequently identified mediators of caregiver stress. Coping and social support may function to diminish the impact of primary and secondary stressors and to limit the process of stress proliferation (Gaugler, Kane, and Langlois 2000; Pearlin et al. 1990). The perception of the availability of informal social support, the receipt of support (particularly from a confidant), and/or a larger network of secondary caregivers are associated with reduced levels of burden in the majority of studies (Dorfman, Berlin, and Holmes 1998; Gaugler, Anderson, et al. 2004; Mui 1995a, 1995b; Sörensen et al. 2006). Finally, emotional or tangible support from the care recipient to the caregiver is associated with reduced caregiver burden (Dorfman, Berlin, and Holmes 1998; Dwyer, Lee, and Jankowski 1994; Ingersoll-Dayton, Starrels, and Dowler 1996; Wright and Aquilino 1998).

Relationship quality between older individuals with illness and disability and their primary caregivers has also been found to mediate the association between problem behaviors and subjective burden, suggesting that when problem behaviors are present there is a likelihood of increased levels of subjective burden because the quality of the relationship is impaired (Lawrence, Tennstedt, and Assmann 1998).

While there is no association between receipt of formal home care (Bull, Maruyama, and Luo 1995; Schwarz and Blixen 1997; Schwarz and Roberts 2000) and caregiver burden, there is an association between unmet need for community services and caregiver emotional strain (Li, Chadiya, and

Morrow-Howell 2005). When unmet needs are defined as how well community services meet the needs of the care receivers, access to resources may be a necessary but insufficient condition for desirable caregiving outcomes. Rather, how well community services meet older adults' service needs may be the factor that reduces caregiving strain.

Research has found that caregivers who believe they have control over their future life and situation are less likely to develop negative mental health outcomes in response to stress (Sörensen et al. 2006). Consistent with these findings, caregiver self-efficacy or feelings of mastery with regard to the tasks of caregiving have been negatively related to levels of caregiver burden in studies that have examined this variable (Spaid and Barusch 1994; Yates, Tennstedt, and Chang 1999). However, a review of the literature notes that in one national study only 41 percent of caregivers reported that they had received instruction in how to perform at least one caregiving task (Schumacher, Beck, and Marren 2006). Among caregivers of older adults with dementia, lack of knowledge influences caregivers to overestimate the abilities of the care recipient, leading to anger, frustration, and depression (Sörensen et al. 2006).

Ethnicity may influence coping style. Several studies have found that African American and Hispanic caregivers of individuals with dementia are more likely than non-Hispanic white caregivers to use religious styles of coping, and they report a more "benign" appraisal of caregiving than non-Hispanic whites (Sörensen et al. 2006:964).

OUTCOMES OF CAREGIVER BURDEN

PHYSICAL AND MENTAL HEALTH OUTCOMES

The progression of caregiver burden may negatively affect caregivers' mental and physical health. In particular, social workers may wish to screen caregivers for depressive symptoms (Bookwala and Schulz 2000; Lawrence, Tennstedt, and Assmann 1998; Yates, Tennstedt, and Chang 1999). Caregivers providing assistance to care recipients with cognitive impairments and/or behavior problems are more likely to have a poor relationship with the care recipient, experience more emotional distress, and endure higher levels of depression than caregivers for care recipients without these symptoms (Bookwala and Schulz 2000; Lawrence, Tennstedt, and Assmann 1998; Yates, Tennstedt, and Chang 1999).

Levels of caregiver depression vary with ethnicity. African American caregivers have lower levels of depression, and Hispanics and Asian Americans higher levels of depression, than non-Hispanic whites (Pinquart and Sörensen 2005). Asian American caregivers may be more depressed than white caregivers because daughters-in-law are expected to assume the caregiving role without regard for personal preferences, and thus may be more likely to have poor relationships with the care recipient than non-Hispanic white caregivers. Asian American caregivers are also more likely than those of other ethnic groups to use emotion-focused coping (i.e., coping that involves regulation of the emotional consequences of stressful or potentially stressful events typically used when stressors are uncontrollable) that does not improve the situation or positively revise the caregiver's perception of stressors (Folkman and Lazarus 1980). Hispanic caregivers may be more depressed than non-Hispanic white caregivers because they care for more-impaired care recipients and have a poorer relationship with the care recipient than non-Hispanic white caregivers, possibly because of strong Hispanic traditions of parental hierarchy and authority that may contribute to intergenerational tensions (Pinquart and Sörensen 2005).

Caregiver burden may also be related to impaired physical health and mortality. Spousal caregivers who experience emotional strain are at increased risk for negative physical health outcomes (such as inadequate time for sleep or self-care) and mortality compared with non-caregiving controls (Schulz and Beach 1999; Schulz et al. 1997).

Non-Hispanic white caregivers report better physical health than African American, Hispanic, and Asian American caregivers. However, caregiving may have less impact on minority caregivers' physical health than other factors independent of caregiving, such as more-restricted access to health care (Williams and Wilson 2001) and the cumulative impact of racial discrimination (Finch et al. 2001).

ELDER MALTREATMENT

Caregiver stress resulting in negative consequences, including burden, is one of the theories applied to explain the etiology of elder maltreatment (Bergeron 2001). Older adults with chronic health problems have been found to be more vulnerable to abuse and neglect, possibly because of caregiver stress and burden (Choi and Mayer 2000). Caregivers who are not prepared to or are unable to provide adequate care may harm the older adult by inappropriately administering medication, not recognizing and correcting safety risks, or mismanaging finances. While some of these situations may not meet the criteria for elder maltreatment, they can nevertheless harm the older adult (Schumacher, Beck, and Marren 2006).

HOSPITAL READMISSION

An inadequate support network is one of the risk factors for hospital readmission (Sevast 2007). Research has found that discrepancies in the implementation of discharge plans for chronically ill older adults and/or inadequate home care are associated with hospital readmission (Proctor et al. 2000; Proctor, Morrow-Howell, and Kaplan 1996). Hospital social workers, pressured by the Diagnosis

Related Group (DRG) system, may not complete an adequate discharge assessment of the older patient. Patients may be discharged "sicker and quicker" to a caregiver who is unable or unprepared to provide care and who also experiences unmet need for community services (Li, Chadiya, and Morrow-Howell 2005; Proctor et al. 2000; Proctor, Morrow-Howell, and Kaplan 1996). Caregivers may become overwhelmed by caregiving responsibilities and experience role overload, a form of subjective burden, contributing to hospital readmission (Proctor et al. 2000; Proctor, Morrow-Howell, and Kaplan 1996; Sevast 2007).

SCREENING AND ASSESSMENT FOR CAREGIVER BURDEN AND SUBJECTIVE WELL-BEING

Caregivers should be screened for their level of stress. Screening measures vary with regard to population (e.g., spouses, adult children), specific illness (e.g., dementia, hip fracture, stroke), definition of caregiver burden as either objective (prevalence), subjective (subjective responses to these stressors), or both. These factors can be measured separately or by obtaining an overall score (Vitaliano, Young, and Russo 1991). Caution is therefore warranted so that the measure selected will be valid for the client.

The Caregiver Strain Index (CSI) is the only current measure of burden developed for clinical use. Its purpose is to identify levels of caregiver strain. The scale takes less than a minute to complete and is orally administered. Thirteen items measure common stressors in caring for an older adult; among them are disturbed sleep, financial strain, physical strain, family adjustment, and confinement. Responses are dichotomous: o = no and 1 = yes. The original sample consisted of family, friends, and neighbors caring for an older adult discharged from a hospital with a diagnosis of heart disease or hip problems. Patients with severe mental impairments were excluded from the sample. A score is obtained by adding all "yes" responses; scores can range from 0 to 13 (Hayslip et al. in press; Robinson 1983). A score of 7 or more indicates a greater level of stress. The CSI has good psychometric properties and is useful as a quick screen for caregivers experiencing higher levels of stress.

The copyright holder is the Gerontological Society of America, Permissions Department, 1030 15th Street, N.W., Suite 250, Washington, D.C. 20005-1503. Phone: 202-842-1275, fax: 202-842-1150. Web site: www.geron.org. There is no cost for use, but permission is required. If reproduction is for publication, costs may vary (Hayslip et al. in press).

If the care recipient has been diagnosed with dementia, the home health care worker should screen for in-home safety issues. The National Institute on Aging Web site posts the booklet *Home Safety for People with Alzheimer's Disease*, which discusses safety tips to prevent injury to the care recipient and the family. Caregivers should also be asked if they fear harm from the behaviors of the care recipient (National Institute on Aging 2006).

The Caregiver Well-Being Scale is a self-administered scale that was developed to measure caregiver strengths in meeting their basic needs and daily activities (Tebb 1995). The 45-item instrument has two subscales, Basic Needs and Activities of Daily Living. The scale measures the caregiver's emotional status, physical needs, spiritual or reflective time, social contacts and supports, and ability to maintain a personal living environment (Berg-Weger, Rubio, and Tebb 2000a). The scale has established psychometric properties for female non-Hispanic white caregivers (Berg-Weger, Rubio, and Tebb 2000a). It can be used by practitioners to identify at-risk family caregivers, caregiver strengths, and areas in which strengths can be enhanced (Berg-Weger, Rubio, and Tebb 2000a). Contact Susan Steiger Tebb, Saint Louis University School of Social Work, 3550 Lindell Boulevard, Tegler Hall, Room 204, St. Louis, Missouri 63103. Phone: 314-977-2730, fax: 314-977-2731, e-mail: tebbsc@slu.edu.

There are currently no valid screening instruments available for clinical use with caregivers of older individuals who have dementia (Sörensen et al. 2006). The American Medical Association Web site posts a "caregiver self-assessment tool" (American Medical Association 2007). This 18-item screen completed by the caregiver poses dichotomous yes/no questions regarding such issues as caregiver isolation, role conflict, satisfaction with social support, and perceived physical and mental health. The Web site provides scoring instructions with cutoff points that indicate high stress and the need for professional help (American Medical Association 2007). Until the instrument's psychometric properties are established, however, scores should be viewed cautiously.

Topics for home health social work screening to supplement these standardized scales, derived from the literature discussed, include the following:

- Is the caregiver in a "high-risk" group for burden? This includes women, spouses, and ethnic minority groups vulnerable to poor physical health.
- What is the duration and intensity of caregiving? Is the caregiver unable or unprepared to provide this care?
- What is the quality of the relationship between caregiver and care recipient, particularly in the presence of care recipient behavior problems and/or a longer duration of caregiving?
- Does the caregiver experience conflicts between the caregiving and work roles?
- What are the caregiver's physical and mental health and self-care activities?
- What is the caregiver's perception of competence or mastery in the caregiving role?

- Does the caregiver lack a confidant and/or experience unmet needs for community services?

FAMILY CAREGIVING CONFLICT

Family conflict is defined as overtly expressed interpersonal disagreement, hostility/anger, or unexpressed emotions such as resentment (Bourgeois, Beach, and Burgio 1996; Semple 1992; Steffen and Berger 2000; Strawbridge and Wallhagen 1991).

Research examining family caregiving conflict indicates that perceptions by care recipients of negative, demeaning behavior by caregivers are associated with depression and less motivation to comply with treatment (Dyeson, Murphy, and Stryker 1999). Family conflict or disagreement related to caring for an impaired elder has been significantly positively associated with caregiver depression, anger, burden, and poor self-reported health (Bourgeois, Beach, and Burgio 1996; Semple 1992; Steffen and Berger 2000; Strawbridge and Wallhagen 1991). Family conflict resolution may influence both the family's ability to provide care for an impaired relative and the well-being of other family members. As a consequence, family conflict, decision making, and conflict resolution may affect the quality of the discharge plan and the patient's length of stay in home health care.

FACTORS CONTRIBUTING TO FAMILY CAREGIVING CONFLICT

Family conflict may focus on the amount of help needed and who will provide help (Davis 1997; Gwyther 1995). Sharing caregiving responsibilities among siblings is not common. In several studies, the majority of caregivers received little or no help from their siblings, a situation that contributed to resentment and conflict (Merrill 1997; Strawbridge and Wallhagen 1991; Suitor and Pillemer 1996).

Parents' knowledge of the conflict in some instances contributed to their involvement in the disagreement and heightened their own sense of being a burden on their children (Merrill 1997). Primary caregivers expressed feelings of confusion and disappointment in these situations, since their view had been that these family members were "supposed" to be the most helpful (Strawbridge and Wallhagen 1991; Suitor and Pillemer 1996).

Family members may also disagree on the severity and/or prognosis of the care recipient's illness or disability (Bourgeois, Beach, and Burgio 1996; Gwyther 1995). Conflict may also focus on the competence of the caregiver (Bourgeois, Beach, and Burgio 1996; Davis 1997; Gwyther 1995; Semple 1992) and may be expressed through unwanted advice or criticism of what the caregiver is doing (Strawbridge and Wallhagen 1991).

Conflict or disagreement may arise between caregiver and care recipient as a result of negative relationships. Research has found that strained relationships predicted greater discrepancies between caregiver and care recipient in perceptions of cooperativeness and sources of formal and informal support. Caregivers whose perception of the caregiving relationship is negative may be more likely to disagree with the care recipient about available sources of support and the cooperativeness of the recipient, suggesting that communication may be impaired when relationships are strained (Lyons et al. 2002). Care recipients who feel overprotected, feel that they are treated as objects, or perceive themselves to be burdens on their caregivers are likely to experience negative relationships with caregivers (Dyeson 2000; Johnson 1996; Thompson et al. 2002).

When the caregiver is an adult child, unique relationship issues may arise. Adult children who are experiencing a role reversal in the relationship with the aging parent may experience discomfort as they try to balance their parent's need for autonomy with their desire to protect the parent's welfare. At the same time, parents struggle with trying to balance their need to depend on their children with their need to maintain their own independence. Conflict arises when adult children confront parents about declining abilities or offer unsolicited help and advice, behaviors that parents may interpret as disrespectful and patronizing. Children who underestimate the parent's ability and take complete control over caregiving decisions are likely to experience conflict in the caregiving relationship with the parent (Haggan 1998; Hummert and Morgan 2001).

ASSESSING FAMILY CAREGIVING CONFLICT
In assessing family caregiving conflicts, social workers may wish to ask the following questions:

- Who initiated the referral to social work?
- Is the primary family caregiver disappointed, angry, or embarrassed?
- How do other family members help the primary caregiver?
- Who helps and who does not help?
- Is family help dependable?
- Is family help adequate?
- How did the family make the decision about current care?
- If there is a current disagreement or difference of opinion in the family about caregiving, how has the family tried to resolve the disagreement?
- What are the care recipient's perceptions of the need for support? What are the caregiver's perceptions of the need for support?
- How cooperative is the caregiver in helping the care recipient? How cooperative is the care recipient in helping the caregiver?

These questions help the social worker to identify the presence and type of family caregiving conflicts as well as the family's approach to decision making and conflict resolution (Gwyther 1995; Lieberman and Fisher 1999).

ELDER MALTREATMENT

PREVALENCE

Social support can be negative as well as positive (Levine 2000). With the exception of self-neglect, the most extreme instance of negative social support is elder abuse, neglect, and exploitation. Estimates of the occurrence of abuse and neglect have varied between 2 and 10 percent (National Research Council 2002; Tomita 2006). This proportion is likely to increase during the next several decades as a larger percentage of the population ages (National Research Council 2002). This figure should, however, be regarded cautiously because research on maltreatment of older adults is limited by unclear and inconsistent definitions, unclear and inadequate measures, lack of population-based data, and lack of prospective data (Clarke and Pierson 1999; Kleinschmidt 1997; National Research Council 2002). It may also be difficult to detect elder maltreatment because victims withhold information out of embarrassment, guilt, fear of abuser retaliation, their value of family privacy, and/or fear of nursing home placement (Bergeron 2000; Tomita 2006; Vandeweerd, Paveza, and Fulmer 2006). Underreporting may also be attributed to failure of professionals to detect abuse, in combination with a lack of knowledge of high-risk indicators of maltreatment (Clark and Pierson 1999; Emlet 1996; Kleinschmidt 1997; Vandeweerd, Paveza, and Fulmer 2006).

TYPES AND INDICATORS OF MALTREATMENT

There is no clear definition of elder maltreatment. This is partly the result of variations and ambiguities in state statutes authorizing reporting and intervention in elder maltreatment and partly the result of unclear operational definitions of elder maltreatment in the existing research (National Research Council 2002). For the purposes of this discussion, the following definitions of the types of elder maltreatment and their accompanying indicators will be used (Tomita 2006).

Physical abuse refers to infliction of physical injury, including acts of assault, battery, and inappropriate use of restraints (Quinn and Tomita 1997; Tomita 2006). Indicators include bruises, scratches, burns, and choke marks; unexplained or repeated accidents; fearful, agitated, or withdrawn behavior when family is present; consistent deference to family members; and/or discussing fears of being harmed or hurt (Quinn and Tomita 1997).

Sexual abuse refers to any form of nonconsensual sexual contact. Sexual abuse may be indicated when older adults report being victims of unwanted sexual invitations or contact, genital irritation, injury or scarring, fear in the presence of a specific person, fear of pelvic examinations, and trauma in the pelvic area (Tomita 2006).

Emotional/psychological abuse refers to the use of threats, humiliation, or similar verbal and nonverbal behaviors to willfully cause mental anguish (Tomita 2006).

Financial abuse is defined as "taking or misappropriation of an older person's property, possession or financial assets" (Wilber and Reynolds 1996:64). Financial abuse is indicated when an older adult trusts family members or other individuals to protect his or her best interests, but the outcome serves the best interests of the perpetrator instead (Wilber and Reynolds 1996). Indicators of financial abuse include documents (e.g., power of attorney, will, joint tenancy, deed to an elder's house) that the client does not understand; care of the older adult that is inconsistent with his or her financial resources; a caregiver who is reluctant to spend money on care; isolation of the older adult from family; and pressure by housekeepers or other trusted social network members to sign over assets (Quinn and Tomita 1997).

Neglect refers to a situation in which the basic needs of the older adult exceed what is being provided. The client may be deprived of nutrition, medical attention, and/or a safe, well-maintained environment. Neglect by the caregiver may be intentional and willful or unintentional or the result of lack of knowledge. Indicators of neglect may include poor client hygiene (e.g., decayed teeth, body odor, unclean clothing and bed linens, vermin and rodents in the house), inadequate housing (e.g., broken windows, plumbing malfunction, and electricity problems), disconnected utilities, absence of edible food in the house, and malnutrition. Like abuse, neglect can result in death (Quinn and Tomita 1997; Tomita 2006).

Self-neglect is the failure by the older adult to provide adequate care with regard to the basic necessities of life, such as food, clothing, shelter, medical care, and medications. The lack of these necessities can threaten the health and safety of the older adult and ultimately lead to increased risks of mortality and institutionalization (Lachs et al. 1998; Tomita 2006). Indicators of self-neglect include poor hygiene, poor nutrition, dehydration, inappropriate clothing for weather conditions (e.g., wearing a housecoat outside during the winter), nonadherence to medical regimens, unpaid bills, and exposure to environmental hazards (e.g., forgetting to turn off the stove, decrepit housing conditions) (Leff and Sonstegard-Gamm 2006).

CHARACTERISTICS OF VICTIMS AND PERPETRATORS

The majority of cases reported to adult protective services involve neglect and self-neglect (Tomita 2006). The victims of abuse are most often female (National Research Council 2002; Tomita 2006; Vladescu et al. 1999). No additional characteristics of abuse victims have been substantiated (Tomita 2006). Family members are the most frequent perpetrators of elder maltreatment (National Research Council 2002; Tomita 2006). When the source of information has been reported cases, adult children are the most frequent perpetrators (Brownell, Berman, and Salamone 1999; National Research Council 2002; Tomita 2006; Vladescu et al. 1999). When the sources are random samples or studies of domestic violence services, spouse abuse is more frequent than abuse by adult children (National Research Council 2002). Caution is warranted in drawing conclusions on information about the victims and perpetrators of elder maltreatment, as studies are limited by the absence of random samples and control groups (Tomita 2006).

RISK FACTORS/RISK INDICATORS FOR ELDER MALTREATMENT

Risk factors may be causes of maltreatment, they may be "risk indicators" ("markers" for unmeasured causes, also called confounders), or they may modify the association between causal variables and maltreatment. For example, caregiver depression may be a causal risk factor for neglect because a depressed caregiver may be socially withdrawn, fatigued, or uninterested in providing care. On the other hand, living arrangement is related to an increased likelihood of maltreatment, not because there is a causal association but because sharing living quarters functions as a contextual factor that increases opportunities for maltreatment (National Research Council 2002).

Risk factors associated with elder maltreatment that have been validated by existing evidence (in the form of clinical accounts and limited empirical research) include living arrangement, social isolation, dementia, intra-individual abuser characteristics, and abuser dependency (National Research Council 2002). Living arrangement is a risk factor for elder maltreatment because it results in more opportunities for interaction, with tension and maltreatment as consequences. Living alone has been associated with protecting older adults from abuse/neglect (Lachs et al. 1997). Shared living arrangements with immediate family, but without a spouse, is a risk factor for violence toward older adults with Alzheimer's disease (Paveza et al. 1992). Unlike other forms of maltreatment, living alone is a risk factor for self-neglect among community-dwelling older adults (Abrams et al. 2002).

Social isolation is associated with maltreatment because identification of maltreatment is less likely in families that have strong social networks and whose members are likely to notice maltreatment and express disapproval or involve formal sources of help such as social service agencies or the police (Choi and Mayer 2000; Kleinschmidt 1997; Lachs and Pillemer 1995; National Research Council 2002). Self-neglect has been found to be associated with being unmarried and with reduced social ties among community-dwelling older adults in two studies (Abrams ct al. 2002; Choi and Mayer 2000). Possibly older adults who live alone and are socially isolated lose the ability to care for themselves and become self-neglecting (Choi and Mayer 2000)

Dementia is a third risk factor for maltreatment. The estimated prevalence of elder maltreatment in samples of dementia caregivers is between 5 and 14 percent. This figure is higher than the estimated range in the general population, between 2 and 10 percent, implying that older individuals with dementia are at higher risk for maltreatment (National Research Council 2002).

However, there is no consistent research explaining the contribution of dementia to the risk of elder abuse, possibly because caregiver violence is strongly related to the experience of violence from the care recipient. Caregivers of older adults with Alzheimer's disease are more likely to exhibit violent behavior when they experience violence or disruptive behavior from the care recipient (Compton, Flanagan, and Gregg 1997; Pillemer and Suitor 1992; Vandeweerd, Paveza, and Fulmer 2006). Thus it is not dementia itself that is a risk factor for abuse but the disruptive behavior associated with dementia (National Research Council 2002). Additional risk factors related to maltreatment of older adults with Alzheimer's disease include high levels of internal abuser stress (depression, substance abuse, burden of care), caregiver and patient isolation, severe dependency by the care receiver, and lack of reciprocity in the caregiver/care receiver relationship (Vandeweerd, Paveza, and Fulmer 2006).

Among community-dwelling older adults, cognitive impairment has been found to be strongly significantly associated with self-neglect (Abrams et al. 2002). Cognitively impaired older adults may have difficulty caring for themselves because of deficits in memory and judgment (Abrams et al. 2002).

Mental health problems may also be associated with older adults' experiences of elder maltreatment. A few studies have found that depression is more common in elders who are abused compared with non-abused controls (Wolf 1999–2000). Older adults calling a statewide abuse hotline were also more likely to use behavioral health services than those not using the hotline (Schonfeld, Larsen, and Stiles 2006). Depression been associated with self-neglect among community-dwelling older adults, possibly because depression is associated with reduced energy and reduced motivation to perform self-care tasks (Abrams et al. 2002).

Intra-individual characteristics of abusers such as emotional problems, hostility, mental illness, and substance abuse have been found to be strongly supported as risk factors for elder maltreatment (Brownell, Berman, and Salamone 1999; Kleinschmidt 1997; Lachs and Pillemer 1995; National Research Council 2002; Quayhagen et al. 1997; Reay and Browne 2001; Reis and Nahmiash 1998; Tomita 2006). The impact of alcohol abuse may be different, depending on the type of abuse. Specifically, physical abuse is twice as likely as neglect to be associated with caregivers' daily consumption of alcohol (Reay and Browne 2001).

Abuser dependency is the last risk factor that is validated by the existing empirical evidence (National Research Council 2002). Abusers have been found to be dependent on the older victim for financial assistance, transportation, and emotional support (National Research Council 2002; Reis and Nahmiash 1998; Tomita 2006).

Community-dwelling individuals who self-neglect are likely to have a past history of strokes and hip fractures and to be low-income men (Abrams et al. 2002). Evidence for an association between alcohol abuse and self-neglect among community-dwelling older adults has also been found (Choi and Mayer 2000).

CULTURAL/ETHNIC FACTORS

African Americans and Hispanics tend to be overrepresented in state reports of elder maltreatment (Tatara 1999), possibly because state welfare systems are biased toward enrollment of low-income minority cases of maltreatment (Lachs et al. 1997). Conversely, maltreatment is underreported in some ethnic groups, such as Japanese Americans, because of cultural norms that emphasize the importance of the social group over the individual, resulting in the silencing of abuse victims (Tomita 1999).

Research has found differing definitions of elder maltreatment between ethnic groups, possibly because cultural norms regarding caregiving vary between groups (Hudson et al. 1998; Hudson et al. 1999; Moon and Benton 2000; Moon and Williams 1993; National Research Council 2002; Tomita 2006). Ethnic groups also differ in tolerance of abuse, propensity to blame the victim, knowledge of sources of formal and informal help, and attitudes toward reporting (Moon and Benton 2000; Moon and Evans-Campbell 1999; Moon, Tomita, and Jung-Kamei 2001).

These findings suggest that home health social work assessment and screening of older adult clients and their families for maltreatment must include an awareness of differences among ethnic groups with respect to definitions of maltreatment, tolerance of maltreatment, attitudes toward the victim, knowledge of formal and informal services, and willingness to report (National Research Council 2002; Tomita 2006).

SCREENING FOR ELDER MALTREATMENT

A noted, older adults may be reticent to reveal maltreatment to professionals (Tomita 2006). Clients who are experiencing maltreatment may be referred to a home health social worker for other problems. In this situation, the social worker should be capable of observing aspects of the client's presentation that may indicate maltreatment. The possible indications include:

- injuries and bruises that the older adult attempts to hide
- frightened and/or withdrawn behavior
- a calm demeanor when alone and agitation in the presence of others
- use of self-denigrating statements ("I am a burden to everyone")
- poor personal hygiene
- a home environment infested with pests and waste (Kahan and Paris 2003; McInnis-Dittrich 2005)

If maltreatment is suspected, the worker should proceed with a screening. During an interview of an older client for suspicion of maltreatment, privacy and confidentiality should be facilitated by asking family members to leave the room temporarily. The client is more likely to give honest responses if their fear of retaliation from family, who may be perpetrators, is minimized (Carney, Kahan, and Paris 2003; Kahan and Paris 2003; McInnis-Dittrich 2005; Tomita 2006).

The goals of assessment/screening are to evaluate whether maltreatment is occurring, and if indicated, the patient's cognitive ability to exercise self-determination by accepting or rejecting intervention (Kahan and Paris 2003).

With the exception of self-neglect, there are currently several rapid-assessment instruments to use in screening for maltreatment of older adults (Fulmer et al. 2004; National Research Council 2002; Wolf 2000). The Indicators of Abuse Screen (OAI) (Reis and Nahmiash 1998) is a 29-item screen with established psychometric properties that was developed specifically for use by social service practitioners who visit the older adult at home (National Research Council 2002). This instrument is appropriate if the suspected perpetrator is the caregiver. It is administered after a psychosocial assessment and is inexpensive, brief, and straightforward (Reis and Nahmiash 1998). The 29 problem-focused items are organized into three categories: (a) abuse caregiver characteristics: personal; (b) abuse caregiver characteristics: interpersonal; and (c) abused care receiver characteristics. The items are rated on a 5-point Likert scale from 0 = nonexistent to 4 = yes/severe. The three categories provide the practitioner with information about problem areas for intervention and prevention. For example, if a caregiver is identified as having a substance abuse problem in the category of caregiver personal characteristics, a referral to a community program for treatment of substance abuse may be indicated. An "abuse alert" score of 16 or more is considered "indicative" but not "definitive" in indicating a positive screen; the practitioner is advised to use clinical judgment in evaluating risk for scores below 16 (Reis and Nahmiash 1998:479).

The scale is copyrighted by the Gerontological Society of America and can be obtained by contacting Susan Sweeney, Associate Production Editor,

Gerontological Society of America, 1030 15th Street N.W., Suite 250, Washington, D.C. 2005-1503. Phone: 202-842-1275, ext. 108, fax: 202-842-2087, e-mail: ssweeney@geron.org.

If the social worker suspects that the abuser is not the caregiver but another family member, the Two Question Abuse Screen can be administered (McFarlane et al. 1995). This scale consists of two questions that are answered either yes or no. If the answer to both questions is "yes," further risk assessment can be evaluated with the Vulnerability to Abuse Screening Scale (VASS) (Schofield et al. 2002; Schofield and Mishra 2003). The VASS, a self-report instrument completed by the suspected victim, consists of four factors: vulnerability, dependence, dejection, and coercion. Each factor has three items that directly measure maltreatment or variables associated with maltreatment. Vulnerability measures physical and psychological abuse; dependence measures lack of autonomy; dejection measures depression, social isolation, and neglect; and coercion measures physical and psychological abuse (Schofield et al. 2002; Schofield and Mishra 2003). The instrument is easy to administer and uses a dichotomous scale consisting of yes/no choices. It has modest reliability and validity (Schofield and Mishra 2003).

The Two Question Abuse Screen is copyrighted by the Emergency Nurses Association. Information about using the scale can be obtained by contacting res@ena.org; phone 847-460-4119. The VASS is copyrighted by the Gerontological Society of America. Copyright release can be obtained by contacting Susan Sweeney, Associate Production Editor, Gerontological Society of America, 1030 15th Street N.W., Suite 250, Washington, D.C. 2005-1503. Phone: 202-842-1275, ext. 108, fax: 202-842-2087, e-mail: ssweeney@geron.org. Further information about the scale is available from Margot Schofield, Ph.D., School of Health, University of New England, Armidale, New South Wales 2351, Australia. E-mail: mscholfi2@metz.une.edu.au.

When an older adult is self-neglecting, the worker attempts to balance respect for the client's autonomy with societal concerns about protecting vulnerable older adults from harm (Tomita 2006). An individual's competence to make decisions about care is a priority for evaluation (Abrams et al. 2002; Leff and Sonstegard-Gamm 2006; Tomita 2006). This evaluation may include a mental status exam and the procedure for evaluating decision-making capacity (presented in chapter 2 in the discussion of ethical conflicts related to autonomy). If the worker is concerned about the client's competence, communication of the worker's evaluation to the patient's physician is indicated to obtain a psychiatry consult.

If the client is capable and understands the consequences of refusing help, he or she has a right to reject services (Leff and Sonstegard-Gamm 2006; Tomita 2006). If the client is willing to cooperate, screening for alcohol abuse and depression (discussed in chapter 5) is also recommended (Abrams et al. 2002; Choi and Mayer 2000).

ASSESSMENT OF ELDER MALTREATMENT

If a screen is positive, the suspected victim can be interviewed alone, using an outline of suggested questions (Carney, Kahan, and Paris 2003). It is advisable to integrate the questions into the interview in a calm and relaxed manner.

If the social worker has not already evaluated the client's mental status (when the client is the suspected victim of abuse/neglect by a perpetrator), this should be completed at this time. Any concerns of the older adult about the consequences of disclosing mistreatment, such as retaliation, loss of the relationship with the abuser, or removal from the home, should also be discussed (Kahan and Paris 2003; Tomita 2006).

After the evaluation of the older adult, an assessment of the suspected perpetrator is indicated. Before this interview, it is important to reassure the older adult that confidentiality will be maintained. The social worker can begin the interview by using some variation of the following: "I have been assessing your mother's current functioning and situation to determine what services she needs. I would like to ask you about your perception of how things are going" (Tomita 2006:234). This statement can be followed by questions about:

- knowledge of the victim's situation
- expectations of the suspected victim
- difficulties in caring for the suspected victim
- degree of financial dependence on the suspected victim (Tomita 2006:234)

When older adults self-neglect, they are unlikely to perceive the risks that are obvious to the practitioner. They may wish to protect their independence and usual routines and consequently may not be motivated to change (Leff and Sonstegard-Gamm 2006).

A focus on understanding how the client's self-neglect developed over time may help provide information for intervention (Tomita 2006). For some clients, self-neglect has been a lifestyle, while others experience risk factors that result in self-neglect over time (e.g., loss of social support, physical and mental impairment, an absence of meaningful roles). Significant areas for assessment include recent losses, history or symptoms of mental illness, the client's values and goals, and relationships with family (Abrams et al. 2002; Leff and Sonstegard-Gamm 2006; Schonfeld, Larsen, and Stiles 2006).

REPORTING REQUIREMENTS

In evaluating suspected elder maltreatment, it is important to know whether reporting is mandatory in your state and to communicate the limits of confidentiality to the elder and the family at the beginning of the contact. Nearly all states provide the reporter with immunity from civil or criminal liability for reporting abuse or neglect (Emlet 1996). If reporting is not mandatory, the worker should be knowledgeable about agency policy and procedures. Any investigation or service provided to the victim if maltreatment is suspected also requires the consent of the victim, if he or she is competent to make this decision (Drake and Freed 1998). In most states the appropriate agency to which to refer an elder if abuse/neglect is suspected is the adult protective service agency in the area. These agencies may also collaborate with the Area Office on Aging, a Social Security office, legal services, mental health agencies, and medical facilities (Naleppa and Reid 2003). A protocol for screening and assessment of elder maltreatment is available for $17 by going to the following Web site: http://www.nursing.uiowa.edu/centers/gnirc/documents/RTDC-CatalogueSept2006.pdf and completing the order form for the "Elder Abuse Prevention" guidelines.

RISK FOR NURSING HOME PLACEMENT

RISK FACTORS ASSOCIATED WITH PLACEMENT

Home health care social workers assessing caregivers and care recipients for nursing home placement should be knowledgeable about the factors associated with risk for placement and the elements of the nursing home decision-making process that are relevant to practice.

HIGH-RISK CAREGIVERS AND CARE RECIPIENTS

Among caregivers of community-residing older adults, risk for nursing home placement is associated with:

- caring for older adults who live alone
- difficult or problem behavior
- an earlier hospitalization
- high levels of ADL and cognitive impairment in the care recipient, while the caregiver perceives few gains in the caregiving role
- higher caregiver burden
- poor caregiver physical and mental health
- inadequate access to formal and informal support (Chenier 1997; Freed-

man 1996, Freedman et al. 1994; Gaugler et al. 2003; Gilley et al. 2005; Mahoney, Eisner et al. 2000; Naleppa 1996; Yaffe et al. 2002).

The single study of older adults and their caregivers utilizing in-home care found three caregiver characteristics—living separately from the care recipient, time conflicts between caregiving and work, and caregiver burden—to be associated with a higher likelihood of nursing home placement (Tsuji, Whalen, and Finucane 1995).

THE DECISION-MAKING PROCESS

Before initiating discussions about nursing home placement with the caregiver and the care recipient (when the care recipient has the decision-making ability to participate in discussions), the social worker, in collaboration with other members of the home health care team, should discuss whether the caregiver can provide adequate care for the care recipient in the community or whether the option of a nursing home should be considered, given the available support and the level of caregiver and care recipient impairment. If a nursing home seems to be a viable option, the worker and the relevant medical staff should share their assessment with the caregiver and the family so they can make an informed choice (Mastrian and Dellasega 1996).

Social workers may also wish to assess the presence of factors that research suggests contribute to a positive transition experience (Davies and Nolan 2003; Nolan and Dellasega 2000). Areas for assessment include first, whether the family and client have had sufficient time to make a decision about placement. The nursing literature suggests that while professional providers may perceive nursing home placement as an obvious choice, caregivers and care recipients may not have anticipated or discussed placement. The caregiver may need some time to accept the deterioration in his or her own ability to provide care and in the care recipient's capacity to live independently (Mastrian and Dellasega 1996). The worker's assessment here may also focus on how realistic the caregiver is about her or his own personal and social resources to provide adequate care, the physical and mental status of the care recipient, and the caregiver's knowledge of available and accessible resources on a continuum of care from home care to nursing home (Abel-Vacula and Phillips 2004; Mastrian and Dellasega 1996; Penrod and Dellasega 1998).

The social worker can also help the caregiver identify the important decision makers. Because the care recipient is frequently excluded from the process (McAuley, Travis, and Safewright 1997; Reinhardy 1992, 1995; Reinhardy and Kane 1999; Salamon and Rosenthal 2004) and because the participation of the care recipient is associated with positive post-placement outcomes (Reinhardy

1992, 1995; Reinhardy and Kane 1999), the worker may wish to assess barriers to open discussion of options for living arrangements.

Possible obstacles may be the caregiver's guilt with respect to the cultural stigma of institutionalization, expectations of family responsibility for care, and hostility toward nursing homes as profit-driven enterprises (Davies and Nolan 2003). Adding to the reluctance of the caregiver may be the emotional and psychological resistance of the care recipient to nursing homes, with the view that they are places to go to die. The care recipient may have told the caregiver, "Don't ever put me in a nursing home" (Davies and Nolan 2003; Mastrian and Dellasega 1996). The caregiver may thus perceive the involvement of the care recipient in decision making as stressful (Davies and Nolan 2003).

Third, the meaning of the placement decision for the caregiver may have an influence on his or her ability to make a decision that is perceived as a positive one. Placement may be associated with feelings of failure, fear of loneliness, sadness that placement signifies the end of a life spent together, disorientation, anxiety, and relief (Hagen 2001; Kellett 1999; Nolan and Dellasega 2000; Penrod and Dellasega 1998; Ryan and Scullion 2000).

Finally, the caregiver's knowledge regarding the process of nursing home placement, financial resources for placement, and the availability of informal social support during this stressful period is also a recommended topic for assessment in the course of a positive decision-making process (Davies and Nolan 2003; Mastrian and Dellasega 1996; Reuss, Dupuis, and Whitfield 2005; Ryan and Scullion 2000).

It should be noted that not all caregivers experience negative reactions to placement. If caregivers felt that the relative wanted to move and was in the right nursing home or that there was no other reasonable alternative, they experienced primarily positive emotions about the move (Dellegasa and Nolan 1997).

ETHNICITY AND NURSING HOME PLACEMENT

The ethnicity of the care recipient influences the use of nursing home care, such that ethnic minority clients are less likely to use nursing homes than non-Hispanic whites, as is indicated by the research when other relevant variables are taken into account (Borrayo et al. 2002; Cagney and Agree 1999; Gaugler et al. 2003; Wallace et al. 1998). Research has found that the same variables—Medicaid eligibility, caregiver burden, the care recipient's cognitive impairment, age of care recipient, and gender of care recipient (men were more likely to be institutionalized earlier) were associated with placement among non-Hispanic white and African American caregivers of older individuals with dementia, suggesting that the stress process model is applicable to the African American context (Gaugler, Leach et al. 2004).

Home care social workers assessing African American clients for their readiness to engage in decision making for nursing home placement may wish to assess family structure and the primary decision makers, the influence of family values, preferences for and knowledge of long-term-care options, financial resources, and preferences regarding facility location staff and programming. Connecting clients with facilities that have bed availability and that match their expectations is critical in completing successful referrals for ethnically diverse clients (Johnson and Tripp-Reimer 2001).

◈ ◈ ◈

In performing a social assessment the social worker attempts to answer the question, Does the individual have enough support to remain in the community after an acute episode or to continue living in the community with a chronic condition? The concept of unmet service needs refers to unavailable, insufficient, inadequate, and/or inappropriate assistance from formal and informal resources to compensate for care recipient ADL/IADL impairments. There are two approaches to measuring unmet service needs: function-specific and service-specific. A function-specific approach is recommended for the purposes of home health social work assessment.

The client's social support system influences level of unmet service needs. In assessing this factor, the social worker evaluates the client's social network and social support.

An assessment of the client's environmental resources should focus on environmental safety and the client's knowledge of and access to public programs and resources.

Caregiver burden, defined as the emotional, psychological, physical, and financial demands of caregiving, and the subjective appraisal of how these tasks influence the caregiver's well-being or a positive appraisal of caregiving are two distinct dimensions of caregiving that may be experienced simultaneously. The purpose of the home health social worker's assessment of burden and well-being is to identify sources of stress and/or satisfaction to support the caregiver and the care recipient.

Family conflict is defined as overtly expressed interpersonal disagreement, hostility/anger, or unexpressed emotions such as resentment. Family conflict resolution may influence the quality of care and family well-being. Family patterns of decision making and the distribution of caregiving responsibilities are important areas for assessment.

Elder maltreatment is difficult to define, since there is no commonly accepted standard. Types of elder maltreatment include physical abuse, sexual abuse, emotional or psychological abuse, financial abuse, neglect, and self-neglect.

Goals of assessment/screening are to determine the presence of maltreatment, to evaluate the victim's ability to make decisions about accepting intervention, and to communicate the limits of confidentiality to the client, within the parameters of state and local elder abuse reporting laws.

In assessing caregivers and care recipients for nursing home placement, the home care social worker should collaborate with other home care providers to determine whether the well-being of the care recipient will be impaired by continued residence in the community. If the assessment is positive, the worker's goal is to assess those factors that obstruct or support a positive decision-making experience for the caregiver and the care recipient.

Ethnicity has been found to influence nursing home placement, with African American caregivers less likely to place a relative than non-Hispanic white caregivers. In discussing long-term care with ethnically diverse clients, social workers should assess the influence of family structure, who the primary decision makers are, the family's values and preferences for and knowledge of long-term-care options, financial resources, and preferences regarding facility location, staff, and programming.

7

SOCIAL WORK INTERVENTIONS WITH THE INDIVIDUAL
IN HOME HEALTH CARE

THIS CHAPTER discusses a number of concerns that arise during the course of home health social work interventions:

- medication management
- advance directive planning
- alternative health care beliefs and medical practices
- depression and suicide
- anxiety disorders
- substance abuse

As noted in chapter 2, social work interventions for mental and emotional problems are circumscribed by Medicare reimbursement policies.

With regard to the criterion of the "best available" research, the literature cited in this chapter is generally methodologically sound and current, particularly with regard to "reminder packaging," CAM management practices, and psychosocial interventions for disease self-management through self-efficacy, depression, suicide, anxiety, and substance abuse. The discussion of advance directives is derived from a conceptual model and scholarship.

MEDICATION MANAGEMENT

The topic of medication management is presented in this book in two places. This chapter deals with interventions with the individual. Chapter 8 describes interventions with a primary focus on the social environment. The following discussion presents interventions implemented by the home health care social worker to reduce or eliminate psychosocial barriers to medication adherence by older adults.

COORDINATION OF MULTIDISCIPLINARY TEAM

Social workers can provide coordination to the multidisciplinary team in the community to reduce medication non-adherence due to psychosocial factors (Erickson and Muramatsu 2004; Hughes 2004). An intervention plan to address barriers to adherence (e.g., simplification or modification of the medication regimen when client forgetfulness is the problem; education of client and family about illness and efficacy of medication) can be developed by working with the patient's primary-care physician, home care nurses, pharmacist, psychiatrist, physical and occupational therapists, the client, and significant others (Erickson and Muramatsu 2004; Hughes 2004; Osterberg and Blaschke 2005).

When clients have difficulty communicating with professionals, the social worker can help the client develop a list of questions and concerns to bring to a visit with a professional. If the client consents, the worker can provide this information to professionals for the client (Erickson and Muramatsu 2004). In particular, since a therapeutic relationship with a physician or nurse is one of the most significant factors influencing adherence, the social worker may wish to communicate to the medical professional client issues that interfere with the development of this relationship (Hughes 2004; Ryan 1999).

INCREASED OR ENHANCED INVOLVEMENT OF CLIENTS IN TREATMENT DECISIONS

While some patients may be reluctant to be involved in decisions about medication regimens, the social worker may wish to explore their reasons for non-participation. If the client is not participating because of lack of confidence or feelings of intimidation by professionals, the social worker can implement strategies to increase client confidence in interacting with professionals (Belcher et al. 2006). One such strategy is to role-play or coach clients in order to prepare them to share their preferences and beliefs with others who are involved in their care (Erickson and Muramatsu 2004; Hughes 2004; Osterberg and Blaschke 2005).

If a client is not cognitively impaired, the social worker can instruct him or her in how to keep a detailed log of medication usage, side effects, barriers to taking the medication as prescribed, and effect of the medication on symptoms. The log can be shared with a physician or nurse to tailor medication regimens to the client's responses. Workers can also follow up by phone to encourage and remind clients to fill out the log and share it with professionals (Erickson and Muramatsu 2004).

DEPRESSION AND MEDICATION ADHERENCE

If a GDS screen is positive and the client's responses to questions indicate a possible diagnosis of depression, the worker should communicate the results of the screening to the patient and complete a referral to a psychiatric nurse and/or the primary-care physician for a comprehensive assessment and treatment plan, since depression can affect medication adherence by reducing motivation and energy and increasing forgetfulness (Erickson and Muramatsu 2004).

ENHANCING ADHERENCE BY LINKING CLIENTS WITH SUPPORTS

To reduce non-adherence that results from forgetfulness, busy lifestyles, or complex medication regimens, the social worker can provide access to medications organized in "reminder packaging." The term refers to any organization of medications such as pillboxes, blister packages, bottles, or single-use containers that organize medication according to the time and day it is to be taken (Erickson and Muramatsu 2004; Heneghan, Glasziou, and Perera 2006; Osterberg and Blaschke 2005). If the patient consistently forgets to reorder medications, the social worker can ask family or other social supports to assume the task of reordering or to remind the patient to reorder. When barriers to transportation influence non-adherence, informal supports can pick up medications and provide transportation to the physician's office or pharmacy (Erickson and Muramatsu 2004).

INTERVENTIONS FOR PLANNING ADVANCE DIRECTIVES

It has been argued that home care is the best setting for advance care planning for several reasons: family members are more available than in a clinic setting; such discussions are difficult and they take more time than a typical clinic visit; families and patients prefer to have such a discussion outside of an acute-care setting and before a crisis; and Medicare reimbursement is available for social work services under the home care benefit (Norlander and McSteen 2000).

During the intake interview, the nurse case manager can identify clinical indicators of life-threatening illnesses and/or cognitive impairment resulting from depression or dementia that suggest that patients will benefit from advance care planning. A holistic approach to advance care planning that incorporates physical, psychosocial, and spiritual factors, implemented by either the social worker or the nurse case manager, is recommended (Norlander and McSteen 2000).

Before any discussion of advance care planning takes place, an assessment of the patient's capacity to make these decisions should be completed. Dementia patients and their significant others are most likely to be capable of participating in these discussions during early stages of the disorder. A relationship based on communication and trust between patients, families, workers, and other health care providers will promote the best care for persons with dementia, as severely demented individuals may have difficulty communicating their wishes about quality of life to surrogates (Rempusheske and Hurley 2000).

Practitioners may fear that they will deprive the patient of hope by introducing a discussion of advance care planning. While patients and families do need hope, avoidance of the discussion may allow patients to maintain an overly optimistic view of their condition and pursue unnecessary aggressive treatment, rather than enabling them to experience a more comfortable and peaceful death. Practitioners also want to communicate that patients will not be abandoned and that the focus of care will be on optimizing the quality of their lives. Helpful and supportive phrases for initiating advance care planning include the following:

- "Making decisions before a crisis is a gift you can give to your family."
- "Have you ever thought about what kind of care you would want if you could not speak for yourself?"
- "This is an opportunity to develop a written health care directive."
- "Advance care planning gives you some control over your future." (Norlander and McSteen 2000:538)

Norlander and McSteen (2000) have piloted a tool for home care social workers and nurses to apply in conducting what they have labeled "kitchen table discussions." The following are key areas for discussion:

- What is the patient's understanding of the illness?
- Does the patient view the illness as life-threatening?
- Does the patient expect a cure or improvement?
- Is the patient's understanding of the illness different from that of the family or physician?
- What are the patient's personal experiences with death?
- What are his or her fears?
- What are the patient's goal and values?
- What are the patient's concerns about spirituality?
- Does the family support the patient's goals and values?
- Is there conflict or disagreement between the patient's wishes and those of family members?
- What are factors inhibiting the patient's willingness to plan?

- Does the patient fear that advance directives will deprive him or her of end-of-life care?
- Does the patient worry that directives are "binding"?
- Does the patient view directives as unnecessary because he or she expects to rely on the family to decide?
- Is the patient interested in filling out an advance directive?
- What does the patient know about different types of advance directives?
- Who will be the health care proxy?
- Does the health care proxy have a thorough understanding of the patient's wishes?
- Is the patient having difficulty communicating health care wishes to the physician?
- Does the patient want help in discussing advance care planning with the physician?

Research has found that patients are less concerned about discussions of life-sustaining treatment but more concerned about clinical outcomes that they consider personally acceptable. The questions they want answered are whether they will be able to engage in valued life activities as a result of the introduction or withholding of life-sustaining treatments (Rosenfeld, Wenger, and Kagawa-Singer 2000). It is unlikely that social workers are competent to answer such questions, and thus any detailed discussion of advance directive scenarios requires the presence of a nurse or a referral to a physician.

Social workers differ in their comfort level and willingness to engage in such discussions, depending on their own personal experiences with death, dying, and loss. Role-playing the discussion with a colleague or completing an advance directive can be helpful in anticipating and understanding these feelings (Norlander and McSteen 2000).

POWER OF ATTORNEY

A discussion of advance planning for financial and legal tasks is appropriate with older adult clients with chronic illnesses since, as mentioned previously, these conditions can affect cognitive status and the ability to perform such IADL tasks as financial management. The topic is more urgent when the client has a diagnosis of Alzheimer's disease, dementia, or stroke that impairs cognition. By completing this process while the patient is still sufficiently cognitively intact to voluntarily make decisions, families avoid future time-consuming and expensive legal proceedings and decisions that may not be consistent with the patient's wishes (Aneshensel et al. 1995).

A power of attorney document is a contract between the client and an individual of his or her choice that gives the other person the legal authority to manage the client's financial affairs (American Association of Retired Persons [AARP] 2007; Arnason, Rosenzweig, and Koski 1995; Overeynder 2003a). The client who creates the power of attorney is referred to as the *principal*, while the person appointed by the client to carry out their wishes is the *agent*. A power of attorney can be created only if the principal has the mental ability to understand what the contract means and is consenting voluntarily. If the client was previously assessed as manifesting cognitive impairment, the worker (possibly in collaboration with a psychiatrist or psychiatric nurse) should evaluate the client's decisional capacity to enter into this agreement (Arnason, Rosenzweig, and Koski 1995; Bassuk and Lessem 2001).

A power of attorney can be very broad, granting the agent authority to handle all financial transactions, or very narrow, authorizing the agent to sell a car or manage a checking account. The client decides on the amount of supervision over financial affairs to delegate to the agent. The client may have difficulty understanding a discussion about power of attorney if he or she does not understand the distinction between advance directives (e.g., living wills and durable power of attorney for health care) and power of attorney for finances. The social worker can discuss these distinctions with the client to facilitate client decision making.

Anyone (family, friends, attorney) whom the client chooses can be appointed as the agent. Several considerations are relevant with respect to the selection of an agent. The individual should be someone the client trusts and who lives close to the client so that he or she will be accessible when the client needs help. If the authority granted to the agent is broad, the agent should be someone who has the necessary time to fulfill the responsibility. It is possible to appoint more than one person as agent for a power of attorney. If two or more people are appointed, the client decides whether they are required to act jointly (requiring both of their signatures at all times) or whether they can act separately. The social worker can facilitate discussions between the client and significant others about who is the most appropriate person to assume this role.

The advantage of the power of attorney document is that the client chooses the agent and can communicate his or her wishes to the principal about how affairs should be handled. The power of attorney also reduces the client's stress related to managing financial tasks. The disadvantage is that the principal may not be trustworthy and, as a consequence, may take action to harm the client. This possibility is one argument for appointing two people so that they can monitor each other's actions (Arnason, Rosenzweig, and Koski 1995; Overeynder 2003a). It should be noted, however, that the power of attorney can be revoked by a mentally competent client at any time (Bassuk and Lessem 2001).

The client, with the worker's assistance, will also need to choose which type of power of attorney to execute. A regular power of attorney is valid only while the client has the ability to direct the agent and supervise the agent's actions. A durable power of attorney remains valid after the client becomes incapable of directing the agent. A springing power of attorney has the same authority as a durable power of attorney with the exception that the agent will not become active right away but at some future time when an event or situation determined by the client in advance occurs. The client can appoint the power of attorney in advance, but the agent would act in the client's place only when the "springing" event occurs (American Association of Retired Persons [AARP] 2006; Arnason, Rosensweig, and Koski 1995; Overeynder 2003a).

Standard forms to create a power of attorney document can be purchased in stores. These forms must be completed, notarized, and filed with the county clerk's office in the client's county of residence. The social worker can assist the client in understanding and completing the form. Since legal implications can be costly if the worker participated in a process in which guidance given to the client was not accurate, workers should be well trained in the use of these forms. If the worker has doubts about his or her competence to respond to client questions, legal advice should be sought (Bassuk and Lessem 2001).

INTERVENTIONS TO ADDRESS HEALTH CARE BELIEFS AND CAM MANAGEMENT PRACTICES

The worker's goal when client explanatory models and management practices differ from those of mainstream health care providers is to act as a culture broker, undertaking a role as the professional on the health care team who understands both the client's and the medical provider's explanatory models and health care practices and works to develop a shared model that maximizes the benefits of both systems for the client. As a culture broker, the worker acts as a mediator, improving communication and resolving conflict between clients and providers when there is the potential for disagreement about treatment. A second function is advocating with providers and/or health care systems that dismiss client preferences on the assumption that conventional medical beliefs and practices are superior. The worker also acts as a consultant, providing information to medical providers about complementary and alternative beliefs and practices and the process of negotiating treatment plans when client and practitioner hold dissimilar assumptions (Carrillo, Green, and Betancourt 1999; Hall, Stone, and Fiset 1998).

Since the majority of clients who use CAM do not disclose their practices to their physicians or presumably other medical providers (Institute of Medicine 2005), it is important to encourage clients to tell physicians/nurses about the use of CAM therapies and underlying explanatory systems. In particular, clients from cultures that consider questioning or confrontation rude may not ask questions of or challenge the provider but may later express their discomfort through non-adherence. If the client can discuss CAM practices with medical providers, adherence can improve and safety issues and interactions between conventional medications and herbal/vitamin supplements can be addressed (Institute of Medicine 2005).

In discussions with the client about disclosure of alternative practices and beliefs to medical providers, a nonjudgmental attitude that does not assume the superiority of conventional medicine over client models and the adoption of a supportive, reassuring tone may facilitate disclosure (Cook, Becvar, and Pontious 2000). These practices and models can then be compared to relevant aspects of the medical model to highlight similarities and differences between the client's model and those of conventional medicine. The discussion of the medical model should be in simple and straightforward language, using the client's terminology and concepts as appropriate (Carrillo, Green, and Betancourt 1999). The goal in comparing the two models is to develop a plan of care that does not threaten or change the client's health care beliefs but combines them with the practices of conventional medicine with the goal of further benefit to the client (Carrillo, Green, and Betancourt 1999; Hall, Stone, and Fiset 1998; Jackson 1993).

Finally, as the professional in home care with expertise related to influence of cultural and socioeconomic factors on health outcomes, the worker can function as a consultant to the health care team regarding the process of developing a shared plan with the older client.

INTERVENTIONS TO ENHANCE SELF-EFFICACY

Interventions that enhance self-efficacy and are applicable in home health care social work practice include performance accomplishment, vicarious experience, verbal persuasion, and reinterpretation of symptoms (Bandura 1997; Lorig 2003).

PERFORMANCE ACCOMPLISHMENT

Performance accomplishment refers to the performance of a behavior. It is the most influential of the four methods of enhancing self-efficacy because "it is difficult to argue that someone cannot do something when they are doing it" (Lorig and Holman 2003:4). To increase client performance accomplishment, the worker and the client break out complex tasks to create a hierarchy of progressively difficult sub-tasks until the client has mastered the entire task. This strategy helps the client avoid early failure, which can undermine self-efficacy

(Bandura 1997; Van de Laar and Van der Bijl 2001). For example, to improve the self-efficacy of a client in communicating with medical providers such as physicians or nurses, the older adult client can agree to perform the following sub-tasks: writing a list of questions and concerns to discuss with the provider; asking a third party (e.g., family member, friend, social worker) to be present during the visit to facilitate the client's accurate recall of provider recommendations; writing down obstacles to implementation of the care plan (e.g., medication non-adherence) to discuss with the provider.

Self-efficacy is also influenced by setting specific, challenging goals. Goals are motivating because they focus attention on the discrepancy between perceived performance and a higher personal standard. Specific goals provide explicit standards to regulate performance by identifying the type and amount of effort required to attain them. Goals that are perceived as challenging but achievable will elicit higher levels of motivation (Bandura 1997; Van de Laar and Van der Bijl 2001). Successful client goal achievement is most effective in increasing self-efficacy if the worker attributes the success to the client's performance rather than to luck or to the help of the professional (Bandura 1997; Van de Laar and Van der Bijl 2001). For example, a challenging goal might be to achieve 80 percent medication adherence in thirty days by developing an individualized care plan with the medical provider.

VICARIOUS EXPERIENCE

Vicarious learning or learning by observing the behaviors of another person is applied when social workers or other home care professionals, who are regarded by the client as competent models, role-play to model the behavior for the client and then switch roles while the client enacts the behavior (Bandura 1997; Van de Laar and Van der Bijl 2001). For example, to demonstrate effective communication techniques, the worker might assume the role of the client while the client assumes the role of the provider.

VERBAL PERSUASION

Verbal persuasion is the most frequently used method for strengthening a client's self-efficacy. An individual is more likely to maintain a sense of self-efficacy, particularly when struggling with difficulties, if significant others express confidence in his or her capacities. People who are persuaded verbally that they are capable of mastering a task are more likely to try hard and persevere.

Persuasion is most effective with individuals who have a moderate level of self-efficacy. It is also most effective and least likely to be misleading when it is close to, but a little beyond, an individual's current capabilities. Unrealistic encouragement that does not accurately match the individual's capabilities is likely to lead to failure and will also contribute to the worker's loss of credibility. This strategy has limited power when used alone; it is most effective when combined with other strategies (Bandura 1997; Van de Laar and Van der Bijl 2001). For example, with a client who has adequate social skills and wishes to request that the physician simplify the medication regimen, the worker can use verbal persuasion by saying, "I am confident that you have the skills to communicate your concerns to your physician."

REINTERPRETATION OF SYMPTOMS

People may base their interpretation of symptoms on their personal beliefs about disease. Sometimes when these beliefs are reinterpreted (not labeled as wrong), clients gain access to new avenues for addressing symptoms. Clients may believe that disease symptoms can be modified only by traditional medical interventions such as medication or surgery. The worker can reinterpret symptoms by attributing disease to psychosocial factors (e.g., inadequate nutrition, lack of exercise, or reactions to stress). This strategy increases self-efficacy by suggesting additional options for symptom management (Bandura 1997). For example, the worker might suggest to an older diabetic client that an appropriate diet and progressive muscle relaxation in combination with medication might improve diabetic symptoms.

Clients develop self-efficacy by combining feedback from each of the four interventions outlined above. However, the influence of different interventions on forming self-efficacy beliefs will vary for different people in different situations (Bandura 1997; Lorig 2003; Lorig and Holman 2003; Van de Laar and Van der Bijl 2001).

DEPRESSION

There is no published social work research on the role of the social worker in providing home care to patients experiencing a *DSM-IV* diagnosis of depression, subsyndromal depression, or dysthymia. In general, an older client is assigned to a psychiatric nurse in home care when the client's primary diagnosis is depression or dysthymia, psychiatric symptoms are acute, and there is a secondary medical diagnosis. In this situation, the psychiatric nurse is responsible for assessment, education about and monitoring of psychotropic medications, psychotherapy, and other skilled nursing services. If the nurse identifies psychosocial issues that are barriers to recovery or stabilization for the patient, he or she refers the patient to the home health social worker. The social worker is responsible for completing a psychosocial assessment, linking the client with community resources, providing advocacy, and assisting with long-term-care planning. Social work counseling can be provided if it is focused on enhancing resources, decreasing social barriers to treatment, and/or ameliorating family/caregiver conflict. Social work counseling focused on treating the patient's psychiatric symptoms is not reimbursed under Medicare guidelines, as this is considered a duplication of the psychiatric nurse's interventions. Documentation by the social worker can clarify this distinction (Byrne 1999).

A client may be assigned to a social worker, as opposed to a psychiatric nurse, when the client has a primary medical diagnosis and subsyndromal depression that interferes with the plan for care. For example, an appropriate client for social work might be a client referred to home care for physical therapy. The physical therapist observes that the patient displays depressive symptoms and thus makes a referral to social work. The patient is assessed by the social worker as experiencing an adjustment disorder with depressed mood, resulting from loss of functioning following a stroke. The social worker's focus in this case might be on providing counseling to reduce depressive symptoms and facilitate adjustment to the consequences of stroke (Byrne 1999).

BARRIERS TO TREATMENT

Research indicates that psychological barriers to treatment, such as minimizing the severity of the illness, and perceived stigma are obstacles to adherence to antidepressant drug treatment across the life cycle (Sirey et al. 2001). However, older adult clients may be more sensitive than younger adults to the stigma associated with a diagnosis of depression (Unützer et al. 1999). Social workers can reduce obstacles to medication adherence by discussing the older patient's perception of the illness and the consequent need for care. In addition, home care workers can reduce stigma by explaining depression as a medical problem for which there are effective treatments and medications. This information may reduce fear that depression indicates character flaws or moral weakness, increase motivation for treatment, and help clients and family identify early signs of relapse (Culpepper 2002). The worker's exploration with the client of the anticipated outcome of seeking care, when to disclose his or her illness, and to whom may also increase treatment adherence (Sirey et al. 2001).

EFFECTIVE COUNSELING INTERVENTIONS
FOR DEPRESSED OLDER ADULTS

Psychosocial interventions are effective for the aged, particularly older adults who reject medication or who are coping with low levels of social support or stressful situations such as acute or chronic illness (Gellis 2006; Lebowitz et al.

1997). Evidence supports the efficacy of cognitive therapy, cognitive-behavioral therapy, and problem-solving therapy (a form of cognitive-behavioral therapy) as alternatives to, or in combination with, antidepressant drug treatment for depressed community-residing older adults (Bartels et al. 2002; DeRubeis et al. 1999; Gellis 2006; McCusker et al. 1998; Schulberg, Pilkonis, and Houck 1998). To benefit from these psychotherapies, clients should be cognitively intact, have minimal comorbid psychopathology, and not be suicidal (Gatz et al. 1998).

While time constraints may not allow a home care social worker to implement a full course of such treatments, the basic principles of these approaches can be applied in counseling older adults with depression. In general, cognitive therapy involves identifying negative automatic thoughts and formulating counterarguments to disprove those thoughts (Culpepper 2002). For example, a patient who has had a stroke and is dependent on his wife for daily care may think that he is a burden to his wife (Dyeson 2000). Discussing the basis of the client's thinking, his sense of loss of control, and asking the client to counter the thought (for example, by saying something like "Everyone is dependent to some degree on others throughout life. It is a strength to recognize and accept help when it is needed") are appropriate interventions.

The basic principles of problem-solving therapy can also be applied within the time constraints of home health social work practice. Problem-solving therapy assumes that problem-solving coping is a moderator of the relationship between stressful events (such as chronic illness) and psychological distress (Nezu et al. 1999). Problem-solving therapy focuses on enhancing problem-solving ability and skills, reducing emotional distress, increasing the patient's sense of control by teaching a set of coping skills that can be generalized, and improving the overall quality of life of the patient (Nezu et al. 1999). For example, a patient with low self-efficacy related to arranging for help with shopping can be instructed to use visualization to change a feeling of helplessness to a one of competence by picturing him/herself successfully solving the problem. The worker in this instance might say, "Imagine yourself solving the problem. How does it feel? What do you do to solve the problem? How does it feel to resolve the problem successfully?" (Nezu et al. 1999:19). Workers can also educate clients about the steps for effective problem solving (defining the problem, deciding what needs to be accomplished, listing possible solutions, choosing and implementing the best solution, evaluating the outcome) (Nezu et al. 1999; Nezu et al. 2003).

PHARMACOLOGIC INTERVENTIONS

Attitudes of older adults toward treatment influences acceptance of and adherence to treatment. Research suggests that community-residing depressed older adults prefer psychotherapy/counseling over medication, and several studies have found no difference in effectiveness between antidepressant medication and psychotherapeutic intervention in older adults (Gellis 2006; McCusker et al. 1998; Schulberg, Pilkonis, and Houck 1998).

However, changes in patient status may require a change in treatment. If the social worker provides short-term counseling to a patient and the patient continues to display depressive symptoms or the patient's symptoms become more severe, the social worker should consult with the physician and the psychiatric nurse to schedule an evaluation of the patient for antidepressant medication (Byrne 1999). Antidepressant medications are effective and safe for depressed older adults and can be taken by patients with a comorbid medical illness (Bartels et al. 2002; Gellis 2006; Unützer et al. 1999). The social worker may then stay involved with the patient to obtain resources, while the psychiatric nurse provides medication teaching and counseling (Byrne 1999).

REFERRALS TO INFORMAL AND FORMAL SUPPORTS

Frail older adult home care clients with medical conditions and comorbid depression present some specific challenges for social workers in making decisions about appropriate referrals for mental health services. Homebound older adults with comorbid physical and mental health problems, compromised decision-making ability, varying levels of family and professional support, and financial concerns may be overwhelmed by the burden of coping with multiple outpatient service providers. Issues related to transportation and navigation of a complex delivery system may complicate access to specialty mental health care for these clients and their significant others (Bruce, Van Citters, and Bartels 2005; U.S. Department of Health and Human Services, Centers for Medicare and Medicaid Services 2005a, 2005b).

A small number of empirical studies, including two randomized controlled clinical trials, suggests that home-based mental health services are most effective for older adults whose access to traditional outpatient mental health providers may be limited by the factors mentioned above (Bruce, Van Citters, and Bartels 2005). These services may be located in or coordinated by a community-based mental health center and include a multidisciplinary geriatric team of social workers, nurses, and psychiatrists who complete an in-home assessment and develop a care plan (Bruce, Van Citters, and Bartels 2005; Lipsman 1996).

Informal social support among home health care clients has been found to be associated with levels of depression that in turn are related to emotional and social well-being. Among older adult women receiving home health care, depression has been found to mediate the relationship between social support and emotional well-being. A higher number of social support providers predicted less depression and better emotional well-being. In addition, greater satisfaction with social support predicted less depression, which in turn predicted better emotional well-being (Friedman et al. 2005).

Interventions to increase the perception of satisfaction with social support may target conflicted relationships between caregivers and care recipients. Dyeson (2000) found an association between chronically ill older adults' negative feelings of dependency on caregivers that indirectly affected care recipient depression. In some situations, negative dependency may be a response to short-tempered caregivers who are angry and frustrated (Dyeson 2000). This association between feelings of negative dependency and depression, as well as the frustration and anger of the caregiver may be reduced by social worker–initiated discussions about what caregiver and care recipient would perceive as a positive, meaningful interaction and by increasing the frequency of those interchanges. For example, a reciprocal behavior by the care recipient directed toward the caregiver, such as being a good listener and providing emotional support in a crisis, may improve the self-esteem of the care recipient and reduce the caregiver's stress by conveying the message that the relationship is reciprocal (Dyeson 2000).

A second resource for social support is referral to visiting clergy for older adult home care clients with a past history of religious involvement (Millstein et al. 2003). Research suggests a protective effect of religious involvement and participation on levels of depression and emotional and social well-being (Friedman et al. 2005; Millstein et al. 2003). A limitation of these studies is that they can establish only association, not causation. Thus, lack of religious involvement and attendance may have brought on depression and lower levels of emotional and social well-being, or depression and lower levels of emotional and social well-being may have inhibited religious involvement and attendance (Millstein et al. 2003).

Additional interventions suggested in the literature for this population include referrals to resources, programs, and services that apply sliding fee scales or provide supplemental coverage for costs to reduce the financial burden of Medicare copayments for mental health services (a rate of 50 percent) (Unützer et al. 1999). Referrals to community resources that assist with medication costs, food, clothing, utility payments, and transportation expenses can address the financial burden for the caregiver and the care recipient. In some instances, when the client is severely depressed and has no social supports, making a transition to long-term care (for example, a nursing home) may be advised (Banazak 1997).

ETHNICITY AND TREATMENT FOR DEPRESSION

Minority populations and low-income populations may be particularly vulnerable to barriers to referral for mental health care. Minority populations have historically been underrepresented in their utilization of mental health settings. Low-income individuals who belong to an ethnic minority may experience numerous instrumental barriers to care, such as inadequate finances, lack of insurance, lack of transportation, and heavier child care responsibilities than non-Hispanic white and higher-income individuals. And, as a result of the historical abuse of African Americans by the health care delivery system, African Americans may also have a fear of being forcibly hospitalized. These observations suggest the importance of cultural competence in referring minority clients to mental health providers (Unützer et al. 1999).

SUICIDE

If a client reports suicidal ideation with a plan and lethal means, a decision must be made about whether the client is in imminent danger of harm. If the social worker's judgment is that the client is at high risk for suicide, hospitalization should be initiated by calling 911 and remaining with the patient until the emergency assistance arrives (Rauc, Brown, and Bruce 2002).

If the patient expresses suicidal ideation but does not have a plan, is not psychotic, is not depressed, has good judgment and few risk factors, and does not have access to a lethal method, permission to contact family members or a friend should be obtained and those parties should be informed about the patient's suicidal ideas. The worker can also assess their opinions about psychiatric hospitalization and their ability to care for the patient in the next few days. If on the basis of this information outpatient care seems sufficient, an appointment with an outpatient clinician can be made.

There is no strong empirical evidence that a "no-suicide contract," in which the patient agrees not to harm her- or himself, is effective in preventing suicide (Jacobs, Brewer, and Klein-Benheim 1999; Szanto et al. 2002). A no-suicide contract with a new client with whom the worker does not have a strong relationship is of little value, since the foundation of the contract is the strength of the bond between the worker and the client (Szanto et al. 2002).

The agency director or clinical supervisor, as well as the patient's primary-care physician and family members, should be notified of any actions taken. It is essential that the social worker be familiar with and follow agency policies and procedures with regard to protocols for assessment, hospitalization, and maintenance of the suicidal patient in the community (Salvatore 2000).

ANXIETY

If a screen for an anxiety disorder is positive, strategies similar to those discussed in relation to depression can be applied to communicate the results of the screening to clients. Older adult clients with anxiety disorders, similar to depressed clients, may feel less stigmatized about participating in assessment and treatment if they view their condition as an illness, rather than as a moral or character flaw (Culpepper 2002). The worker can assure patients that there are pharmacological and psychosocial interventions that have been proven effective in reducing these symptoms, and when clients have a panic disorder, the worker can emphasize to clients that they are not "going crazy" (Busch 1996).

COUNSELING INTERVENTIONS

Progressive muscle relaxation, guided imagery, deep-breathing exercises, distraction, role playing and rehearsal, and in-home cognitive-behavioral therapy are recommended interventions for anxiety disorders in older adults (Banazak 1997; Bartels et al. 2002; Gellis 2006).

Home health care social workers can use tapes, written material, and verbal instruction to take clients through the steps of progressive muscle relaxation. Guided imagery asks the client to imagine a relaxing mental picture and focus on the calm feelings and thoughts associated with the image. Deep-breathing exercises (concentrating on inhaling and exhaling in long, slow breaths) may calm anxiety by reducing physical symptoms of accelerated heartbeat and shortness of breath that accompany panic attacks. The client can be instructed to practice those techniques that are helpful so that they become automatic behaviors in the presence of anxiety.

Distraction counters anxiety by focusing concentration on a routine task. The worker can suggest that the client imagine a pleasant experience or find a pleasurable activity that is engrossing enough to shift his or her attention from anxiety. Role playing reduces anxiety by asking the client to think of a possible stressor and imagine the most extreme and severe consequence. The client is asked to describe his or her fears in experiencing this scenario. Asking the client to visualize several alternative outcomes and practice different behaviors in responding to the stressor may result in learning adaptive responses and increase control in response to anxiety (Banazak 1997).

As noted in the discussion of interventions for depression, time constraints do not permit the application of cognitive-behavioral therapy in home care, but the worker can use the basic principles of the therapy to help the client manage anxiety. One approach is to attempt to correct misconceptions about events that cause worry and to identify and examine the automatic thoughts that trigger misconceptions. For example, a patient with generalized anxiety disorder may worry that a minor change in social roles (for example, delegating the task of driving to family members) will lead to a catastrophic car accident. Discussing the basis of these thoughts and pointing out that family members have been driving and no accidents have occurred may be helpful (Culpepper 2002).

Patients who require continued intervention at discharge from home care can be referred to a community-based agency that provides in-home cognitive-behavioral therapy (Gellis 2006).

ENVIRONMENTAL INTERVENTIONS

A client with an anxiety disorder may also require more formal and informal support. While older clients may not express their concerns to family members or medical personnel, their ability to live safely in the community without an increase in support may be threatened as they become increasingly anxious, avoidant, and preoccupied with minor physical symptoms. At this point the patient may experience functional decline, increased dependence on family/friends, and more frequent visits to physicians and/or emergency room departments for minor symptoms. Such an increase in the severity and level of anxiety can indicate the need for higher levels of assistance from family, a referral to a case manager, or relocation to a more-structured environment such as assisted living (Banazak 1997; Busch 1996). Families who feel restricted by the increased dependency of the anxious patient may also benefit from respite services (Farran et al. 1998).

When clients with subsyndromal levels of anxiety develop more acute symptoms, they should be referred to the psychiatric nurse and/or the primary-care physician for assessment and possible pharmacological treatment with anxiolytic medications or tranquilizers, including benzodiazepines.

SITUATIONS IN WHICH THE CAREGIVER HAS A PSYCHIATRIC DIAGNOSIS

When the family caregiver of an older patient impaired by a *DSM-IV* diagnosis is also affected by anxiety, depression, or some other psychiatric condition, the social worker may provide help with long-term decision making for the patient and family member to determine whether the patient requires relocation to a nursing facility, more community support, or different sources of informal support. Treatment for the impaired relative should also be discussed.

SUBSTANCE ABUSE FEEDBACK ON SCREENING

Because of the complex interaction of social, psychological, and physiological factors, developing an assessment of and an individualized treatment plan for the older adult client with a substance abuse problem is a complex process requiring the expertise of a multidisciplinary team of physicians, nurses, psychiatrists, and social workers. The role of the home care social worker is therefore limited to screening home care patients for problems and communicating these results, when positive, to professionals and clients. The following are recommendations for communicating the results of a positive screen to an older client:

- Relate the findings to a health problem, as older adults are likely to respond more positively to this way of framing the problem than if it is characterized as a mental health problem. For example, the worker might say, "The results of your screening raise the possibility that alcohol may be one of the reasons your diabetes is hard to control."
- Immediately state: "If this is the case, it is treatable. Giving up or cutting down on drinking or your use of librium will help you maintain your independence, make it less likely that you will be hospitalized so frequently, reduce the likelihood of future hip fractures, and help you avoid getting so confused." The goal is to connect reduction or cessation of substance use with improvement in the future quality of the older adult's life. Because it is unlikely that most problem drinkers can address their problem by reducing use, it is advisable to emphasize abstinence by making a statement similar to the following suggestion, "Though I strongly recommend that you stop altogether, cutting down is a good start."
- Discuss options. "I could refer you to your primary-care physician for a complete assessment so that you can get a better understanding of what is occurring with your health." If the patient is an at-risk drinker, another option might be, "Try to cut down on your drinking to one beer a day to see if this will help control your diabetes. Would you be willing to try this if you might feel better?"
- If the situation appears dangerous and the patient is alcohol dependent and may require inpatient detoxification, the psychiatric nurse and the primary-care physician should be notified (Levin, Kruger, and Blow 2004:12).

❖ ❖ ❖

The interventions of the home care social worker are circumscribed by Medicare payment policy defining reimbursable social work activities as related to psychosocial factors influencing the patient's medical condition. Within these parameters, the home care social worker provides interventions with individual clients in a variety of issues.

When medication management is a problem, the worker identifies barriers to adherence and mobilizes resources to reduce obstacles that compromise adherence.

Social work interventions with clients and families to implement advance care planning include evaluating the patient's capacity to make these decisions, clarifying goals and attitudes toward advance directives, discussing spirituality, and facilitating communication between the patient and his or her physician or health care proxy.

When the client's explanatory models of the illness and his or her health care practices differ from those of mainstream medicine, the social worker functions as a "culture broker"—the professional on the health care team who mediates, advocates, and consults with both systems to develop a shared model of care.

The role of the social worker in intervening with clients in home health care also includes enhancing self-efficacy through short-term cognitive and behavioral interventions. Performance accomplishment, vicarious learning, persuasion, and reinterpretation of symptoms are techniques that enhance self-efficacy and indirectly improve disease management.

When patients are admitted to home care with a medical illness but subsequently develop symptoms of depression, the social worker can screen the patient for depression and, if indicated, communicate the results of a positive screen to the patient and to medical providers for assessment and treatment planning. In such cases, social work interventions include mobilizing resources, brief counseling, and facilitating communication between caregivers and clients to reduce symptoms of depression.

If a client has a primary medical diagnosis and a subsyndromal diagnosis of depression, a social worker provides brief counseling, modifying the techniques of cognitive-behavioral therapy, cognitive therapy, and problem-solving therapy to the home health care setting. When clients are suicidal, the social worker should use crisis intervention techniques that are consistent with agency procedures and policies.

Workers link clients with resources, advocate, provide brief counseling, and facilitate communication between caregivers and patients with a *DSM-IV* diagnosis of depression when psychosocial factors present barriers to treatment or adjustment to illness.

When clients are admitted to home care with medical illness but subsequently display symptoms of an anxiety disorder, the worker's interventions include screening for a *DSM-IV* diagnosis and, if indicated, providing feedback to the patient and medical providers, who can use the information to complete an assessment and treatment plan. For clients with an admitting diagnosis of a medical illness and symptoms of anxiety, the worker's interventions include relaxation techniques, brief counseling, mobilization of family support, and, if necessary, relocation to a more-structured environment. If a caregiver is impaired by a *DSM-IV* diagnosis, the social worker's role can include mobilizing community support, assisting with relocation to a safer environment, such as a nursing facility, and referring the caregiver for longer-term treatment.

Substance abuse interventions require feedback to the patient on a positive screen, followed by a referral for a comprehensive assessment and the development of a treatment plan by a medical provider. If the patient appears to be alcohol dependent and may require detoxification, the psychiatric nurse and the primary-care physician should be notified immediately.

MRS. DANEFELD

Betty Danefeld, an 82-year-old widow with hypertension, coronary artery disease, and type II diabetes, was brought to the hospital emergency room from home by her daughter, Rachel (age 50), who was her primary caregiver and with whom she lived. She was admitted with complaints of "dizziness" accompanied by chest tightness and shortness of breath. She had not fallen or lost consciousness but complained of tiredness, short-term memory loss, and "not feeling well." She did not report any feelings of depression or suicidal ideation. She had entered the hospital from the emergency room five times for similar episodes in the last year. She did not have a regular physician, and during each admission she received care from a different doctor. She had Medicare coverage and received survivor Social Security benefits from her husband, but she had not applied for Medicare Part D.

All tests to diagnose her condition were negative, but she continued to report the same symptoms. The physician treating her for this admission noted a new condition: anemia.

Her daughter, Rachel, worked full-time as an administrative assistant to a middle manager in a local company, had been divorced for two years, and had three children, aged eight, ten, and twelve. She did not visit her mother in the hospital and arrived to take Mrs. Danefeld home two hours after she was formally discharged.

Mrs. Danefeld was discharged to home with six medications, three of which were new prescriptions, to control her coronary artery disease, hypertension, diabetes, and the new diagnosis of anemia. A referral was made to home health care to monitor medication adherence and diet.

During the first visit, the home health care nurse noted that Mrs. Danefeld had "forgotten" the discharge instructions about taking her medication. Discussion with the daughter and her mother revealed that Mrs. Danefeld had lost her husband of fifty-six years six months before the onset of her symptoms, and she had moved from a different city to live with her daughter after the death. She had two sons as well, but both sons had demanding full-time jobs, lived far away, and stated that they could not care for her.

Rachel appeared tense and angry during the interview, and in discussion with the nurse she displayed little understanding of her mother's illnesses and the prescribed medication regimen. She worried about the expense of covering her mother's medications because Mrs. Danefeld's Social Security check was inadequate to meet these costs. She also expressed "disappointment" that her mother was "not willing" to be more active with babysitting and small household tasks. The nurse decided to make a referral to social work for an assessment of social and emotional factors related to the patient's illness, the need for care, the response to treatment, adjustment to care, appropriate action to obtain community resources, and counseling services needed.

On the initial social work visit, with Mrs. Danefeld and Rachel present, Mrs. Danefeld reported that she had led an active social life in her old home, including membership in a Unitarian church, but she did not know anyone in her new location and had not joined a church because she had "lost interest" in socializing with people. She said she was "too tired." She spent most of the day going back and forth from bed to a chair in the living room, though she reported sleeping only intermittently. Mrs. Danefeld confided that she felt she was a "burden" to her daughter because she did not help out more, as was expected. The daughter remained silent in response to this statement, though the worker invited her feedback. Both the daughter and the patient confirmed a previously "distant" relationship. The social worker also noted that Mrs. Danefeld had a history of "dizzy spells" of unknown etiology during her childhood, following the death of her father when she was ten years old.

Questions:

1. What problems does this situation present?
2. What interventions are appropriate?

8

SOCIAL WORK INTERVENTIONS WITH SOCIAL SYSTEMS IN HOME HEALTH CARE

THIS CHAPTER focuses on interventions with social systems or interventions with systems that are separate from but influence the older adult receiving home care, such as the family system, the immediate physical environment of the home, the community resource system, and the system of programs at the wider societal level. More specifically, this chapter will discuss interventions to:

- reduce or eliminate unmet service needs through information and referral activities to link clients with community resources and social programs
- reduce or eliminate caregiver burden
- reduce or eliminate family conflict related to caring for a relative with an illness
- minimize harm to victims of elder maltreatment
- assist clients and older adults to delay placement and/or provide education and support during relocation to a nursing home

Chapter 7 also discussed interventions with social systems. The decision to include content in one or the other of these two chapters was made by differentiating the primary target of social work intervention. When interventions were focused primarily on the individual, the material was included in chapter 7; when interventions were focused primarily on social systems, the content was included in this chapter.

The "best available" research presented here varies in methodological quality, though all literature is current. The topics of intervention for unmet service needs and caregiver burden are supported by strong methodology, but the "best available" research on interventions for family conflict, elder maltreatment, and nursing home placement varies in quality from weak to strong. The area with the strongest research support related to these topics is interventions for delaying nursing home placement.

INTERVENTIONS: UNMET SERVICE NEEDS

Social work interventions to address clients' unmet service needs are likely to focus on information and referral activities, for several reasons (Dyeson, Murphy, and Stryker 1999; Kadushin and Egan 2006). Increased use of community services has been associated with a decrease in unmet needs (Yordi et al. 1997). Caregivers and elders transitioning from one care setting to another (for example, from hospital discharge to home) report a need for and an absence of information and referral services (Naylor 2002; Weaver, Perloff, and Waters 1998). Community-dwelling elders and their caregivers also place a high priority on information and referral regarding community-based services (Young, McCormick, and Vitaliano 2002).

The activities of information and referral are related in that the worker provides information so that the client is aware of all options and can make an informed choice to use or not to use a referral (McCallion et al. 2004). The purpose of a referral is to link the client with a program, service, or professional that will assist him or her with an unmet need when this a mutually agreed-upon goal of the worker-client contract (Compton, Galaway, and Cournoyer 2005; Shaefor and Horejsi 2006). A referral is appropriate when the agency and/ or the worker cannot provide the help the client needs (Shaefor and Horejsi 2006). In home health care, a referral may be made to another member of the health care team within the agency or to a program service or provider outside of the agency.

INTERVENTIONS TO INCREASE CLIENT KNOWLEDGE
OF RESOURCES/PROGRAMS

Providing information is an important component of information and referral. Research has found that client knowledge of services is associated with increased use of services (McCallion et al. 2004; Rinehart 2002). This suggests that providing information about services and how to access them is an important social work activity (Rinehart 2002; Toseland et al. 1999; Toseland et al. 2002). While there is no definitive figure on the prevalence of lack of knowledge about services among home care clients, one study showed that almost three-fourths of caregivers of individuals with dementia wanted more knowledge about a needed service (Toseland et al. 1999). Several studies have also found that clients who have completed fewer years of formal education are less knowledgeable about services (McCallion et al. 2004; Ozawa and Tseng 1999; Toseland et al. 2002), possibly because formal education provides skills that are helpful in accessing information. This implies that client literacy levels should be considered in distributing written material and in describing services to clients (McCallion et al. 2004). The following are some guidelines for home health care information and referral.

The association between client knowledge and use of services suggests that home care social workers need to maintain detailed information about programs, services, and professionals that are relevant to practice. These resources may be organized in a database maintained by the individual agency and/or a community clearinghouse for information and referral (Compton, Galaway, and Cournoyer 2005; Shaefor and Horejsi 2006).

While referrals will vary according to the care needs of the individual client as determined by the care plan, the literature suggests that, at a minimum, home health care social workers should be familiar with a number of specific types of resources. Inadequate financial resources are a significant issue for home care clients. Social workers should be knowledgeable regarding local, state, and federal services and programs to alleviate financial strain (Dyeson, Murphy, and Stryker 1999; Gelfand 1999). In particular, medication noncompliance and hospital readmission are influenced by lack of resources to purchase medications, suggesting that workers should be knowledgeable about the Medicare prescription drug benefit and pharmacy assistance programs (Li, Morrow-Howell, and Proctor 2004). Familiarity with financial assistance programs for food, utilities, and home maintenance is also a priority for home care social workers (Dyeson, Murphy, and Stryker 1999; Gelfand 1999).

A thorough knowledge of Medicaid and Medicare policies regarding coverage for medical equipment, social care (e.g., personal care), and institutional care is recommended (Borrayo et al. 2002; Dyeson, Murphy, and Stryker 1999). Familiarity with the state's case management programs is also important, as these programs have been associated with increased use of home and community-based services such as homemakers and day care (Fox et al. 2000; Newcomer et al. 1999).

FAMILY INFLUENCE ON REFERRALS

The family is likely to be a factor in the success of a referral (Shaefor and Horejsi 2006; Smerglia and Deimling 1997). The support of the family has been found to mediate the use of formal services by caregivers (Cotrell and Engel 1998). This mediating role is particularly important for services that lack a "norm" for use. For example, decisions about utilization of nursing and other medical services are made by physicians. On the other hand, it may be difficult for caregivers to decide when their level of strain is high enough to justify the use of respite care or day care. Family members may also function to provide feedback to legitimize the need for a service and emotional support to reduce caregiver guilt (Cotrell and Engel 1998).

If the client is cared by for by a caregiver, both the care recipient and the caregiver should be involved in decisions about referrals (with the care recipient's permission). Caregivers and care recipients may have discrepant opinions about need for assistance, with caregivers slightly more likely to view care recipients as more dependent than care recipients view themselves (Lyons et al. 2002). It is possible that this divergence in opinion could influence the perspectives of caregivers and care recipients regarding the need for a formal referral. Therefore, the opinions of both about the need for formal services should be elicited. It should be noted that even care recipients with moderate levels of cognitive impairment can express preferences reliably and accurately (Lyons et al. 2002). Including both the client and the family in decisions about referrals is therefore good practice. While this approach may be more time-consuming, it can also be more cost-effective and efficient if it facilitates the success of a referral and promotes client rehabilitation and stabilization in the community.

BARRIERS TO SUCCESSFUL REFERRALS

In making a referral, the social worker must also be aware of the obstacles or barriers that may prevent clients from using resources. Barriers related to characteristics of the service delivery system may present obstacles to the client's acceptance of formal help (Kosloski, Montgomery, and Youngbauer 2001; Toseland et al. 1999; Toseland et al. 2002). Issues may include:

- negative client attitudes about quality of the program or staff (e.g., are staff adequately trained?)
- security (e.g., the trustworthiness and honesty of staff)
- costs
- eligibility criteria
- inability to access programs because of transportation problems (Choi 1999; Kosloski, Montgomery, and Youngbauer 2001; Schoenberg and Coward 1998; Toseland et al. 1999)

The emotional implications for older adults of accepting formal help may represent another barrier. Older adults may view the use of formal services as signifying a loss of autonomy, independence, privacy, and self-image in the context of a life stage often characterized by many losses (Forbes and Hoffart 1998; Roe et al. 2001). To address concerns about characteristics of the delivery system, the social worker should describe the proposed service in detail (e.g., cost, duration, frequency, eligibility requirements, staff training, etc.), then elicit and address any client misgivings. It may be useful to discuss the client's experiences with agencies or with resources that were rejected in the past to understand the previous interactions and avoid a repetition of failure. The worker should also make every effort to refer clients only to programs and providers that are competent and ethical (Shaefor and Horejsi 2006). Discussing the client's preferences with the referral agency so that services are arranged to accommodate these preferences (to the extent that this is realistic) may facilitate the use of the service (Kosloski, Montgomery, and Youngbauer 2001; Pedlar and Biegel 1999). In addressing affective reactions to referrals, workers may wish to be sensitive to the client's emotions and attitudes about accepting help and to facilitate the client's ability to retain control and choice in the decision to accept formal help (Roe et al. 2001).

Caregivers' attitudes may also represent barriers to completed referrals. Family caregivers have been found to prefer informal care, believe it is their responsibility to provide care, and worry that formal caregivers will not provide as high a quality of care (Dorfman, Berlin, and Holmes 1998; McCallion et al. 2004; Pedlar and Biegel 1999; Smyth and Milidonis 1999). Family members may also view caregiving as integral to being a "good" spouse, parent, or sibling, and so they may not be receptive to information and referral because they do not identify themselves as "caregivers" (National Family Caregiver Association 2001). Interventions with caregivers are most effective if the worker and the caregiver discuss whether he or she is making an informed choice. Are resources available to provide care? Is the decision to reject services related to an attitude that services are not acceptable (McCallion et al. 2004)? If the reason for service refusal is that services are not acceptable, it may be advisable to focus on a care plan that is consistent with client beliefs by placing an emphasis on strengthening the client's informal supports. This approach may reassure caregivers that their values and attitudes are not being challenged, build trust and rapport, and lead to a more receptive response by the caregiver to the integration of formal services as part of the care plan (Smyth and Milidonis 1999). If the reason for negative attitudes toward a referral is lack of identification with the caregiving role, using the term "caregiver" in discussions with the client and defining the role of caregiver as distinct from that of wife, daughter, or sibling may facilitate the process of caregiver self-identification, contributing to a more receptive attitude to referral acceptance (National Family Caregiver Association 2001).

To maximize the amount of assistance a client receives, the worker should also discuss the client's preferences regarding the integration of informal sources of support into the care plan (Boaz and Hu 1997; Shaefor and Horejsi 2006). An overlooked source of support may be non-kin caregivers (e.g., an unrelated individual who provides some form of unpaid help to a care recipient once a week), such as neighbors, friends, or members of religious congregations (Barker 2002; Lubben and Gironda 2003). Non-kin caregivers may function as primary caregivers or may supplement the help provided by family and formal providers. It may be that non-kin caregivers have more-flexible schedules than employed family members or agency providers and so are able to assist with tasks that other members of the support network cannot perform (Barker 2002). Identifying sources of informal support may be particularly important for individuals who have a higher level of unmet needs because they live alone and/or are unmarried.

The level of directiveness of the worker in coordinating and linking clients with resources is likely to be determined by the coping capacities of the client (Cox 1997; Toseland et al. 2002). Therefore, when a client is unable to cope with the demands of obtaining resources, the worker may take a more active role and arrange for services, eliciting the client's suggestions regarding resources (Montoro-Rodriguez, Kosloski, and Montgomery 2003; Toseland et al. 2002). Caregivers with good coping skills and/or who are knowledgeable about resources may be given the name of a referral source and assigned the "task" of contacting that source; here the worker acts as a consultant (Abramson 1992; Bass et al. 2003; Hash 2003; McCallion et al. 2004).

REFERRALS FOR SPECIFIC PROBLEMS

FALL HAZARD INTERVENTIONS
Research does not support the efficacy of intervention by disciplines (such as social work) that lack specialized training relevant to home modification (Gillespie et al. 2003). When an assessment for home hazards indicates the presence of situations that may result in risk of falls or the client has a history of falls, research suggests that the social worker should collaborate with occupational and physical therapists, nurses, and physicians to develop intervention plans (Gillespie et al. 2003). Since the risk of falling is related to multiple factors at both the individual and the environmental levels, multidisciplinary intervention planning is most effective (Gillespie et al. 2003).

Social workers can intervene by linking clients with sources of coverage for home modification. In general, there are few programs that cover these costs. However, there are some exceptions to this general rule. The worker should contact the local Area Agency on Aging or the local Center for Independent Living for eligibility information and resources to connect clients to funding, if it is available (Overeynder 2003b).

The worker may also discuss with the client who may have actually experienced a fall or may be at risk for a fall the desirability of obtaining an emergency response system, a resource specifically developed for situations in which the client has fallen and cannot get help. The client who uses this service wears a transponder around the neck that is the size of a small button. The transponder is linked to a twenty-four-hour telephone service that activates emergency services when the client presses the button to call for help. Emergency telephone services are easily installed and are not expensive (King 2003).

The home health social worker can also function as a consultant to other disciplines, such as occupational and physical therapy. These professionals may elicit negative reactions from clients when they behave as "experts" and prescribe a plan for home modification. A "prescribed" plan is likely to be less effective than a collaboratively developed plan that incorporates the older adult's preferences. This suggestion derives from the fact that older adult clients are likely to experience their home as more than a physical space. "Home" may evoke a strong sense of attachment, be a repository of past history and memories (good and bad), a source of identity, a space for privacy, and a place where the older adult can exercise control and experience competence through daily rituals, customs, the regulation of social behavior, and the arrangement of decor and furnishings (Lawton 1999). A collaborative approach may reduce the client's tendency to perceive suggestions for environmental change as a threat to his or her competence and ability to control the home environment (Lawton 1999). The social worker who is aware of these psychological factors can educate therapists so they will be able to interact more effectively with their clients in developing a plan for home modification.

INTERVENTIONS TO ADDRESS MEDICATION ADHERENCE

Social workers can reduce medication non-adherence related to financial obstacles by educating clients about Medicare Part D, the federal program that covers medication for Medicare recipients. This educational process should also include the client's primary caregiver. Involving a member of the client's natural support system is necessary when clients are impaired by illness or cognitive deficits that are obstacles to understanding information. The booklet *Medicare and You 2006* (issued every year), which can be printed from the government Web site: www.medicare.gov, provides a clear and readable explanation of the program. Unless the client is familiar with how to use a computer, this means of access is unlikely to be a viable option. If the client can print the booklet, the social worker can go through the booklet with the client to answer questions and clarify information. An alternative for clients who cannot use a computer might be for staff at the home care agency to print the booklet from the Web site, make copies, and spend some time with the client discussing the program and answering questions. The client can then keep the booklet as a reference tool. Other options for education are calling the Medicare helpline (1-800-633-4227) and/or suggesting that the client or caregiver contact the local Area Agency on Aging (www.eldercare.gov will provide phone numbers). Finally, Medicare recommends calling the State Health Insurance Assistance Program for information. Of particular importance in providing this education is to discuss government subsidies with low-income patients who have not applied but may be eligible and to refer the client to a local agency that can help the client/caregiver select the best drug plan if the client's medications are not covered by his or her current plan.

Social workers can play an important role in the physician's treatment of the patient by identifying patients whose non-adherence is the result of cost factors and encouraging clients to discuss this problem with their physician or by sharing this information with the physician with the client's consent. Because patients report barriers to discussing medication cost problems with their physicians (e.g., embarrassment, feeling pressed for time during outpatient visits), the physician may be unaware of under-use of medications due to finances as a factor associated with poor clinical outcomes and may increase the dose or augment medication, thus unintentionally exacerbating the problem (Piette, Heisler, and Wagner 2004; Piette et al. 2005). Physicians who are aware of patient problems with the affordability of medication can pursue strategies such as discontinuing ineffective medications and prescribing lower-cost generic drugs when possible (Tseng et al. 2004).

Patient depression has also been associated with non-adherence in situations of medication cost pressures (Piette et al. 2005). Social work administration of a depression screen and, if the screen is positive, referral to the interdisciplinary team for follow-up is also an intervention that may increase adherence.

THE INFLUENCE OF ETHNICITY/CULTURE ON INFORMATION AND REFERRAL

The literature indicates that home and community-based services (e.g., respite adult day care, senior centers, transportation, homemakers) are more likely to be used by ethnic minorities if their programs are responsive to ethnic minorities (Choi 1999; Hooyman and Kiyak 2005; Kosloski et al. 2002; Kuo and Torres-Gil 2001; Young, McCormick, and Vitaliano 2002). One study comparing non-Hispanic whites, African Americans, Hispanics, and Asian Americans found that African Americans were significantly more likely than any other group to be discharged from home health care without any formal or informal support (Peng, Navaie-Waliser, and Feldman 2003). Among African American older adults the absence of informal support has been found to be associated with an increased need for formal services (Cagney and Agree 1999). Non-Hispanic whites had a significantly greater risk of poor psychological functioning (e.g., depression and anxiety) at discharge from home health care than did other groups (Peng, Navaie-Waliser, and Feldman 2003). The practice implications of these findings for home health care social workers attempting to make a successful referral are summarized below.

Barriers to access of informal and formal resources should be explored with African American elders to facilitate continuing care after home health care discharge. Non-Hispanic white elders may require referrals to community agencies to address depression and/or anxiety after home health care discharge. For all groups, referrals should be made to agencies that provide services consistent with cultural/ethnic lifestyles. For example, nutrition programs should offer ethnic foods, and adult day care programs should make culturally appropriate recreational activities available. Staff of any agency/program for which a referral is made should be bilingual in English and the client's language to eliminate language barriers. To assist clients in understanding services and to provide outreach, print material (brochures, fact sheets, etc.) should be in the client's language. If possible, to enhance accessibility, agencies/programs should be located in the client's community. Acceptability is likely to be fostered if agencies/programs are under the auspices of the client's cultural group. For example, African American clients may be more likely to use an agency's Meals on Wheels program if it is provided by a church in their neighborhood. It is important for a worker to be aware of the variation in needs at discharge and responses to referrals between ethnic groups.

At the level of the agency, home care administrators can support workers in their efforts to make referrals by networking with natural support systems in the community such as ethnic civic organizations, neighborhood organizations, and community advocates. For example, African Americans may be more likely to have positive attitudes toward home health care if agencies link with black churches to inform the community about their services.

INTERVENTIONS WITH FAMILIES

CAREGIVER BURDEN: THE KNOWLEDGE BASE

Research on interventions to address caregiver burden focus primarily on Alzheimer's disease. This literature is so extensive that several meta-analyses have been completed (Acton and Kang 2001; Bourgeois, Schulz, and Burgio 1996; Brodaty, Green, and Koschera 2003; Yin, Zhou, and Bashford 2002). A smaller body of research exists on interventions to reduce caregiver burden among caregivers of individuals with other physical and mental impairments (Sörensen, Pinquart, and Duberstein 2002). The following discussion focuses on interventions to reduce caregiver burden for all caregivers of older adults with disability and illness. However, the paucity of research on interventions for caregivers of the physically and/or cognitively impaired without a diagnosis of Alzheimer's disease suggests that this discussion should be interpreted with caution.

There is no research on effective social work interventions to reduce caregiver burden in home health care under the prospective payment system. The following discussion combines information on generic social work interventions for home care clients within the PPS environment (Egan and Kadushin 2005; Kadushin and Egan 2006; Lee 2002; Malinowski 2002) with research on effective interventions for caregiver burden among caregivers to community-dwelling physically and/or mentally impaired elders to suggest potential interventions for home care social workers.

In selecting interventions to address caregiver burden, an important consideration is the high level of variability among individuals in their response to a stressor. Some individuals may cope adequately, while others feel overwhelmed. A finding that has been replicated in the caregiving research is that different constellations of variables influence the caregiving situation for each individual. Because each person responds differently to different sources of stress, each person will require a unique combination of interventions.

Two concepts—stress proliferation and stress containment—help to identify individual variation in responses to caregiving and potential points for intervention. As discussed in chapter 6, the concept of stress proliferation suggests that stressors directly associated with caregiving (primary stressors) may affect other roles (secondary stressors). For example, a caregiver who invests thirty hours a week in caregiving tasks may be absent from work frequently, contributing to stress in relation to the work role. To address the potential for stress proliferation, interventions need to have a dual focus: on problems immediately related to caregiving and on the consequences of these problems for other areas of the caregiver's life (e.g., work and family roles). In other words, to reduce the potential for stress proliferation, interventions should target both immediate and emergent problems.

Stress containment refers to the process by which resources available to the caregiver, such as social support or caregiving skill, reduce the impact of the stressor on the caregiver. Clinical interventions with caregivers can therefore be effective if the immediate and emergent stressors that affect the caregiver are identified and if strategies to contain these stressors are implemented (Aneshensel et al. 1995; Schulz 2000).

However, caregivers of care recipients with Alzheimer's disease benefit less from existing interventions than do caregivers of individuals with other illnesses. There is no strong support for the effectiveness of respite care, support group interventions, short educational programs, and brief interventions that are not supplemented with long-term contact in reducing caregiver burden among caregivers of these individuals (Acton and Kang 2001; Brodaty, Green, and Koschera 2003).

The following discussion of social work interventions assumes that social workers are constrained by time and resources. Therefore, social work interventions are likely to be short-term efforts. Some workers may have no more than one in-person contact with the client to complete an assessment and negotiate an intervention plan with the client. Follow-up phone calls may supplement this single contact to implement and monitor the plan (Malinowski 2002).

INTERVENTIONS TO REDUCE PRIMARY STRESSORS

Caregivers are likely to be referred to home care when a new diagnosis or a change in an impaired relative's condition requires an increase in caregiver involvement (e.g., more time and/or more tasks) and/or the mastery of new caregiving activities, contributing to an increase in caregiver strain (Archbold et al. 1995). These are sources of strain related to the caregiving role, and therefore it can be assumed that at the point of initial admission to home care, the majority of caregivers require assistance in reducing primary stressors because of an increase in objective care-related demands and the caregivers' subjective appraisal of these demands (Aneshensel et al. 1995; Pearlin et al. 1990).

Within the limited time available for client contact, social worker provision of knowledge and education about appropriate community resources and linking or coordinating referrals to services and programs are likely to be the most significant practice activities to reduce caregiver strain (Egan and Kadushin 2005).

However, caregiver strain will not be reduced if services are not matched to the needs and preferences of older adults and their caregivers. The input of clients in developing a service plan is helpful in clarifying their expectations and preferences, including what services are provided and how often. It is also helpful in connecting client needs to services and to expected outcomes (Li, Chadiha, and Morrow-Howell 2005).

INTERVENTIONS TO REDUCE PRIMARY STRESSORS THAT FOCUS ON EDUCATION/KNOWLEDGE

KNOWLEDGE OF RESOURCES AND PROGRAMS

The intervention of education/knowledge addresses primary stressors by decreasing uncertainty and enhancing coping and mastery, thereby contributing to stress containment (Palmer and Glass 2003; Schulz et al. 2002). Caregivers, both new and experienced, may lack knowledge about appropriate community resources and how to obtain these resources (Dyeson, Murphy, and Stryker 1999; England 2001; Grant 1996; Kadushin and Egan 2006; Toseland et al. 1999; Weaver, Perloff, and Waters 1998).

In one study, home care professionals reported that they frequently had contact with patients and caregivers who were uninformed about services and eligibility requirements (Coleman 2004). Information about financial and legal issues related to assuming caregiving responsibilities in the form of government or privately funded programs and grants that reduce out-of-pocket expenses for social care (e.g., personal care, homemaker services, assistive devices, and respite) is essential, since Medicare does not cover in-home custodial care (help with bathing, dressing, using the bathroom, eating, etc.), provides limited coverage for assistive technologies and personal care, and offers no coverage for home modifications (Code of Federal Regulations 1999).

Home care social workers should be familiar with the services and eligibility requirements for services and programs available through their Medicaid state plans, the Older Americans Act, the National Family Caregiver Support Program, general revenue from state funding, local United Way agencies, religious organizations, social service agencies, and the Area Agency on Aging (Coleman 2004; Kassner 2006). Helpful Web sites include National Association for Home Care, www.nahc.org; Alzheimer's Association, www.alz.org; American Association of Retired Persons, www.aarp.org; the ElderCare Locator, www.elder.gov; the Family Caregiver Alliance, www.caregiver.org; and Medicaid, www.cms. hhs.gov/medicaid/consumer.asp. The community Area Agency on Aging is a good resource for obtaining information about state and federal sources of funding at one location.

An emerging trend in providing family caregiver support is consumer-directed care. As already noted, consumer-directed care is based on a model of transferring decision making about services from providers and payers to consumers and their families (Feinberg, Wolkwitz, and Goldstein 2006). The majority of research published to date compares traditional and consumer-directed care for public program beneficiaries with disabilities. The data suggest that many outcomes are significantly more positive in consumer-directed programs than in traditional programs and that there are no differences between the two types of programs on other outcomes (Doty 2004). For example, in one study that compared traditional care with consumer-directed care, the latter was associated with reduced caregiver financial, emotional, and physical strain (Foster et al. 2005). Research has also found that low-income caregivers in rural areas using consumer-directed care, compared to those receiving traditional care, were significantly more satisfied with services and more often reported that these services allowed them to prolong the time they provided in-home care, thus avoiding nursing home placement (Perkins, Lapore, Sambahar, Jackson and Ball 2004, cited in Feinberg, Wolkwitz, and Goldstein 2006).

As noted in the discussion of caregiver burden, caregiving may conflict with paid employment. Research suggests that caregivers in consumer-directed programs in which they are paid report more positive outcomes than caregivers in consumer-directed programs in which they are unpaid or in traditional programs (Doty 2004).

The limited research available has not found significant problems with abuse/neglect, fraud, or financial exploitation in consumer-directed programs (Doty 2004; Feinberg, Wolkwitz, and Goldstein 2006). Home care social workers should be aware of opportunities for consumer-directed care in their communities and consider this as one option for referral for caregivers who are eligible during discharge planning from home care.

The Family Medical Leave Act provides unpaid leave for qualified caregivers who care for an ill spouse or parent. The act requires establishments with fifty or more employees to provide up to twelve weeks of unpaid job-protected leave per year for specific reasons, among which is caring for an ailing parent or spouse. To be eligible, an employee must have worked for an employer for at least twelve months and for at least 1,250 hours that year (Waldfogel 2001). While family leave is associated with caregiver emotional and physical well-being, problems include restricted coverage of employees under the act and financial problems in taking leave that is unpaid (Waldfogel 2001). Information about the Family Medical Leave Act can be provided by employers to caregivers in the labor force who are balancing work and caregiving responsibilities.

Another resource for working family caregivers is workplace eldercare programs. Among employers with one hundred or more employees, 25 percent offer caregiver workplace programs. Flexible hours and time off have been identified as the most important supports an employer can provide to caregivers. Availability of workplace eldercare programs is limited, since most employees work for small companies. The utilization rate for these programs is also low (2 percent of less of the workforce) because of the stigma associated with bringing family issues into the workplace, workplaces that discourage employees from using eldercare programs, lack of fit between available programs and caregivers' needs, and inadequate knowledge among caregivers regarding what community-based services and programs to access. However, eldercare workplace programs are one resource to support working caregivers. Home care social workers can suggest that workers check with their employers to obtain information about available employer-provided programs (Wagner 2003).

When information about disease cause and progression, administration of medications, symptoms of adverse reactions to medications, and special diets are priority learning needs, social workers may wish to request consultations with other agency staff who have the appropriate technical expertise (Bull and McShane 2002; Kuhn 1998).

INTERVENTIONS TO REDUCE PRIMARY STRESSORS THAT FOCUS ON REFERRAL TO RESOURCES

REFERRAL TO PERSONAL CARE

A realistic and appropriate intervention to address primary stressors within the time limits of home health care social work is a focus on reduction of environmental stressors through referrals to programs and services and/or home modification. An activity that has been identified as causing discomfort for caregivers to frail elders following hospital discharge is providing assistance with bathing and toileting because of the intimate nature of these tasks (Proctor, Morrow-Howell, and Kaplan 1996). While there is no outcome research linking personal care with caregiver burden, this finding suggests that personal care provided by private or publicly funded programs may reduce caregiver distress by partly relieving caregivers of this responsibility. Sources of coverage for personal care include Medicare home care. Home health aides provide limited personal care (Federal Conditions of Participation 1999). Medicaid programs with a personal care option, state Medicaid waiver programs, and the Family Caregiver Support Program cover personal care in some localities when Medicare home health aide services are terminated (Coleman 2004; Federal Conditions of Participation 1999; Feinberg, Newman, and Fox-Grage 2005).

RESPITE: LONG-TERM AND SHORT-TERM

Caregivers identify what they need most as "a little time for myself," or respite care (Feinberg, Newman, and Fox-Grage 2005). Respite is designed to allow the care recipient to receive safe care while the caregiver takes some time off. Respite is provided either in the home (Bass, Noelker, and Rechlin 1996) or outside of the home in a structured setting such as a day care facility. It may extend for a few hours (generally in-home or adult day care) to a few days or weeks (generally an out-of-home arrangement) (Hokanson 2003a, 2003b; Schneider 2003). A homemaker is an in-home option to provide respite from the daily demands of caregiving (Bass, Noelker, and Rechlin 1996). Adult day care is a cost-effective alternative to in-home care that provides the care recipient with an opportunity to participate in structured activities and socialize with peers (Schneider 2003). Long-term respite is used by family members to go on a vacation, attend to family matters, or just take time out for themselves. It is provided in nursing homes, hospitals, adult respite homes, foster homes, or by family and friends. The care recipient may benefit from the socialization opportunities offered by long-term respite (Hokanson 2003a).

The worker should be familiar with local community resources that offer respite care and sources of coverage for care. The local Area Office on Aging and the ElderCare Locator (www.eldercare.gov) provide information about community respite services (Hokanson 2003a, 2003b). The National Family Caregiver Support Program (www.aoa.gov) offers limited coverage for respite services to caregivers (U.S. Department of Health and Human Services, Administration on Aging 2003). Before engaging in a detailed discussion of respite services, it is important to provide information about community and federal sources of coverage, eligibility requirements, and the client's finances to pay for respite, since funding for this type of care is limited (Hokanson 2003a).

Use of respite care (both short- and long-term care) is associated with reduction in levels of burden (McNally, Ben Shlomo, and Newman 1999; Sörensen, Pinquart, and Duberstein 2002). It has been suggested that respite may be most effective in alleviating burden if caregivers use the time to engage in social and recreational activities with friends and family. Social workers may wish to encourage clients' caregivers to use the time freed by respite to socialize with friends and kin in social activities as opposed to spending that time on chores or errands related to caregiving. Social activities facilitate the maintenance of socially supportive relationships after respite has ended and may therefore produce long-term benefits (McNally, Ben-Shlomo, and Newman 1999; Thompson et al. 1993).

Respite is also effective in partially alleviating a secondary stressor, conflict between employment and caregiving roles, by providing coverage during the caregivers' work hours (Aneshensel et al. 1995; Foster et al. 2005). Therefore, respite may address both primary and secondary stressors.

In referring clients to respite services, the social worker should be aware of several issues. While caregivers of both physically and cognitively impaired care recipients indicate that they want respite, they generally delay the initiation of services until the individual is significantly impaired and the caregiver is burdened (Cox 1997; Zarit et al. 1999). Further, the rate of respite service use (the amount of service used) is low despite need for the service (Zarit et al. 1999).

Therefore, the social worker may be faced with a dilemma: a caregiver who is burdened, but who may be unlikely to use respite service early enough or frequently enough to benefit from it (Zarit et al. 1999). Caregivers who state that their level of distress or burden has been increasing may be telling the social worker that they have begun to think about respite (Cox 1997; Kosloski, Montgomery, and Youngbauer 2001). While strain may motivate caregivers initially to consider respite services, actual use and continued participation are determined by additional factors.

Caregivers may be hesitant to use respite care if arranging and managing care is so complicated that the psychological and financial reserves of an already burdened caregiver are depleted (Worcester and Hedrick 1997). If the choice is in-home respite, and the care recipient has developed a good relationship with a homemaker or a home health aide, the worker can contact the appropriate party (either the agency or the individually contracted worker) to determine the feasibility and cost of extending the original service contract to include respite (Cotrell 1996).

If the choice is adult day care, the worker can provide information about available local programs (Hokanson 2003b; Schneider 2003). Reliability, or the extent to which the caregiver can depend on services being available when needed, and program utility to the caregiver (cost, availability of transportation, hours service is available, etc.) are associated with service use (Kosloski, Montgomery, and Youngbauer 2001).

Spousal/partner caregivers may have difficulty discussing overnight respite with the care recipient due to concerns about guilt, abandonment, and/or the impact of the experience on the spouse (Cotrell 1996; Worcester and Hedrick 1997). The worker may need to take an active role in introducing this topic. Arranging a family meeting in which concerns and opinions of all who are involved can be heard is important (Hokanson 2003a).

When long-term respite is provided on an out-of-home basis, educating the family members about adjustment to relocation is a recommended strategy. The literature suggests that preparation for the change and control over the choice to move are associated with positive outcomes after relocation (Reinhardy 1995; Reinhardy and Kane 1999). It may be helpful to emphasize activities that the care recipient may enjoy in long-term respite facilities beyond simple custodial care (Hokanson 2003a). Providing information about facilities (when there is a choice) can enhance care recipient choice and control over the move (Hokanson 2003a).

Consumer-directed care is also an option for providing in-home or out-of-home respite, depending on state coverage (Feinberg, Wolkwitz, and Goldstein 2006).

INTERVENTIONS THAT ALTER THE ENVIRONMENT

Interventions that alter the environment (e.g., installing grab bars, providing shower chairs) to enhance the ability of impaired elders to perform ADL tasks without assistance or with a reduced amount of help from the caregiver are also associated with a reduction in caregiver stress (Gitlin et al. 2003; Overeynder 2003b). Social workers can provide information about coverage by public and private services and programs of assistive devices and other resources to make homes handicap-accessible by contacting the local Area on Aging or the local Center for Independent Living (Dyeson, Murphy, and Stryker 1999; Overeynder 2003b). The National Family Caregiver Support Program offers limited coverage for home modification (U.S. Department of Health and Human Services, Administration on Aging 2003). A referral by the home care social worker to an occupational therapist is recommended to develop a plan for home modification.

INTERVENTIONS TO REDUCE PRIMARY STRESSORS THAT FOCUS ON THE SITUATION ITSELF

Research suggests that support groups and psycho-educational groups are effective in reducing burden related to primary stressors among caregivers of individuals with chronic illnesses (Sörensen, Pinquart, and Duberstein 2002) and also reduce burden related to secondary stressors that affect other areas of the caregivers' life (Aneshensel et al. 1995; McCallion and Toseland 1995). Support groups provide understanding, information, and mutual aid by developing relationships among group members. Caregivers who are likely to benefit from a referral to a support group are isolated individuals (e.g., elderly spouses with shrinking support networks) or those assuming the caregiving role for the first time (Sörensen, Pinquart, and Duberstein 2002).

Psycho-educational groups are based on structured educational programs that generally apply a cognitive-behavioral framework and social learning model to help caregivers acquire and enact the caregiving role (Gallagher-Thompson et al. 2000; Hepburn et al. 2001; Ostwald et al. 1999). Appropriate caregivers for referral to psycho-educational groups include adult children who are experiencing family conflict, spouses/partners with caregiving problems who will not confide in others and reject nursing home placement (McCallion and Toseland 1995), those who are inexperienced (Hepburn et al. 2001), and individuals with poor problem-solving skills (Roberts et al. 1999).

The worker should be familiar with community resources that provide these services and the local funding for services so that the client can make decisions about what services are accessible and affordable.

INTERVENTIONS TO ADDRESS SECONDARY STRESSORS

INTERVENTION PROVIDED BY THE HOME CARE SOCIAL WORKER

While it is more likely that caregivers referred to home care are experiencing primary stressors, it is also possible that they are simultaneously experiencing secondary stressors in the form of a deteriorating caregiver/care recipient relationship, particularly in the presence of problem behaviors related to caregiver burden and depression (Lawrence, Tennstedt, and Assmann 1998). If the quality of the relationship is not addressed, it is unlikely that referrals to resources such as respite care will be successful in reducing adverse outcomes of caregiving by simply giving the caregiver time off (Lawrence, Tennstedt, and Assmann 1998).

Caregivers who are experiencing shifts in family roles, secondary to the impact of illness, may perceive concerns related to "role reversal" (Haggan 1998; Hummert and Morgan 2001; Kane et al. 1999). Family members may experience frustration in making decisions that are unfamiliar, and the care recipient may feel that important issues are being decided without his or her input or

consent. The home care social worker can intervene by providing basic information about the effects of dementia, Alzheimer's disease, or stroke to explain
the reason that the care recipient behaves in a disturbing and embarrassing
manner (England 2001; Grant et al. 2004a, Grant et al. 2004b). This information may be helpful in reducing caregiver frustration, anger, and depression
by educating caregivers about the care recipient's limited ability to change or
regulate behavior. Reducing unrealistic expectations of the care recipient by the
caregiver can reduce caregivers' negative reactions. If the caregiver can blame
the disease, and not the care recipient or him/herself, the ability to manage feelings, problem-solve, and empathize with the patient is likely to be enhanced,
contributing to stress containment (Aneshensel et al. 1995; Grant et al. 2004a,
2004b; Sörensen et al. 2006).

This information can be applied to engage caregiver and care recipient in an
evaluation of the limits of the care recipient's abilities and the caregiver's willingness and capability to provide care. What roles can the care recipient continue to
perform that have meaning for him or her and the caregiver? How can roles be
redefined so that the dignity and self-respect of the care recipient are preserved?
What skills does the caregiver need to learn or what emotional support is required
for continued caregiving? (Dyeson 2000; Glass et al. 2000; Haggan 1998; Kane et
al. 1999; Yates, Tennstedt, and Chang 1999). These interventions are unlikely to
be successful without some follow-up after the termination of home health care
by a case management or social service program (Kane et al. 1999).

Another approach to improving the quality of the caregiver/care recipient relationship is to evaluate with the caregiver and the care recipient whether the care
recipient can provide some emotional or tangible support to the caregiver and
what type of support the care recipient is willing and able to provide. Intervening
with caregivers and care recipients to devise strategies to increase reciprocity in
the relationship through the care recipient's performance of tasks such as babysitting, light housework, or provision of companionship may mediate the effects of
burden (Dorfman, Holmes, and Berlin 1996; Dwyer, Lee, and Jankowski 1994;
Ingersoll-Dayton, Starrels, and Dowler 1996; Wright and Aquilino 1998). When
care recipients are too impaired to provide the caregiver with support, the social
worker should encourage the caregiver to maintain or build contact with family
or friends to lower levels of caregiver strain (McInnis-Dittrich 2005).

FAMILY CONFLICT

FAMILY MEETINGS

Organizing a family meeting is a useful intervention to address family conflict.
Family meetings can be used to enhance communication between family members and to increase support to the caregiver and the care recipient (Lieberman

and Fisher 1999). To obtain the cooperation and consent of the family to a family meeting, the worker can present the meeting as an opportunity for the older adult or caregiver to exercise more control over care by participating in decision making (Ringham 2001). Individuals invited to a family meeting can include family members as well as providers from other home care disciplines who are knowledgeable about the older adult's or caregiver's need for support (nurses, physical therapists, occupational therapists, home health aides) (Ringham 2001).

One common issue contributing to family stress that can be addressed effectively in a family meetings is excessive burden on one caregiver. The expression of feelings of being overburdened by the caregiver can provoke strong emotional reactions (e.g., feelings of guilt and anger among family members). To ensure that the views of all family members are heard, the social worker can function as a facilitator. A discussion of dividing caregiving tasks may lead to increased family tension. One strategy for defusing such tension is to note that positive conflict resolution may produce more care for the care recipient and more cohesion and closeness among family members (Hokanson 2003c; Lieberman and Fisher 1999). The worker may also wish to discuss the possibility of introducing formal services, such as respite care and/or long-term-care placement, if appropriate.

The meeting should end with the establishment of a family care plan. If the decision is for the older adult to remain with the same caregiver, it is important for the plan to include some provision for respite—that is, some block of personal time during which caregiving responsibility is covered by someone else (family member, adult day care, respite care) (Hokanson 2003c). The plan should be documented so that it can be communicated to providers from other home care disciplines who work with the older adult.

INTERVENTIONS: CONFLICT BETWEEN ADULT CHILDREN AND PARENTS
When family conflict between adult children is present as a consequence of increased parental dependency, home care social workers can provide brief direct services to the adult children. Communication between adult children and their dependent and/or ailing parent can be facilitated if the adult child resists complete paternalism and, if possible, appropriately supports parental control over behaviors and decisions. This strategy allows the parent to avoid a loss of dignity and self-respect (Haggan 1998; Hummert and Morgan 2001).

To maintain appropriate parent-child boundaries, it may be advisable for social workers to discuss with adult children the desirability of making recommendations but not decisions for parents. In other words, while the parent may be dependent on the adult child, the parent assumes as much personal control over decisions as possible. In situations in which adult child caregivers are uncomfortable in a relationship with a dependent parent, the home health care social worker can help the adult child discuss the emotional issues that are affecting the quality of the relationship (McInnis-Dittrich 2005).

INTERVENTIONS FOR ELDER MALTREATMENT

The primary goal of the social worker's intervention with older adults suspected of being victims of maltreatment is protecting their safety. The first priority of the worker is to answer the question, Is the elder at imminent risk for harm? If the answer is affirmative, the worker should report the situation to the state agency providing protective services. Adult protective services agency staff can advise the social worker on the protocol for intervention during this type of crisis. The worker should also be aware of agency protocols to direct and protect their staff in dangerous situations (Allan 1998; McInnis-Dittrich 2005).

If a problem is an emergency related to financial abuse, the worker must act quickly to prevent the depletion of the elder's assets. Several options are available to the worker to pursue with the client. The first would be reporting the abuse to the appropriate adult protective service agency. While the investigation is being completed, the worker can determine who has legal responsibility for managing the older adult's finances. These individuals should be contacted, with the consent of the client, to discuss the situation and solicit their assistance in interrupting the financial abuse. If a representative payee or a conservator is the alleged perpetrator, the worker may wish to obtain the advice of an attorney on how to proceed in order to stop the abuse. When the client manages his or her own affairs, the worker can develop a plan with the client to be transported to the bank, or if he or she is unable to travel, bank personnel can be asked to visit the client at home to prevent further abuse (McInnis-Dittrich 2005; Quinn and Tomita 1997).

There are several issues that workers may wish to address in reporting elder maltreatment to adult protective services. When state laws mandate reporting of elder maltreatment by social workers, but clients do not want incidents to be reported, the worker is required to report but should attempt to preserve his or her relationship with the client through the following strategies (Capezuti, Brush, and Lawson 1997; Welfel, Danzinger, and Santoro 2000). Unless the client will be placed at risk, the client should be informed that a report will be made, and he or she should be included in the reporting process to the extent that cognitive capacity to participate will allow. Client perceptions of the process and consequences of reporting can be explored to provide support. While the worker should have provided a general explanation of the process and consequences of reporting in the first interview as part of explaining the limits of confidentiality, it can be helpful to discuss the practical and emotional consequences of reporting in this specific situation, to the best of the worker's knowledge (Freed and Drake 1999; Marshall, Benton, and Brazier 2000; McInnis-Dittrich 2005; Welfel, Danzinger, and Santoro 2000). This is important because clients are likely to be unfamiliar with reporting laws and because they may be concerned about the consequences of the reporting process for both themselves and the alleged abuser. This discussion can offer an opportunity to correct client misconceptions, provide support, and help clients understand the next step in the process. Clients may fear that reporting will mean automatic removal from their homes and separation from their families; they may be concerned about the affordability of an increase in formal services or new living arrangements; and they may also be worried about whether abuse will escalate once it is disclosed. In order to provide support, social workers will need to be familiar with the literature on elder abuse, as well as the specifics of the reporting laws in their state (one journal devoted specifically to the subject of abuse and neglect is the *Journal of Elder Abuse and Neglect*) (Bergeron and Gray 2003; Freed and Drake 1999; McInnis-Dittrich 2005; Welfel, Danzinger, and Santoro 2000).

The worker's report, submitted to the adult protective services (APS) worker, can be a significant document in advocating for the client by assisting the APS worker in making an assessment and an effective care plan. The report is particularly important because most APS workers are not health professionals, but they must make decisions about, and intervene with, older adults who have complex medical, mental, and physical problems. The content of the report is likely to be influenced by the reporting laws in the state and agency policies and/or procedures. Consistent with the emphasis on confidentiality in the *Code of Ethics*, and to convey to the client that the worker respects his or her privacy, the report should include only information relevant to the incident of abuse/neglect. It is recommended that the report also include the victim's and the worker's perceptions about any danger to the victim and/or to the investigating caseworker that may be provoked by the report. When there is the potential for danger directed at the investigating worker, the report may contain the home health care worker's suggestions about how the follow-up contact can be conducted without the alleged perpetrator's knowledge. If the worker fears retaliation by the perpetrator when making future visits, he or she may request the assistance of the APS worker.

Though reports can be made anonymously, it is recommended that the worker document the report (e.g., recording the caseworker's name and number, the time, date, and nature of information provided) and keep reports in a locked file to ensure confidentiality. The worker may also wish to request a follow-up call from the investigating caseworker about actions taken or services provided. If the client denies the abuse, the report should include clear documentation of the data on which the worker based her/his assessment. This is necessary to prevent potential liability, since all adult protective service laws provide immunity from prosecution only for those who report in "good faith." The worker must demonstrate action with good intention and affirm that the report reflects what he or she believes to be reasonably true (Capezuti, Brush, and Lawson 1997; Freed and Drake 1999; Roby and Sullivan 2000; Welfel, Danzinger, and Santoro 2000).

Once a report is submitted, the worker is obligated to follow up with the client, preferably by making a home visit to ensure that necessary services are being provided. Because of the fragmented service delivery system for maltreated older adults, this is a particularly important step (Freed and Drake 1999; Quinn and Tomita 1997; Welfel, Danzinger, and Santoro 2000). If follow-up reveals that the client refused protective services, and/or if the report is substantiated but social services provided under the auspices of APS are inadequate for the situation, the worker is obligated to provide education about, and referral to services, including homemaker services, respite care, adult day care, and case management services. A referral to Medicaid and/or a case management program under the auspices of a Medicaid waiver program in the state may be necessary to facilitate the delivery of these services. If the family is not eligible for such services, the social worker can attempt to decrease caregiver stress by involving other members of the informal support system. Alcohol and substance abuse counseling may be appropriate for referrals for both the abuser and the older adult. In addition, the caregiver and the perpetrator may benefit from individual counseling.

For older adults who are experiencing financial exploitation, the designation of a representative payee can be arranged. Information about financial management services offered by community agencies may be helpful. Finally, the option of alternative living arrangements such as assisted-living facilities, board and care homes, or nursing homes can be explored, particularly if the worker has some evidence that the perpetrator's behavior is intractable (Allan 1998; Choi and Mayer 2000). If the client refuses all services, the worker should provide names and telephone number of community services should an emergency arise (Allan 1998).

When older adults are self-neglecting, interventions may range from persuasion to advocacy to finding a surrogate decision maker. An older adult who is competent to make decisions about self-care and understands all of the available options has a right to refuse services (Leff and Sonstegard-Gamm 2006; Tomita 2006). Involuntary interventions such as guardianship or conservatorship are indicated when older adults are incapable of making relevant decisions and they face imminent harm (Tomita 2006).

Recommended interventions with older adults who self-neglect include focusing on the establishment of trust and rapport as the first priority (Leff and Sonstegard-Gamm 2006; Tomita 2006). Knowledge of the older adult's level of cognitive functioning can be applied to provide information and feedback (Leff and Sonstegard-Gamm 2006; Tomita 2006). Concrete assistance with a goal identified by the client that is congruent with the worker's primary purpose of protecting the client from harm, regardless of the current presenting problem, is likely to contribute to the development of trust and rapport (Leff and Sonstegard-Gamm 2006; Tomita 2006). Client-centered techniques such as motivational interviewing may be useful in negotiating change. Motivational interviewing includes the following strategies:

- Express empathy and recognize that change is difficult and ambivalence is normal. For example, "I understand that accepting Meals on Wheels would be a big change in your life. This is a very difficult decision for you. What do you hope will happen? What are you most afraid of?"
- Develop discrepancy by helping the client realize there is a conflict between behavior and personal goals and values. An example: "You mentioned you do not eat much and feel weak and exhausted. When you were eating regular meals before this time, you said you had more energy and you were able to enjoy a more active life."
- Roll with resistance by avoiding arguments and identifying areas for overcoming barriers to change by involving the client in brainstorming acceptable strategies. For example, "You are concerned about letting a stranger into the house. What are your ideas about how the meals could be delivered without letting a strange person into the house? Could the delivery person leave the meals outside on your doorstep and just ring the doorbell? Would you feel comfortable if the meals were delivered and you opened the door but did not let the person into the house?"
- Support client self-efficacy and control. For example, "You have told me about many difficult challenges that you have overcome in your life before this time. I believe you can do this with my support, and the support of the nurse" (Leff and Sonstegard-Gamm 2006).

Because of the complexity of situations of abuse and neglect it is recommended that these cases be handled through a multidisciplinary approach, involving all appropriate disciplines (Capezuti, Brush, and Lawson 1997; Lachs and Pillemer 2004).

NURSING HOME PLACEMENT

DELAYING PLACEMENT

Those who enter nursing homes from home health care do so largely for social reasons, such as caregiver stress (Gaugler et al. 2003; Tsuji, Whalen, and Finucane 1995). When workers and other members of the home health care team identify, through screening or assessment, a caregiver and care recipient who are vulnerable to placement but could delay or postpone placement if they had access to increased formal and informal support, interventions should target early introduction of community-based services and increased family support.

Among the frail elderly at risk of nursing home placement whose diseases are not confined to dementia, several demonstration projects that provide comprehensive community-based care and case management have been associated with postponed institutionalization (Fischer et al. 2003; Friedman et al. 2005). Within the parameters of the traditional delivery system, however, the literature suggests that formal services may serve a more limited function in postponing placement. Community services may be used as an interim step toward institutionalization, reflecting the inability of the informal caregiving system to adequately meet the needs of an extremely disabled client. Early intervention, before the caregiver and the informal support system are exhausted and depleted and the client has deteriorated to a level that precludes community living, is recommended to improve the impact of formal services on placement delay (Bauer 1996; Jette, Tennstedt, and Crawford 1995).

Among caregivers of individuals with dementia, research has found that the introduction of in-home services (e.g., personal care or chore services) early in the caregiving career is related to delayed placement, while adult day care is associated with postponement of institutionalization at any time during the caregiving career. It is thought that in-home care delays placement by providing respite while the caregiver accommodates life routines to the caregiving role; adult day care also reduces strain by offering respite (Gaugler et al. 2005).

Because of the stressful nature of assisting care recipients with ADL tasks such as toileting and bathing, placement can be postponed if the family supports the caregiver in performing these tasks. Overnight respite provided by the family to the caregiver is also associated with delayed placement, possibly because the caregiver can avoid the disruptive nighttime behavior of the care recipient (Gaugler et al. 2000).

INTERVENTIONS TO ASSIST CLIENTS WITH DECISION MAKING FOR NURSING HOME PLACEMENT

The goals of the home health care social worker in helping the family and older adult make decisions about nursing home placement are:

- Plan a family meeting
- Identify and reduce family conflict
- Clarify feelings toward placement
- Provide information for an informed choice

- Include caregivers and care recipients in decision making (Dellasega and Nolan 1997; Gaugler et al. 2001; Mastrian and Dellasega 1996; Nolan et al. 1996).

A family meeting is recommended to structure decision making and planning about placement so that all family members can participate in the process. The goal of the meeting can be identified as improving care for the older adult in the present situation. The social worker should identify the family decision makers and others who will be involved in making the placement decision during this meeting so that the decision maker(s) are always involved (Mastrian and Dellasega 1996). The worker should be aware of family conflict; if it is present it will increase the difficulty of searching for a nursing home (Gaugler et al. 2001). One strategy is to help families collaborate on a decision by emphasizing a goal that all family members and the older adult can share: to improve the health and well-being of the older adult.

Clarification of the caregiver's and the care recipient's feelings toward placement by empathizing with and supporting emotional reactions can help the caregiver and the care recipient with placement by addressing some of the affectively charged images and meanings associated with nursing homes (Penrod and Dellasega 1998). Providing professional validation for the placement decision by emphasizing the safety needs of the older adult and/or representing placement as the only reasonable alternative may also be helpful in assisting a caregiver to feel more comfortable with placement (Dellasega and Nolan 1997; Rodgers 1997; Salamon and Rosenthal 2004). Caregivers who feel they are "good caregivers" are more likely to make a decision in favor of placement (Schur and Whitlatch 2003). Fostering a collaborative relationship with family and friends can also provide validation for the placement decision (Mastrian and Dellasega 1996; Ryan and Scullion 2000) and is associated with less difficulty during the placement process (Gaugler, Kane, and Langlois 2000).

Home care social workers should be aware of the need to provide practical information and support. Providing information about area nursing homes and helpful Web sites such as Nursing Home Compare site (www.medicare.gov/NHCompare/home.asp) (Harrington et al. 2003), the AARP Web site (www.AARP.com), and Family Care of America (www.familycareamerica.com) may help to educate families about available resources.

Including caregivers and care recipients in decision making is an important component for a successful transition (Davies and Nolan 2003; Reinhardy 1992, 1995; Reuss, Dupuis, and Whitfield 2005). Caregivers may resent providers who do not acknowledge their expertise. Collaboration with family caregivers and recognition of their perspectives can encourage caregivers to feel they have control over the process of placement (Gaugler, Kane, and Langlois 2000; Reuss, Dupuis, and Whitfield 2005).

Family participation is also facilitated when information is presented in clear, simple language and families have time to assimilate this content (McAuley, Travis, and Safewright 1997). When dealing with several decision makers, the social worker should also be conscious of giving out consistent information. Families under stress may need to hear information more than once and may try to validate information by asking different professionals the same questions. They will be reassured if they receive the same information from everyone. Team meetings are recommended to ensure consistency in information given to clients (Mastrian and Dellasega 1996).

Caregivers and care recipients are likely to continue to experience conflicting feelings after placement. Because the home care worker's time may be largely consumed with assisting the family with the emotional and practical tasks of the transition to care, issues that require long-term follow-up are better addressed through a referral to nursing home staff or a local support group (Davies and Nolan 2004; Mastrian and Dellasega 1996; Reinhardy 1995).

❖ ❖ ❖

Social work interventions to address unmet client service needs emphasize the activities of information and referral. The worker's skill in education and referral is influenced by knowledge of relevant programs, services, and professionals, involvement of clients in decision making, accommodating worker directiveness to client coping capacities, and matching clients to culturally preferred resources.

In selecting interventions to address caregiver burden arising from the objective demands of caregiving, the worker's objective is to contain stress by providing education and referrals to respite care and to professionals and programs that alter the home environment. Home health social workers can attempt to reduce stress related to the situation through education, referral to support and psychoeducation groups, and provision of short-term counseling to the client.

When family conflict is present between adult children and older, impaired parents, effective interventions include enhancing communication in the parent-child dyad and organization and conduct of family meetings.

When an older adult is at imminent risk of harm, the duty of the home health social worker is to consult with the interdisciplinary team, file a report with the local protective services agency if indicated, involve the client to the extent that he or she is capable of decision making, and monitor the outcomes of the reporting process.

Interventions to delay nursing home placement include introduction of formal and informal services before the impairment of caregiver and care recipient is so severe that the care recipient can no longer remain safely in the community. If placement is unavoidable, effective interventions include convening family meetings to increase cooperation and decrease conflict, individual counseling to clarify affective reactions to placement, providing professional validation of the placement decision, providing information and support to the caregiver and care recipient during the placement process, and referring the family to a support group after placement, when indicated.

MR. AND MRS. CERRILO

Anthony Cerrilo is an 85-year-old man with Alzheimer's disease, congestive heart failure, and hypertension who was discharged to his wife's care with a referral to home health following a hospitalization for a severe urinary tract infection. The nurse's initial assessment was obtained from information provided by his 78-year-old wife, Marie, because Mr. Cerrilo was confused and disoriented at the time of the visit. Mrs. Cerrilo stated that before the hospitalization her husband had been ambulatory with a walker, was able to follow directions, and required supervision and assistance with some ADL tasks such as dressing and toileting. Mr. Cerrilo is now bedridden and incontinent and needs total care with ADL tasks. Mrs. Cerrilo has congestive heart failure and severe arthritis, and in the judgment of the nurse she is currently unable to provide adequate care. The nurse observed that Mr. Cerrilo was soaked in urine and had decubuti.

Mr. and Mrs. Cerrilo have been married for 50 years but have no children. They have lived in the same home for the past 40 years. The Cerrilos receive Social Security, a small pension, and have minimal savings.

Mr. Cerrilo's family immigrated to the United States from Italy when he was 15 years old and his two sisters were 16 years old and 18 years old, respectively. Mrs. Cerrilo was born in the United States, though she is also of Italian descent. In the interview with the nurse, Mrs. Cerrilo confided that she wants to continue to care for her husband at home and believes that his sudden decline is the result of "old age" and his recent infection. Mr. Cerrilo's two sisters live in the same neighborhood but are too old and infirm to assist with care. Mr. Cerrilo's family has maintained strong bonds, and the sisters call frequently.

Though Mrs. Cerrilo is devoted to her husband's care, the nurse's assessment is that she is unable to provide appropriate care. Mrs. Cerrilo is resistant to a home health aide and refuses to consider nursing home placement. She is visibly exhausted, has not been able to leave the house to go to church or her weekly bingo game for months, and has not seen her doctor in a year. The nurse decides to make a referral to the home health social worker for a clinical assessment of social and emotional issues related to the need for care, counseling for long-range planning and decision making, and information and referral to community resources.

During the initial visit Mrs. Cerrilo confided to the worker that she had promised her husband and his two sisters that she would never put him in a nursing home. She became tearful at this point and stated that she has felt frustrated and lonely since her husband's illness. They have been devoted and committed to each other during their entire marriage; Mr. Cerrilo has been the "head of the family," making all of the decisions for the couple. Now Mrs. Cerrilo has had to take on many responsibilities for which she was unprepared—balancing the checkbook, paying bills, talking to doctors. She deeply misses her husband's companionship and the comfort of being dependent on and cared for by him. Sometimes all of this becomes overwhelming. She feels guilty that she has done something "wrong" to cause her husband's sudden decline and worries that she is not providing the "right care." She also feels angry and guilty because Mr. Cerrilo's sisters object to her acceptance of home health care, telling her "it's her duty" as a wife to care for her husband without any help from strangers.

Questions:

1. What are the problems in this situation from the perspective of home health social work?
2. What interventions should the social worker plan and implement?

9

EVALUATING SOCIAL WORK PRACTICE
IN HOME HEALTH CARE

IT MUST be noted that while the profession has endorsed practitioners' evaluating their own practice for more than two decades, in 1996 only one in six social work journals that published health-related content included research on practice evaluation (Auslander 2000). It has been suggested that practitioner resistance to doing practice evaluation results from a confusion of thought—assuming that practice evaluation is clinical research—or from inadequate information on how to evaluate practice. Conversely, it is suggested that while some social workers do evaluate their practice, most have little time or interest in publishing (Bloom, Fisher, and Orme 2003; Corcoran, Gingerich, and Briggs 2001). This chapter seeks to provide the knowledge and skills that make evaluation of the individual's practice in home health feasible, valuable, and interesting. The discussion differentiates between the social worker's practice and program evaluation; program evaluation is outside the scope of this practice text.

Evaluating social work practice in general (Bloom, Fisher, and Orme 2003; Corcoran, Gingerich, and Briggs 2001), and particularly the practice of social work in health care, receives increasing attention in this era of managed care (Auslander 2000; Berkman 1996; Kayser, Hansen, and Groves 1995; Schneider, Hyer, and Luptak 2000). The emphasis on efficient and cost-effective service provision mandates that social workers in health care practice take on the task of evaluating services in three areas:

- proving the "value added" of social work to the organization
- demonstrating that social work is cost-effective
- evaluating the impact—the effectiveness—of social work interventions on patient outcomes

In social work practice in home health, the challenge of achieving these three goals increases because of the role of social work in the host setting—one that is also a medical hierarchy (Auslander, 1996, 2000; Kayser, Hansen, and Groves 1995)—of home care agencies. The combination of the demands of managed care in home health care services and the role of the social worker in this setting make it increasingly important that practice evaluation deal with all three goals.

WHY IS PRACTICE EVALUATION IN HOME HEALTH IMPORTANT?

Providing evidence of the value added by having social workers in home health agencies is particularly important given the findings that significant numbers of workers in home health are not full-time, regular employees and that workers in home health practice may have experienced reductions in the scope, hours, or status of their positions in recent years (Egan and Kadushin 2005).

TARGETS FOR EVALUATION

The value-added aspect of social work in home health might be related to the coordination and documentation of coordination of the activities of the worker, both within the agency and between the agency and outside community resources and/or managed-care systems to facilitate achievement of agency goals (Auslander 2000). It has also been suggested that this coordination, "oiling the wheels" or helping to maintain staff and community relations, fosters increased status and influence of social workers in agencies (Rizzo and Abrams 2000) and is an area that needs evaluation (Auslander 2000).

In order to evaluate this aspect of social work in home health, the worker would collect data on the satisfaction of community resources with respect to contacts, referrals, and follow-through by the social worker and of managed-care agents concerning the social worker's coordination activities. Inside the agency, evaluating the "value-addedness" of the social worker might be accomplished through assessment of intra-agency activities, such as

- the social worker's participation on the health care team
- the team's understanding of the expertise of the social worker in the agency
- comparisons of non–social work clients with social work clients, measured by the number of effective discharges and/or the number of crises while in care

These targets speak to the "value-addedness" of social work and relate, as has been recommended, to the need for social worker to substantiate how social work contributes to the agency's goals and mission (Auslander 2000; Rizzo and Abrams 2000).

The second area of evaluation for social work in home health involves the cost consciousness of health care in general and the influence of financial priorities in home health. This emphasis on cost-effectiveness can be understood in terms of cost-benefit evaluation of social work services to the agency. In other words, does the productivity of the social worker prove a benefit to the agency in relation to the cost to the agency of employing the social worker? An evaluation of the cost benefits of social work may include:

- cost comparisons of the social worker by patient outcomes
- analysis of the cost of the social worker to the agency by the worker's tasks

Early in the history of cost consciousness in health care, researchers (for example, Coulton, Keller, and Boone 1985) first attempted to prove the "worth" of social work in hospitals by having social workers record the number of services provided and the acuity of need (i.e., the number of patient problems) to which they were responding in relation to the length of hospital stay. More recently, social work cost-benefit evaluation resulting from cost-containment efforts in health care takes the form of justifying the presence of the social worker in terms of reducing costs to the agency, most notably by reducing the length of hospital stays (Berkman et al. 1988). In light of the reduction in length of stay related to the Medicare prospective payment system that reimburses home health care agencies for a sixty-day episode of care, this way of thinking is relevant.

In the home care setting, analysis of the worker's efficiency in assessing, intervening, and referring home health patients and/or their families within the designated episode of care speaks to the worker's efficiency. The following questions are pertinent to this aspect of evaluation:

- Does the worker successfully complete the process of social service delivery within the episode?
- What, if any, unmet psychosocial needs are present at the conclusion of the episode?
- In terms of cost-effectiveness, does the worker complete needed work with the patient and/or family without exceeding the capitated rate for that patient episode?

Data to evaluate efficiency might include a checklist of the psychosocial problems identified in assessment and/or by the other home care staff and whether or not the social work services/interventions were delivered within an episode of care (i.e., sixty days). Did the worker make needed referrals? And did the patient and/or family utilize—follow up—with those referrals? The last point relates to identifying unmet psychosocial needs and the worker's ability to complete work within the episode and within the capitated fee of home health as well. Workers alone, or in conjunction with patients, could complete these checklists for each patient. When individual client checklists are combined, the practitioner has the data to evaluate social work efficiency for the agency. Incorporating the checklist in practice facilitates the documentation of worker efficiency mandated by managed care. When included in the client database, reports from patients and families about the social work services provide further evaluative data.

Practice evaluation for intervention effectiveness is the component of evaluation that utilizes systematic collection of data to establish whether a social worker's intervention achieved a desired patient or family outcome (Corcoran, Gingerich, and Briggs 2001). Its primary purpose is to provide information to the practitioner and the client about client change. It is distinguished from clinical research, which seeks to develop scientific knowledge using rigorous methodologies (Corcoran, Gingerich, and Briggs 2001).

THE PROCESS OF PRACTICE EVALUATION

Practice evaluation involves identifying target client problems (i.e., the condition or issue of concern), designating a goal or objective that, if achieved, would indicate that the target problem had been resolved, and developing observations or selecting validated measurements related directly to the target problem and to the goal or objective (Alter and Evans 1990). Both the target problem and the goals/objectives must:

- be identified in the process of assessment
- be described in client terms
- be observable
- be measurable in some way

Goals identify the outcome of the worker's interventions—the desired outcome of the client system, which some researchers refer to as the outcome that has clinical importance to the client (Briggs and Corcoran 2001). Goals should be

- clearly stated
- client-centered
- specific as to who is the target of the intervention

This last point is particularly prescient in home health, since the person with whom the worker is intervening may not be the singular or direct focus of needed change. For example, intervening through education to help a family caregiver modify the behavior of the patient regarding self-care activities would have as its goal knowledge acquisition by the caregiver and a behavior change in the patient (Pinkson et al. 2003). To evaluate the effectiveness of the educational intervention, the worker would want to develop goal(s) with the family and client for both the family caregiver and the patient.

MEASUREMENT, METHODS, AND DESIGN IN PRACTICE EVALUATION

Multiple techniques have been documented to measure practice effectiveness. Each of these techniques is applicable regardless of the design of the practice evaluation (which is discussed below). Measurement methods that are useful for practice evaluation include standardized measures, goal attainment scaling, and self-anchored scales.

While the use of standardized measures is integral to scientific clinical research, their use in practice evaluation is not always necessary or applicable (Corcoran, Gingerich, and Briggs 2001). Several available sources include these standardized measures, among them rapid assessment instruments (RAIs) (see, for example, Berkman and Maramaldi 2001; Bloom, Fischer, and Orme 2003; Corcoran and Fischer 2001; McMurtry, Rose, and Cisler in press). It is recommended that the standardized scales, or their subscales, that are selected for practice evaluation be brief, easily implemented, and easily scored (Briggs and Corcoran 2001).

Goal attainment scaling (GAS) is a method of measurement that easily shows client change in relation to service goals. The traditional goal attainment scale ranges from 1 to 5, with 1 designated as the least favorable outcome and 5 as the most favorable. Intermediate numbers represent a less than expected outcome (2), the expected outcome (3), and a greater than expected outcome (4). The worker and the client/patient system describe each level of the scale clearly, from the client's perspective and in observable terms jointly. The numbering system may reflect lowest to highest positive integers, as in the above example, or negative to positive integers, as in -2 to +2. The important point is that the descriptions of each level of outcome and the numbering system are meaningful to the client and to the worker. A separate GAS should be developed for each goal or objective of service. (For examples of GAS, see Bloom, Fischer, and Orme 2003 and Alter and Evans 1990.)

A third form of measurement for practice evaluation is self-anchored scales (SARS), which are very useful when the target problem is an internal state. The worker and the client in relation to a target problem develop a self-anchored scale. A range of levels of the target problem is then identified and points are assigned along usually a 4- or 5-point Likert scale (Bloom, Fischer, and Orme

2003). For example, a caregiver who feels resentment might identify the following levels:

- Worst (level 1): Sometimes I am so angry I just can't go in that room again
- Somewhat better (level 2): I just hate having to clean mother up
- Better (lever 3): I can't stand to be around here
- Good (level 4): I feel good when I take care of mother
- Best (level 5): She smiles back at me when I wash her face

Given that the home health environment is a medical model of service, it is beneficial to include measurements directly related to the target problems identified. As an illustration, a caregiver reporting resentment, as in the above discussion, might logically experience physical problems related to that resentment (headaches, hypertension exacerbation, sleeplessness, etc.) and be receiving medical care for those problems, such as tranquilizers or hypertension medications. Monitoring the caregiver's physical symptoms, like blood pressure or presence of headaches, on a weekly or biweekly basis and his or her internal state (through a caregiver SARS, as above) and the use of medical interventions (medication) throughout the course of social work interventions are recommended (Auslander 2000; Bloom, Fischer, and Orme 2003).

Because the purpose of practice evaluation is to provide feedback to the worker and to the client(s) and/or family as to whether or not and to what extent the interventions have achieved goals/objectives, the design methodologies recommended focus in one way or another on before-intervention evaluation and during or after-intervention evaluation—most typically single-subject designs.

DESIGN

The single-subject design in practice evaluation ideally allows the worker to gain knowledge related to the effectiveness of interventions with each client or client system with whom he or she works (Alter and Evans 1990; Bloom, Fischer, and Orme 2003). The classic single-subject design is an AB, or before-and-after design, in which data are collected prior to intervention, at "baseline" A by using one or more of the measures discussed above. During the B, or intervention, phase, data are again collected at multiple points in time. These points in time may represent actual meetings of home health patients and families with the worker, with measurements being completed at the conclusion of the session. It is also useful, particularly with GAS and SARS measures, for the home health client to complete measures on a regular, more frequent basis. For in-depth discussion of more-complex single-subject designs, such as ABAB,

ABCD, or ABACAD designs, see Bloom, Fischer, and Orme 2003. The more-complicated designs are intended primarily for evaluating practice in which the worker and the client meet many times over a protracted period of time; thus those designs may not be applicable to the short-term nature of practice in home health social work.

In some situations collecting measures of target problem indicators completely before intervention is not feasible; every effort should be made, however, to incorporate the collection of baseline data during the assessment. It is also possible to collect such data by asking the client to describe the target problem retrospectively. Finally, some types of intervention, such as educational interventions, may have immediate effect. In this situation, "pre-session" and "post-session" measurements for a single session/meeting intervention can be used and thus approximate the AB design during the B phase. Given the comparative brevity of a patient's episode of care in home health and the brevity of the number of sessions a social worker may meet with the patient and family, follow-up activities via phone are particularly important. Data on post-intervention— B phase—can and should be incorporated into follow-up efforts.

DATA ANALYSIS

Data collected through any of the measurement techniques and design methodologies described above are best analyzed visually (Bloom, Fisher, and Orme 2003; Nugent 2000; Patterson and Basham 2006). Visualization by graphing is particularly helpful for the worker, and it is just as useful for the client, to discern whether the desired change has occurred. Two excellent resources are available for those who seek in-depth details of statistical analysis, as well as techniques for visualizing data in single-system evaluation (Bloom, Fischer, and Orme 2003; Patterson and Basham 2006).

AFTERWORD

THIS BOOK has discussed the complex role of social work in home health care. The content demonstrates the importance of psychosocial factors in addressing the older adult home health care population. As the proportion of older adults in the United States with chronic illnesses and disabilities increases in the future, the need for home care social workers who are knowledgeable in gerontology and health will also grow. Numerous challenges confront home care social workers at this important juncture.

The home health social work role is currently restricted by health care policies and system barriers such as a lack of acceptance of social work as a profession by other home health care disciplines. Perhaps the most significant challenge confronting home health care social work in expanding its professional role is demonstrating the positive impact of social work on the health of older adults. Currently there is little research on social work outcomes in home care. Without this kind of evidence, it is less likely that social work advocacy for revision of existing health care policies and professional status will be successful. Research on social work services in home care has been advocated but remains scant (Benjamin and Naito-Chan 2006; Lee and Gutheil 2003).

Making the case for an expanded social work role in home care will require evidence-based research on the impact of home health care social work on patient outcomes and agency cost-effectiveness, the contribution of psychosocial factors to reducing cost and increasing quality of care, the development and evaluation of screening instruments for "high-risk" social work clients, and the effects of such screening instruments on efficient, effective service delivery (Benjamin and Naito-Chan 2006; Lee and Gutheil 2003). It has been suggested that the funding and evaluation of a small number of demonstration projects to test the impact of selected social work interventions with older home care clients can contribute to the beginning accumulation of an evidence base for substantiating the contribution of social work to efficient, effective patient care (Benjamin and Naito-Chan 2006). Evidence of positive social work outcomes may be a necessary but not sufficient condition to change health care policy and system barriers in the host setting of home care. A knowledge base that demonstrates the unique contribution of the social work profession in home care is a required first step to expanding social work services so that they are more accessible to vulnerable older adults and their families, both now and in the future (Benjamin and Naito-Chan 2006).

APPENDIX

INTERNET RESOURCES

NAME	WEB SITE

GENERAL INFORMATION

NAME	WEB SITE
American Association of Retired Persons	www.aarp.org
National Association of Area Agencies on Aging	www.n4a.org
National Association for Home Care and Hospice	www.nahc.org
U.S. Department of Health and Human Services, Area Agency on Aging	www.eldercare.gov.Eldercare/Public/Home.asp
U.S. Department of Veterans Affairs, Veterans Administration	www.va.gov

ADVANCE DIRECTIVES

NAME	WEB SITE
Compassion in Dying	www.compassionandchoices.org/cid
National Hospice and Palliative Care Organization	www.nhpco.org/templates/1/homepage.cfm
Partnership for Caring	www.partnershipforcaring.com

ASSISTIVE TECHNOLOGY

NAME	WEB SITE
AbleData	www.abledata.com
Area Agency on Aging Elder Care Locator	www.elder.gov/eldercare/Public/resources/fact_sheets/assistive_tech.asp
Family Caregiver Support Act	www.aoa.gov/caregivers
Solutions: Assistive Technologies for People with Hidden Disabilities	www.uiowa.edu/infotech/Solutions.pdf
U.S. Government Disability Information	www.disability.info.gov

CHORE/HOMEMAKER SERVICES

NAME	WEB SITE
Area Agency on Aging ElderCare Locator	www.eldercare.gov/eldercare/Public/network/services.asp
Family Caregiver Support Act	www.eldercare.gov
Medicaid Home and Community-Based Waiver Programs	www.cms.hhs.gov/MedicaidStWaivProgDemoPGI/01_Overview.asp
Medicaid State Plans Personal Care Option Benefit	www.hhs.gov/news/press/2003pres/20031119.html
National Association of Professional Geriatric Care Managers	www.caremanager.org

CONSUMER-DIRECTED HOME CARE

Centers for Medicaid and Medicare Services: Medicaid Waiver Programs	www.chshhs.gov/MedicaidStWaivProgDemoPG
Medicaid State Plans Personal Care Option Benefit	www.hhs.gov/news/press/2003pres/20031119.html

ELDER MALTREATMENT

Area Agency on Aging Elder Care Locator	www.eldercare.gov/eldercare/Public/network/services.asp
National Center on Elder Abuse	www.elderabusecenter.org
National Committee for the Prevention of Elder Abuse	www.preventelderabuse.org

FAMILY MEDICAL LEAVE ACT

U.S. Department of Labor Compliance Assistance Family and Medical Leave Act	www.dol.gov/esa/whd/fmla

FINANCIAL SUPPORT

Medicaid	www.cms.hhs.gov/medicaid/geninfo
Medicare	www.medicare.gov
Medicare Part D	www.medicare.gov/pdphome.asp
Medicare Plans—The Original Plan and Medicare Advantage Plans	www.medicare.gov/Choices/Overview.asp
Medicare and Prescription Drug Costs— Help for Low-Income Beneficiaries	www.ssa.gov/prescriptionhelp
Old Age Survivors Disability Insurance	www.ssa.gov
Representative Payee Program	www.ssa.gov/payee
Supplemental Security Income	www.ssa.gov
U.S. Department of Veterans Affairs, Veterans Administration	www.vba.va.gov/survivors/index.htm
U.S. Department of Veterans Affairs, Veterans Administration	www.va.gov/healtheligibility/coveredservices Standard Benefits.asp
U.S. Government Benefits	www.GovBenefits.gov

HOME CARE SERVICES

Centers for Medicare and Medicaid Services	www.cms.hhs.gov
Health Insurance Association of America	www.hiaa.org
LifePlans Incorporated	www.lifeplanproverpathway.com
MetLife	www.metlife.com/Applications/Corporate/WPS/CDA/PageGenerator
National Association for Home Care and Hospice	www.nahc.org
U.S. Department of Health and Human Services, Agency for Children and Families Social Services Block Grant Program	www.acf.hhs.gov/programs/ocs/ssbg
U.S. Department of Veterans Affairs, Veterans Administration	www.vba.va.gov

HOME SAFETY/MODIFICATION

Administration on Aging, National Energy Assistance and Referral Project	www.aarp.org
Area Agency on Aging Elder Care Locator	www.elder.gov/eldercare/Public/resources/fact_ sheets/home_mod._asp
Family Caregiver Support Act	www.aoa.gov/caregivers
Low-Income Home Energy Assistance Program (LIHEAP)	www.acf.dhhs.gov/programs/liheap/faq.htm
National Resource Center on Supportive Housing and Home Modifications (NRCSHHM)	www.homemods.org
U.S. Department of Energy, Weatherization Assistance Program	www.eere.energy.gov/weatherization

MENTAL HEALTH

American Geriatrics Society	www.americangeriatric.org/links
Centers for Medicare and Medicaid Services	www.medicare.gov/publications/pubs/pdf/10050.pdf
SAMSA Guide to Mental Health Services	mentalhealth.samhsa.gov/publications/allpubs/ cmh94-5001/Default.asp
SAMSA National Mental Health Information Center	www.mentalhealth.samhsa.gov/databases
U.S. Department of Health and Human Services, National Institutes of Health (NIH)	www.nih.gov
U.S. Department of Health and Human Services, Substance Abuse and Mental Health Services Administration	mentalhealth.samhsa.gov/cmhs
U.S. Department of Veterans Affairs, Veterans Administration	www.vba.va.gov

NURSING HOMES

Centers for Medicare and Medicaid Services	www.medicare.gov/publications/pubs/pdf/10050.pdf
Centers for Medicare and Medicaid Services	www.cms.hhs.gov/medicaid/consumer.asp.
Centers for Medicare and Medicaid Services Nursing Home Compare	www.medicare.gov/NHCompare/home.asp

NUTRITION

Meals on Wheels Association of America	www.moaa.org
U.S. Department of Health and Human Services, Administration on Aging, Area Agency on Aging Elderly Nutrition Program	www.aoa.gov/eldfam/Nutrition/Nutrition.asp

RESPITE CARE

Alzheimer's Disease Association	www.alz.org
Area Agency on Aging ElderCare Locator	www.elder.gov/eldercare/Public/resources/ fact_ sheets/respite_care.asp
Family Caregiver Alliance	www.caregiver.org
National Adult Day Care Services	www.nadsa.org
National Alliance for Caregiving	www.caregiving.org
U.S. Department of Health and Human Services, Area Agency on Aging, Family Caregiver Support Act	www.aoa.gov/caregivers

SUPPORT GROUPS/OTHER GROUPS

Alzheimer's Association	www.alz.org
American Heart Association	www.strokeconnection@heart.org
Mended Hearts, Inc.	www.mendedhearts.org
U.S. Agency on Aging	www.aoa.gov/caregivers
U.S. National Institutes of Health National Cancer Institute	www.cancer.gov.cancerrtopics/support

WORKS CITED

Abel-Vacula, C., and K. Phillips. 2004. *Home Health Care Social Work: Guidelines for Practitioners and Agencies*. Wilmette, Ill.: Gail Gill.

Abrams, R. C., M. Lachs, G. McAvay, K. Keohane, and M. Bruce. 2002. Predictors of self-neglect in community-dwelling elders. *American Journal of Psychiatry* 159:1724–1730.

Abramson, J. 1992. Health-related problems. In W. Reid, ed., *Task Strategies: An Empirical Approach to Clinical Social Work*, 225–249. New York: Columbia University Press.

Acton, G.J., and J. Kang. 2001. Interventions to reduce the burden of caregiving for an adult with dementia: A meta-analysis. *Research in Nursing and Health* 24:349–360.

Agree, E. M., and V. A. Freedman. 2003. A comparison of assistive technology and personal care in alleviating disability and unmet need. *Gerontologist* 43:335–344.

Al-Krenawi, A., and J. Graham. 2000a. Culturally sensitive social work practice with Arab clients in mental health settings. *Health and Social Work* 25 (1): 9–22.

——. 2000b. Islamic theology and prayer: Relevance for social work practice. *International Social Work* 43 (3): 289–304.

Allan, M.A. 1998. Elder abuse: A challenge for home care nurses. *Home Healthcare Nurse* 16 (2): 103–111.

Allen, S.M., A. Foster, and K. Berg. 2001. Receiving help at home: The interplay of human and technological assistance. *Journals of Gerontology* 56B (6): S374–S381.

Allen, S.M., and V. Mor. 1997. The prevalence and consequences of unmet need. *Medical Care* 35:1132–1148.

Alter, C., and W. Evans. 1990. *Evaluating Your Practice: A Guide to Self-Assessment*. New York: Springer.

Altman, C. 1999. Gay and lesbian seniors: Unique challenges of coming out in later life. *Siecus Report* 27:14–17.

Alzheimer's Disease and Related Disorders Association. 2006. Fact Sheet. http://alz.org.

American Association of Retired Persons. 2006. *Guardianship*. Retrieved January 6, 2006, from http://www.aarp.org/families/caregiving/caring_parents/a2003-11-07-Guardianship.html.

——. 2007. *Understanding Power of Attorney*. Retrieved January 6, 2006, from http://www.aarp.org/money/financial_planning/estate_planning/a2002-08-12-EstatePlanningPowerofAttorney.html.

American Geriatrics Society, British Geriatrics Society, and American Academy of Orthopaedic Surgeons Panel on Fall Prevention. 2001. Guideline for the prevention of falls in older persons. *Journal of the American Geriatrics Society* 49:664–672.

American Medical Association. 2007. *Caregiver Self-AssessmentQuestionnaire*. Retrieved January 19, 2007, from http://www.ama-assn.org/ama/upload/mm/36/caregivertool-eng.pdf.

American Psychiatric Association. 2000. *Diagnostic and Statistical Manual of Mental Disorders (DSM-IV-TR)*. 4th ed. Washington, D.C.: American Psychiatric Association.

Andersen, M., and P. Collins. 2004. Conceptualizing race, class, and gender. In M. Andersen, ed., *Race, Class, and Gender: An Anthology*, 75–98. 5th ed. Belmont, Calif.: Wadsworth.

Anderson, M. A., M. M. Clark, L. B. Helms, and M. D. Foreman. 2005. Hospital readmission from home health care before and after prospective payment. *Journal of Nursing Scholarship* 37 (1): 73–79.

Aneshensel, C. S., L. I. Pearlin, J. T. Mullan, S. H. Zarit, and C. J. Whitlatch. 1995. *Profiles in Caregiving: The Unexpected Career*. San Diego: Academic Press.

Antonucci, T. C. 2001. Social relations. In J. E. Birren and K. W. Schaie, eds., *Handbook of the Psychology of Aging*, 427–453. San Diego, Calif.: Academic Press.

Appel, S., J. Harrell, and S. Deng. 2002. Racial and socioeconomic differences in risk factors for cardiovascular disease among Southern rural women. *Nursing Research* 51 (3): 140–147.

Applewhite, S. 1995. *Curanderismo*: Demystifying the health beliefs and practices of elderly Mexican Americans. *Health and Social Work* 20:247–253.

——. 1998. Culturally competent practice with elderly Latinos. *Journal of Multicultural Social Work* 30 (1/2): 1–15.

Aranda, M., and B. Knight. 1997. The influence of ethnicity and culture on the caregiver stress and coping process: A sociocultural review and analysis. *Gerontologist* 17 (3): 342–354.

Archbold, P. G., B. J. Stewart, L. L. Miller, T. A. Harvath, M. R. Greenlick, L. Van Buren, et al. 1995. The PREP system of nursing interventions: A pilot test with families caring for older members. *Research in Nursing and Health* 18:3–16.

Arnason, S., E. Rosenzweig, and A. Koski. 1995. *The Legal Rights of the Elderly*. New York: Practising Law Institute.

Arras, J., and N. Dubler. 1994. Bringing the hospital home: Ethical and social implications of high-tech home care. *Hastings Center Report* 24 (Special Supplement): S19–28.

Auerbach, D., R. Bann, D. Davis, S. Sassi, R. Straus, and S. Felsen. 1984. The social worker in home health care. *Caring* 3:71–76.

Auslander, G. 1996. Outcome evaluation in host settings: A research agenda. *Administration in Social Work* 20 (2): 15–27.

——. 2000. Outcomes of social work interventions in health care settings. *Social Work in Health Care* 31 (2): 31–46.

Auslander, W., D. Haire-Joshu, C. Houston, C.-W. Rhee, and J. H. Williams. 2002. A controlled evaluation of staging dietary patterns to reduce the risk of diabetes in African-American women. *Diabetes Care* 25 (5): 809–814.

Axelrod, T. 1978. Innovative roles for social workers in home-care programs. *Health and Social Work* 3:49–66.

Bachelor, A., and A. Horvath. 1999. The therapeutic relationship. In M. A. Hubble, B. L. Duncan, and S. D. Miller, eds., *The Heart and Soul of Change*, 133–178. Washington, D.C.: American Psychological Association.

Balinsky, W., and J. G. Blumengold. 1995. Home care's integration into managed care. *Caring* 15:36–44.

Baltes, M. M., and H. Wahl. 1996. Patterns of communication in old age: The dependence-support and independence-ignore script. *Health Communication* 8:217–231.

Banazak, D. A. 1997. Anxiety disorders in elderly patients. *Journal of the American Board of Family Practice* 10 (4): 280–289. Retrieved June 30, 2003, from the Ovid database.

Bandura, A. 1997. *Self-efficacy: The Exercise of Control.* New York: W. H. Freeman.

Barker, J. C. 2002. Neighbors, friends, and other nonkin caregivers of community-living dependent elders. *Journals of Gerontology* 57B (3): S158–S167.

Barnes, S. 2001. Stressors and strengths: A theoretical and practical examination of nuclear, single-parent, and augmented African American families. *Families in Society* 82 (5): 449–460.

Barranti, R., and H. Cohen. 2000. Lesbian and gay elders: An invisible minority. In R. L. Schneider, N. P. Kropf, and A. J. Kisor, eds., *Gerontological Social Work: Knowledge, Service Settings, and Special Populations,* 343–367. 2nd ed. Pacific Grove, Calif.: Brooks/Cole.

Barry, C. L. 2006. The political evolution of mental health parity. *Harvard Review of Psychiatry* 14:185–194.

Barry, K. L., and F. C. Blow. 1999. Screening and assessment of alcohol problems in older adults. In Peter A. Lichtenberg, ed., *Handbook of Assessment in Clinical Gerontology,* 243–269. New York: John Wiley.

Barry, K. L., D. Oslin, and F. C. Blow. 2001. *Prevention and Management of Alcohol Problems in Older Adults.* New York: Springer.

Bartels, S. J., A. R. Dums, T. E. Oxman, L. S. Schneider, P. A. Areán, G. S. Alexopoulos, and D. V. Jeste. 2002. Evidence-based practices in geriatric mental health care. *Psychiatric Services* 53:1419–1431.

Barton, J. A., and N. J. Brown. 1995. Home visitation to migrant farm worker families: An application of Zerwekh's family caregiver model for public health nursing. *Holistic Nursing Practice* 9:34–40.

Bass, D. M., P. A. Clark, W. J. Looman, C. A. McCarthy, and S. Eckert. 2003. The Cleveland Alzheimer's Managed Care Demonstration: Outcomes after 12 months of implementation. *Gerontologist* 43 (1): 73–85.

Bass, D. M., L. S. Noelker, and C. A. McCarthy. 1999. The influence of formal and informal helpers on primary caregivers' perceptions of quality of care. *Journal of Applied Gerontology* 18:177–200.

Bass, D. M., L. S. Noelker, and L. R. Rechlin. 1996. The moderating influence of service use on negative caregiving consequences. *Journals of Gerontology* 51B (3): S121–S131.

Bassuk, K., and J. Lessem. 2001. Collaboration of social workers and attorneys in geriatric community-based organizations. *Journal of Gerontological Social Work* 34 (3): 93–108.

Bauer, E. J. 1996. Transitions from home to nursing home in a capitated long-term care program: The role of individual support systems. *HSR: Health Services Research* 31 (3): 309–326.

Beck, A., J. Brown, M. Boles, and P. Barrett. 2002. Completion of advance directives by older health maintenance organization members: The role of attitudes and beliefs regarding life-sustaining treatment. *Journal of the American Medical Association* 50:300–306.

Beck, A. T., N. Epstein, G. Brown, R. and A. Steer. 1988. An inventory for measuring clinical anxiety: psychometric properties. *Journal of Consulting and Clinical Psychology* 56 (6): 893–897.

Beers, M. H., and R. Berkow. 2005. *The Merck Manual of Diagnosis and Therapy*. Retrieved July 5, 2005, from http://www.merck.com/mrkshared/mmanual/home.jsp.

Begun, A. 2005. *Alcohol Use Disorders Curriculum*. National Institute on Alcohol Abuse and Alcoholism. Accessed September 15, 2007, at http://pubs.niaaa.nih.gov/publications/Social/main.html.

Belcher, V. N., T. R. Fried, J. V. Agostini, and M. E. Tinetti. 2006. Views of older adults on patient participation in medication-related decision making. *Journal of General Internal Medicine* 21 (4): 298–303.

Benjamin, A. E. 1993. An historical perspective on home care policy. *Milbank Quarterly* 71:129–166.

——. 1999. A normative analysis of home care goals. *Journal of Aging and Health* 11:445–468.

Benjamin, A. E., and E. Naito-Chan. 2006. Home care settings. In B. Berkman and S. D'Ambruoso, eds., *Handbook of Social Work in Health and Aging*, 423–434. New York: Oxford University Press.

Bergeron, L. R. 2000. Servicing the needs of elder abuse victims. *Policy and Practice of Public Human Services* 58 (3): 40–45.

——. 2001. An elder abuse case study: Caregiver stress or domestic violence: You decide. *Journal of Gerontological Social Work* 34:47–63.

Bergeron, L. R., and B. Gray. 2003. Ethical dilemmas of reporting suspected elder abuse. *Social Work* 48 (1): 96–105.

Berg-Weger, M., D. M. Rubio, and S. S. Tebb. 2000a. The Caregiver Well-Being Scale revisited. *Health and Social Work* 25 (4): 255–262.

Berke, D. 2000. Demography is destiny: Forecasting a bright future for home care and hospice. *Caring* 19:20–21.

Berkman, B. 1996. The emerging health care world: Implications for social work practice and education. *Social Work* 41:541–551.

Berkman, B., D. Bedell, E. Parker, L. McCarthy, and C. Rosenbaum. 1988. Preadmission screening: An efficacy study. *Social Work in Health Care* 13 (3): 35–50.

Berkman, B., and P. Maramaldi. 2001. Use of standardized measures in agency-based research and practice. *Social Work in Health Care* 34 (1/2): 115–129.

Beutter, M. B., and R. Davidhizar. 1999. A home care provider's challenge: Caring for the Hispanic client in the home. *Journal of Practical Nursing* 49:26–33.

Billingsley, A. 1992. *Climbing Jacob's Ladder: The Enduring Legacy of African American Families*. New York: Touchstone Books.

——. 1999. *Mighty Like a River: The Black Church and Social Reform*. New York: Oxford University Press.

Bishop, C. 1999. Efficiency of home care: Notes for an economic approach to resource allocation. *Journal of Aging and Health* 11:277–298.

Bishop, C., and K. Skwara. 1993. Recent growth of Medicare home health. *Health Affairs* 12:95–110.

Blackhall, L., G. Frank, S. Murphy, V. Michel, J. Palmer, and S. Azen. 1999. Ethnicity and attitudes towards life sustaining technology. *Social Science and Medicine* 48:1779–1789.

Blanchard, L., G. Gill, and E. Williams. 1991. *Guidelines and Documentation*

Requirements for Social Workers in Home Health Care. Washington, D.C.: National Association of Social Workers.

Bloom, M., J. Fischer, and J. Orme. 2003. *Evaluating Practice: Guidelines for the Accountable Professional.* 4th ed. Boston: Allyn and Bacon.

Blow, F. 1998. *Substance Abuse Among Older Adults, Treatment Improvement Protocol (TIP).* Series 26. Rockville, Md.: U.S. Department of Health and Human Services, Substance Abuse and Mental Health Services Administration, Center for Substance Abuse Treatment.

Blow, F.C., and K. L. Barry. 2002. Use and misuse of alcohol among older women. *Alcohol Research and Health* 26:308–315.

Blow, F. C., L. M. Brockman, and K. L. Barry. 2004. Role of alcohol in late-life suicide. *Alcoholism: Clinical and Experimental Research* 28:48S–56S.

Blow, F.C., K. J. Brower, J. E. Schulenberg, L. M. Demo-Dananberg, J. P. Young, and T. P. Beresford. 1992. The Michigan Alcoholism Screening Test—Geriatric Version (MAST-G): A new elderly-specific screening instrument. *Alcoholism: Clinical and Experimental Research* 16:372.

Boaz, R. F., and J. Hu. 1997. Determining the amount of help used by disabled elderly persons at home: The role of coping resources. *Journals of Gerontology* 52B (6): S317–S324.

Bodenheimer, T., and K. Grumbach. 2002. *Understanding Health Policy: A Clinical Approach.* 3rd ed. New York: McGraw-Hill.

Bookwala, J., and R. Schulz. 1998. The role of neuroticism and mastery in caregivers' assessment of and response to a contextual stressor. *Journals of Gerontology: Psychological Sciences* 53B:P155–P164.

———. 2000. A comparison of primary stressors, secondary stressors, and depressive symptoms between elderly caregiving husbands and wives: The Caregiver Health Effects Study. *Psychology and Aging* 15:607–616.

Borrayo, E.A., J. R. Salmon, L. Polivka, and B. D. Dunlop. 2002. Utilization across the continuum of long-term care services. [Electronic version.] *Gerontologist* 42 (5): 603–612. Retrieved September 11, 2005, from the Ovid database.

Bourgeois, M. S., S. Beach, and L. D. Burgio. 1996. When primary and secondary caregivers disagree: Predictors and psychosocial consequences. *Psychology and Aging* 11:527–537.

Bourgeois, M.S., R. Schulz, and L. Burgio. 1996. Interventions for caregivers of patients with Alzheimer's disease: A review and analysis of content, process, and outcomes. *International Journal of Aging and Human Development* 43 (1): 35–92.

Boyd-Franklin, N. 2003. *Black Families in Therapy: Understanding the African American Experience.* 2nd ed. New York: Guilford.

Brach, C., and I. Fraser. 2000. Can cultural competency reduce racial and ethnic health disparities? A review and conceptual model. *Medical Care Research and Review* 57:181–217.

Branch, L. G. 2000. Assessment of chronic care need and use. *Gerontologist* 40 (4): 390–396.

Briggs, H. E., and K. Corcoran, eds. 2001. *Social Work Practice: Treating Common Client Problems.* Chicago: Lyceum.

Brodaty, H., A. Green, and A. Koschera. 2003. Meta-analysis of psychosocial interventions for caregivers of people with dementia. *Journal of the American Geriatric Society* 51:657–664.

Brotman, S., B. Ryan, and R. Cormier. 2003. The health and social service needs of gay and lesbian elders and their families in Canada. *Gerontologist* 43 (2): 192–202.

Brown, A., and P. Draper. 2003. Accommodative speech and terms of endearment: Elements of a language mode often experienced by older adults. *Journal of Advanced Nursing* 41:15–21.

Brown, C. 2000. Exploring the role of religiosity in hypertension management among African Americans. *Journal of Health Care for the Poor and Underserved* 11 (1): 19–32.

Brown, E. L., M. L. Bruce, G. J. McAvay, P. J. Raue, M. S. Laches, and P. Nassisi. 2004. Recognition of late-life depression in home care: Accuracy of the outcome and assessment information set *Journal of the American Geriatric Society* 52:995–999.

Brown, E. L., G. McAvay, P. Raue, S. Moses, and M. L. Bruce. 2003. Recognition of depression among elderly recipients of home care services. *Psychiatric Services* 54:208–213.

Brownell, P., J. Berman, and A. Salamone. 1999. Mental health and criminal justice issues among perpetrators of elder abuse. *Journal of Elder Abuse and Neglect* 11 (4): 81–94.

Bruce, M. L. 2002. Mental health services: In-home healthcare: Opportunities and challenges. *Generations*, Spring, 78–82.

Bruce, M. L., G. J. McAvay, P. J. Raue, E. L. Brown, B. S. Meyers, D. J. Keohane, D. R. Jagoda, and C. Weber. 2002. Major depression in elderly home health care patients. *American Journal of Psychiatry* 159:1367–1374.

Bruce, M. L., A. D. Van Citters, and S. J. Bartels. 2005. Evidence-based mental health services for home and community. *Psychiatric Clinics of North America* 28:1039–1060.

Bull, M. J., G. Maruyama, and D. Luo. 1995. Testing a model for posthospital transition of family caregivers for elderly persons. *Nursing Research* 44:132–138.

Bull, M. J., and R. E. McShane. 2002. Needs and supports for family caregivers of chronically ill elders. *Home Health Care Management and Practice* 14 (2): 92–98.

Busch, P. E. 1996. Panic disorder: The overlooked problem. *Home Healthcare Nurse* 14 (2): 111–116.

Butler, S. 2004. Gay, lesbian, bisexual, and transgender (GLBT) elders: The challenges and resilience of this marginalized group. *Journal of Human Behavior in the Social Environment* 9 (4): 25–44.

Butler, S., and B. Hope. 1999. Health and well-being for late middle-aged and older lesbians in a rural area. *Journal of Gay and Lesbian Social Services* 9 (4): 27–46.

Byington, M. F. 1932. Teamwork between the nurse and the social worker. *Public Health Nursing* 25:13–16.

Byrne, J. 1999. Social work in psychiatric home care: Regulations, roles, and realities. *Health and Social Work* 24 (1): 65–71.

Cagney, K. A., and E. M. Agree. 1999. Racial differences in skilled nursing home care and home health use: The mediating effects of family structure and social class. *Journals of Gerontology: Social Sciences* 54B:S223–S226.

Cahill, S., K. South, and J. Spade. 2000. *Outing Age: Public Policy Issues Affecting Gay, Lesbian, Bisexual, and Transgender Elders*. New York: Policy Institute of the National Gay and Lesbian Task Force Foundation.

Campinha-Bacote, J. 2002. The process of cultural competence in the delivery of healthcare services: A model of care. *Journal of Transcultural Nursing* 13 (3): 182–184.

Campinha-Bacote, J., and M. Narayan. 2000. Culturally competent health care in the home. *Home Care Provider* 5 (6): 213–219.

Capezuti, E., B. L. Brush, and W. T. Lawson. 1997. Reporting elder mistreatment. *Journal of Gerontological Nursing* 23 (7): 24–32.

Carlat, D. J. 2005. *The Psychiatric Interview*. New York: Lippincott, Williams and Wilkins.

Carmin, C. N., C. A. Pollard, and K. L. Gillock. 1999. Assessment of anxiety disorders in the elderly. In P. Lichtenberg, ed., *Handbook of Assessment in Clinical Gerontology*, 51–90. New York: John Wiley.

Carney, M. T., F. S. Kahan, and B. E. C. Paris. 2003. Elder abuse: Is every bruise a sign of abuse? *Mount Sinai Journal of Medicine* 70 (2): 69–74.

Carney, R. M., K. E. Freedland, S. A. Eisen, M. W. Rich, and A. S. Jaffe. 1995. Major depression and medication adherence in elderly patients with coronary artery disease. *Health Psychology* 14:88–90.

Carrillo, J. E., A. R. Green, and J. R. Betancourt. 1999. Cross-cultural primary care: A patient-based approach. *Annals of Internal Medicine* 130 (10): 829–831.

Centers for Disease Control and Prevention. 2000. *National Home Health and Hospice Survey*. Retrieved October 14, 2007, from http://www.cdc.gov/nchs/nhhcs.htm.

Centers for Disease Control and Prevention, Office of Minority Health. 2002. *Eliminating Racial and Ethnic Health Disparities*. Retrieved February 23, 2005, from www.cdc.gov/omh/AboutUs/disparities.

Chappell, N. L., and R. C. Reid. 2002. Burden and well-being among caregivers: Examining the distinction. *Gerontologist* 42 (6): 772–780.

Chenier, M. C. 1997. Review and analysis of caregiver burden and nursing home placement. *Geriatric Nursing* 18 (3): 121–126.

Chin, J. 2000. Culturally competent health care. *Public Health Reports* 115 (1): 25–38.

Choi, N. G. 1999. Determinants of frail elders' lengths of stay in Meals on Wheels. [Electronic version.] *Gerontologist* 39 (4): 397–404. Retrieved September 11, 2005, from the Ovid database.

——. 2001. Diversity within diversity: Research and social work practice issues with Asian American elders. In N. Choi, ed., *Psycho-Social Aspects of the Asian-American Experience: Diversity Within Diversity*, 301–399. Binghamton, N.Y.: Haworth.

Choi, N. G., and J. Mayer. 2000. Elder abuse, neglect, and exploitation: Risk factors and prevention strategies. *Journal of Gerontological Social Work* 33 (2): 5–25.

Christ, C. H., M. Sormanti, and R. B. Francoeur. 2001. Chronic physical illness and disability. In A. Gitterman, ed., *Handbook of Social Work Practice with Vulnerable and Resilient Populations*, 124–162. New York: Columbia University Press.

Chrits-Christoph, P., and M. B. Connolly. 1999. Alliance and technique in short-term dynamic therapy. *Clinical Psychology Review* 19:687–704.

Ciechanowski, P. S., W. J. Katon, and J. E. Russo. 2000. Depression and diabetes. *Archives of Internal Medicine* 160:3278–3285.

Clark, M. J. 1999. *Nursing in the Community*. Stamford, Conn.: Appleton and Lange.

Clarke, M., and W. Pierson. 1999. Management of elder abuse in the emergency department. *Emergency Medicine Clinics of North America* 17:631–643.

Code of Federal Regulations. 1999. Title 42, vol. 3, parts 430 to end. No. 42CFR484.36. Washington, D.C.: U.S. Government Printing Office via GPO access.

Cohen, M. A. 2003. Private long-term care insurance: A look ahead. *Journal of Aging and Health* 15:74–98.

Cohen, R. A., B. Bloom, G. Simpson, and P. E. Parsons. 1997. Access to health care. Part 3: Older adults. *Vital Health Statistics* 10:1–32.

Coleman, B. 2004. *Navigating the Care System: A Guide for Providers to Help Family Caregivers*. Family Caregiver Alliance. Retrieved June 10, 2007, from www. caregiver. org/caregiver/jsp/home.jsp.

Comas-Diaz, L. 2001. Hispanics, Latinos, or Americanos: The evolution of identity. *Cultural Diversity and Ethnic Minority Psychology* 7 (2): 115–120.

Compton, B. R., B. Galaway, and B. R. Cournoyer. 2005. *Social Work Processes*. Belmont, Calif.: Brooks/Cole.

Compton, S. A., P. Flanagan, and W. Gregg. 1997. Elder abuse in people with dementia in Northern Ireland: Prevalence and predictors in cases referred to a psychiatry of old age service. *International Journal of Geriatric Psychiatry* 12:632–635.

Congress, E. 2004. Cultural and ethical issues in working with culturally diverse patients and their families: The use of the Culturagram to promote cultural competent practice in health care settings. *Social Work in Health Care* 39 (3/4): 249–262.

Cook, C. A. L., D. S. Becvar, and S. L. Pontious. 2000. Complementary alternative medicine in health and mental health: Implications for social work practice. *Social Work in Health Care* 31 (3): 39–57.

Corbett, C. F. 1999. Research-based practice implications for patients with diabetes. *Home Healthcare Nurse* 17:587–598.

Corcoran, K., and J. Fischer. 2001. *Measures for Clinical Practice: A Sourcebook*. Vol. 2. 3rd ed. New York: Free Press.

Corcoran, K., W. Gingerich, and H. Briggs. 2001. Practice evaluation: Setting goals and monitoring change. In H. Briggs and K. Corcoran, eds., *Social Work Practice: Treating Common Client Problems*, 66–84. Chicago: Lyceum.

Cotrell, V. 1996. Respite use by dementia caregivers: Preferences and reasons for initial use. *Journal of Gerontological Social Work* 26 (3/4): 35–55. Retrieved September 11, 2005, from the PsychINFO database.

Cotrell, V., and R. J. Engel. 1998. The role of secondary supports in mediating formal services to dementia caregivers. [Electronic version.] *Journal of Gerontological Social Work* 30 (3/4): 117–132. Retrieved September 11, 2005, from the PsycINFO database.

Coulton, C., S. Keller, and C. Boone. 1985. Predicting social workers' expenditure of time with hospital patients. *Health and Social Work* 10 (1): 35–44.

Council on Scientific Affairs, American Medical Association. 1996. Alcoholism in the elderly. *JAMA* 275:797–801.

Covinsky, K. E., J. D. Fuller, C. B. Johnston, M. B. Hamel, J. Lynn, J. M. Teno, and R. S. Phillips. 2000. Communication and decision-making in seriously ill patients: Findings of the SUPPORT Project. *Journal of the American Geriatrics Society* 48: S187–S193.

Cowles, L. 2003. *Social Work in the Health Field: A Care Perspective*. Binghamton, N.Y.: Haworth.

Cox, C. 1997. Findings from a statewide program of respite care: A comparison of service users, stoppers, and nonusers. *Gerontologist* 37 (4): 511–517.

Cox, D., and M. Ory. 2000. The changing health and social environments of home care. In R. Binstock and L. Cluff, eds., *Home Care Advances*, 35–58. New York: Springer.

Crist, J. 2002. Mexican American elders' use of skilled home care nursing services. *Public Health Nursing* 19 (5): 366–376.

Cuellar, N. 2002. A comparison of African American and Caucasian American female caregivers of rural, post-stroke, bedbound older adults. *Journal of Gerontological Nursing* 28 (1): 36–45.

Culpepper, L. 2002. Generalized anxiety disorder in primary care: Emerging issues in management and treatment. *Journal of Clinical Psychiatry* 63 (supp. 8): 35–42.

Dane, B., and B. Simon. 1991. Resident guests: Social work in host settings. *Social Work* 36:208–213.

Davies, S., and M. Nolan. 2003. "Making the best of things": Relatives' experiences of decisions about care-home entry. *Ageing and Society* 23:429–450.

——. 2004. "Making the move": Relatives' experiences of the transition to a care home. *Health and Social Care in the Community* 12 (6): 517–526.

Davis, L. 1997. Family conflicts around dementia home-care. *Families, Systems, and Health* 15:85–89.

Davitt, J., and L. Kaye. 1996. Supporting patient autonomy: Decision making in home health care. *Social Work* 41:41–50.

DeCoster, V. A. 2001. Challenges of type 2 diabetes and role of health care social work: A neglected area of practice. *Health and Social Work* 26, 26–37.

DeCoster, V., and S. Cummings. 2004. Coping with type 2 diabetes: Do race and gender matter? *Social Work in Health Care* 40 (2): 37–53.

Dellasega, C., and M. Nolan. 1997. Admission to care: Facilitating role transition amongst family carers. *Journal of Clinical Nursing* 6 (6): 443–451.

DeRubeis, R. J., L. A. Gelfand, T. Z. Tang, and A. D. Simons. 1999. *American Journal of Psychiatry* 156:1007–1013.

Desai, M., H. Lentzner, and J. Weeks. 2001. Unmet need for personal assistance with activities of daily living among older adults. *Gerontologist* 41:82–88.

Dhooper, S. 2003. Health care needs of foreign-born Asian Americans: An overview. *Health and Social Work* 28 (1): 63–73.

Dhooper, S. S., and T. V. Tran. 1998. Understanding and responding to the health and mental health needs of Asian refugees. *Social Work in Health Care* 27 (4): 65–82.

DiMatteo, M. R., H. S. Lepper, and T. W. Croghan. 2000. Depression is a risk factor for noncompliance with medical treatment: Meta-analysis of the effect of anxiety and depression on patient adherence. *Archives of General Medicine* 160:2101–2107.

Dittbrenner, H. 1997. Diabetes: Working with the newly diagnosed patient. *Caring* 16:52–61.

Ditto, P. H., J. H. Danks, W. D. Smucker, J. Bookwala, K. M. Coppola, R. Dresser, A. Fagerlin, M. Gready, R. M. Houts, L. K. Lockhart, and S. Zyzanski 2001. Advance directives as acts of communication. *Archives of Internal Medicine* 161:421–430.

Dombi, W. A. 1991. Access to Medicaid home care. *Caring* 10:15–18.

Dorfman, L. T., K. L. Berlin, and C. A. Holmes. 1998. Attitudes toward service use among wife caregivers of frail older veterans. *Social Work in Health Care* 27 (4): 39–63.

Dorfman, L. T., C. A. Holmes, K. L. Berlin. 1996. Wife caregivers of frail elderly veterans: Correlates of caregiver satisfaction and caregiver strain. *Family Relations* 45:46–55.

Dosser, D., A. Smith, E. Markowski, and H. Cain. 2001. Including families' spiritual beliefs and their faith communities in systems of care. *Journal of Family Social Work* 5 (3): 63–78.

Doty, P. 2004. *Consumer-Directed Home Care: Effects on Family Caregivers*. Retrieved June 8, 2007, from www.caregiver.org/caregiver/jsp/home.jsp.

Doty, P., and S. Flanagan. 2002. *Highlights: Inventory of Consumer-Directed Support Programs*. Washington, D.C: U.S. Department of Health and Human Services, Office of Disability, Aging, and Long-Term Care.

Drake, V., and P. E. Freed. 1998. Research applications: Domestic violence in the elderly. *Geriatric Nursing* 19:165–167.

Dreher, B. B. 2001. *Communication Skills for Working with Elders*. New York: Springer.

Dwyer, J. W., G. R. Lee, and T. B. Jankowski. 1994. Reciprocity, elder satisfaction, and caregiver stress and burden: The exchange of aid in the family caregiving relationship. *Journal of Marriage and the Family* 56:35–43.

Dyeson, T. 2000. Burden self-image: A mediating variable of depressive symptoms among chronically ill care recipients. *Journal of Gerontological Social Work* 33 (1): 17–33.

Dyeson, T. B., J. Murphy, and K. Stryker. 1999. Demographic and psychosocial characteristics of cognitively intact chronically ill elders receiving home health services. *Home Health Care Services Quarterly* 18 (2): 1–25.

Egan, M., and G. Kadushin. 2000. The social worker in the emerging field of home care: Professional activities and ethical concerns. In S. Keigher, A. Fortune, and S. Witkin, eds., *Aging and Social Work: The Changing Landscape*, 373–388. Washington, D.C.: NASW Press.

——. 2002. Ethical conflicts over access to services: Patient effects and worker influence in home health. *Social Work in Health Care* 35:1–21.

——. 2005. Managed care in home health: Social work practice and unmet client needs. *Social Work in Health Care* 41 (2): 1–18.

Eleazer, P. G., C. A. Hornung, C. B. Egbert, J. R. Egbert, C. Eng, H. Hedgepeth, R. McCann, H. Strothers, M. Sapir, M. Wei, and M. Wilson. 1996. The relationship between ethnicity and advance directives in a frail older population. *Journal of the American Geriatrics Society* 44:938–943.

Ell, K., and H. Northern. 1990. *Families and Health Care: Psychosocial Practice*. New York: Aldine de Gruyter.

Ellenbecker, C. 1995. Profit and non-profit home care agency outcomes: A study of one state's experience. *Home Health Care Services Quarterly* 15:47–60.

Emanuel, L. L., C. von Gunten, and F. Ferris. 2000. Advance care planning. *Archives of Family Medicine* 9:1181–1187.

Emlet, C. A. 1996. Assessing social function, support, and socioeconomic status. In C. Emlet, J. Crabtree, V. A. Condon, and L. Trend, eds., *In-Home Assessment of Older Adults*, 154–179. Gaithersburg, Md.: Aspen.

England, M. 2001. Expressed information and resource needs of filial caregivers reporting recent experiences of crisis. [Electronic version.] *Educational Gerontology* 27 (2): 139–157. Retrieved September 12, 2005, from the PsychINFO database.

Erickson, C. L., and N. Muramatsu. 2004. Parkinson's disease, depression, and medication adherence: Current knowledge and social work practice. *Journal of Gerontological Social Work* 42:3–18.

Ewing, J. A. 1984. Detecting alcoholism: The CAGE questionnaire. *JAMA: Journal of the American Medical Association* 252:1905–1907.

Fagerlin, A., P. H. Ditto, N. A. Hawkins, C. E. Schneider, and W. D. Smucker. 2002. The use of advance directives in end-of-life decision making. *American Behavioral Scientist* 46:268–283.

Farran, C. J., S. L. Horton-Deutsch, D. Loukissa, and L. Johnson. 1998. Psychiatric home care of elderly persons with depression: Unmet caregiver needs. *Home Health Care Services Quarterly* 16 (4): 57–73.

Fedei, J., H. Komisar, and M. Niefeld. 2000. Long-term care in the United States: An overview. *Health Affairs* 19:40–56.

Federal Conditions of Participation. 1999 CFR Title 42, Vol. 3. *Home Health Agencies.* Accessed September 22, 2007, at http://www.access.gpo.gov/nara/cfr/waisidx_99/42cfr484_99.html.

Federal Interagency Forum on Aging-Related Statistics. 2004. *Older Americans 2004: Key indicators of well-being.* Retrieved May 27, 2005, from http://www.aging-stats.gov.

Feinberg, L. F., S. Newman, and W. Fox-Grage. 2005. *Family Caregiver Support Services: Sustaining Unpaid Family and Friends in a Time of Public Fiscal Constraints.* American Association of Retired Persons. Accessed September 15, 2007, at www.aarp.org/research/houseing-mobility/caregiving/s112_hcbs.html.

Feinberg, L. F., K. Wolkwitz, and C. Goldstein. 2006. *Ahead of the Curve: Emerging Trends and Practices in Family Caregiver Support.* National Center on Caregiving, and Family Caregiver Alliance. Retrieved June 1, 2006, from www.aarp.org/ppi.

Ferry, R. 2001. Why caregiver depression and self-care abilities should be part of the PPS case mix methodology. *Home Healthcare Nurse* 19:23–30.

Fessler, S., and C. Adams. 1985. Nurse/social worker role conflict in home health care. *Journal of Gerontological Social Work* 9:113–123.

Fifield, J., H. Tennen, S. Reisine, and J. McQuillan. 1998. Depression and the long-term. risk of pain, fatigue, and disability in patients with rheumatoid arthritis. *Arthritis and Rheumatism* 41 (10): 1851–1857.

Finch, B. K., R. A. Hummer, B. Kol, and W. A. Vega. 2001. The role of discrimination and acculturative stress in the physical health of Mexican-origin adults [Electronic version.] *Hispanic Journal of Behavioral Sciences* 23:399–429. Retrieved January 19, 2007, from http://hjb.sagepub.com.

Fingerhood, M. 2000. Substance abuse in older people. *Journal of the American Geriatrics Society* 48: 985–995.

Finlayson, R. 1997. Misuse of prescription drugs. In A. M. Gurnack, ed., *Older Adults' Misuse of Alcohol, Medicines, and Other Drugs,* 158–184. New York: Springer.

Fischer, G. S., R. M. Arnold, and J. A. Tulsky. 2000. Talking to the older adult about advance directives. *Clinics in Geriatric Medicine* 16:239–254.

Fischer, L. R., C. A. Green, M. J. Goodman, K. K. Brody, M. Aickin, F. Wei, et al. 2003. Community-based care and risk of nursing home placement. *Medical Care* 41 (12): 1407–1416.

Flaherty, J. H., H. M. Perry, G. S. Lynchard, and J. E. Morley. 2000. Polypharmacy and hospitalization among older home care patients. *Journals of Gerontology* 55A:M554–M559.

Fleming, M. 2002. Identification and treatment of alcohol use disorders in older adults. In Anne M. Gurnack, Roldand Atkinson, and Nancy Osgood, eds., *Treating Alcohol and Drug Abuse in the Rlderly,* 85–108. New York: Springer.

Flowers, N. 2000. In-home assessment and counseling of the elderly. In N. A. Newton and K. Sprengle, eds., *Psychosocial Interventions in the Home,* 275–285. New York: Springer.

Folkman, S., and R. S. Lazarus. 1980. An analysis of coping in a middle-aged community sample. Journal of Health and Social Behavior 21:219–239.

Follman, J. E. 1963. *Medical Care and Health Insurance*. Homewood, Ill.: Richard D. Irwin.

Forbes, S., and N. Hoffart. 1998. Elders' decision making regarding the use of long-term care services: A precarious balance. *Qualitative Health Research* 8 (6): 736–750.

Foster, L., R. Brown, B. Phillips, and B. L. Carlson. 2005. Easing the burden of caregiving: The impact of consumer direction on primary informal caregivers in Arkansas. *Gerontologist* 45 (4): 474–485.

Fox, P., R. Newcomer, C. Yordi, and P. Arnsberger. 2000. Lessons learned from the Medicare Alzheimer Disease Demonstration. [Electronic version.] *Alzheimer Disease and Associated Disorders* 14 (2): 87–93. Retrieved September 11, 2005, from the Ovid database.

Freed, P. E., and V. K. Drake. 1999. Mandatory reporting of abuse: Practical, moral, and legal issues for psychiatric home healthcare nurses. *Issues in Mental Health Nursing* 20:423–436.

Freedman, V. A. 1996. Family structure and the risk of nursing home admission. *Journals of Gerontology* 51B (2): S61–S69.

Freedman, V. A., L. F. Berkman, S. R. Rapp, and A. M. Ostfeld. 1994. Family networks: Predictors of nursing home entry. *American Journal of Public Health* 84 (5): 843–845.

Friedman, L., A. E. Brown, C. Romero, M. Dulay, L. Peterson, P. Weirman, D. Whisnand, L. Laufman, and J. Lomas. 2005. Depressed mood and social support as predictors of quality of life in women receiving home health care. *Quality of Life Research* 14 (8): 1924–1929.

Friedman, S. M., D. M. Steinwachs, P. J. Rathouz, L. C. Burton, and D. B. Mukamel. 2005. Characteristics predicting nursing home admission in the program of all-inclusive care for elderly people. *Gerontologist* 45 (2): 157–166.

Fulmer, T., L. Guadagno, C. Bitondo Dyer, and M. T. Connolly. 2004. *Journal of the American Geriatrics Society* 52:297–304.

Gabbay, S., and J. Wahler. 2002. Lesbian aging: Review of a growing literature. *Journal of Gay and Lesbian Social Services: Issues in Practice, Policy, and Research* 14 (3): 1–21.

Galambos, C. 1999. Resolving ethical conflicts in a managed health care environment. *Health and Social Work* 24 (3): 191–197.

Gallagher-Thompson, D., S. Lovett, J. Rose, C. McKibbin, D. Coon, A. Futterman, et al. 2000. Impact of psychoeducational interventions on distressed family caregivers. [Electronic version.] *Journal of Clinical Geropsychology* 6 (2): 91–110. Retrieved August 11, 2004, from the PsychINFO database.

Gallo, J. J., T. F. Fulmer, G. J. Paveza, and W. Reichel. 2003. *Handbook of Geriatric Assessment*. 3rd ed. Gaithersburg, Md.: Aspen.

Gatz, M., A. Fiske, L. S. Fox, B. Kaskie, K. E. Kasl-Godley, T. J. McCallum, and J. L. Wetherell. 1998. Empirically validated psychological treatments for older adults. *Journal of Mental Health and Aging* 4 (1): 9–30.

Gaugler, J. E., K. A. Anderson, C. R. Leach, C. D. Smith, F. A. Schmitt, and M. Mendiondo. 2004. The emotional ramifications of unmet need in dementia caregiving. *American Journal of Alzheimer's Disease and Other Dementias* 19 (6): 369–380.

Gaugler, J. E., A. B. Edwards, E. E. Femia, S. H. Zarit, M. P. Stephens, A. Townsend, et al. 2000. Predictors of institutionalization of cognitively impaired elders: Family help and the timing of placement. *Journals of Gerontology* 55B (4): P247–P255.

Gaugler, J. E., R. L. Kane, R. A. Kane, T. Clay, and R. Newcomer. 2003. Caregiving and institutionalization of cognitively impaired older people: Utilizing dynamic predictors of change. *Gerontologist* 43 (2): 219–229.

Gaugler, J. E., R. L. Kane, R. A. Kane, and R. Newcomer. 2005. Early community-based service utilization and its effects on institutionalization in dementia caregiving. *Gerontologist* 45 (2): 177–185.

Gaugler, J. E., R. A. Kane, and J. Langlois. 2000. Assessment of family caregivers of older adults. In R. L. Kane, and R. A. Kane, eds., *Assessing Older Persons*, 320–359. New York: Oxford University Press.

Gaugler, J. E., C. R. Leach, T. Clay, and R. C. Newcomer. 2004. Predictors of nursing home placement in African Americans with dementia. *Journal of the American Geriatrics Society* 52:445–452.

Gaugler, J. E., L. I. Pearlin, S. A. Leitsch, and A. Davey. 2001. Relinquishing in-home dementia care: Difficulties and perceived helpfulness during the nursing home transition. *American Journal of Alzheimer's Disease and Other Dementias* 16 (1): 32–42.

Gehi, A., D. Haas, S. Pipkin, and M. A. Whooley. 2005. Depression and medication adherence in outpatients with coronary artery disease. *Archives of Internal Medicine* 165:2508–2513.

Gelfand, D. E. 1999. *The Aging Network: Programs and Services*. New York: Springer.

Gellad, W. F., H. A. Huskamp, K. A. Phillips, and J. S. Haas. 2006. How the new Medicare drug benefit could affect vulnerable populations. *Health Affairs (Millwood)* 25 (1): 248–255.

Gellis, Z. D. 2006. Older adults with emotional problems. In B. Berkman, ed., *Handbook of Social Work in Health and Aging*, 129–139. New York: Oxford University Press.

Gillespie, L. D., W. J. Gillespie, M. C. Robertson, S. E. Lamb, R. G. Cumming, and B. H. Rowe. 2003. Interventions for preventing falls in elderly people. *Cochrane Database of Systematic Reviews*, issue 4.

Gilley, D. W., J. J. McCann, J. L. Bienias, and D. A. Evans. 2005. Caregiver psychological adjustment and institutionalization of persons with Alzheimer's disease [Electronic version.] *Journal of Aging and Health* 17 (2): 172–189.

Giordano, J. A. 2000. Effective communication and counseling with older adults. *International Journal of Aging and Human Development* 51:315–324.

Gitlin, L. N., S. H. Belle, L. D. Burgio, S. J. Czaja, D. Mahoney, D. Gallagher-Thompson, R. Burns, W. W. Hayejm, S. Zhang, R. Schultz, and M. G. Ory. 2003. Effect of multicomponent interventions on caregiver burden and depression: The REACH multisite initiative at 6-month follow up. *Psychology and Aging* 18 (3): 361–374.

Glass, T. A., B. Dym, S. Greenberg, D. Rintell, C. Roesch, and L. Berkman. 2000. Psychosocial intervention in stroke: The Families in Recovery from Stroke Trial (FIRST). *American Journal of Orthopsychiatry* 70:169–181.

Goldberg, H. B., and D. Delargy. 2000. Developing a case-mix model for PPS. *Caring* 19 (1): 16–19.

Goode, R. 2000. *Social Work Practice in Home Health Care*. New York: Haworth.

Grant, J. S. 1996. Home care problems experienced by stroke survivors and their family caregivers. *Home Healthcare Nurse* 14:892–902.

Grant, J. S., G. L. Glandon, T. R. Elliot, J. N. Giger, and M. Weaver. 2004a. Caregiving problems and feelings experienced by family caregivers of stroke survivors the first month after discharge. [Electronic version.] *International Journal of Rehabilitation Research* 27 (2): 105–111. Retrieved September 12, 2005, from the Ovid database.

Grant, J. S., M. Weaver, T. R. Elliot, A. A. Bartolucci, and J. N. Giger. 2004b. Family caregivers of stroke survivors: Characteristics of caregivers at risk for depression. [Electronic version.] *Rehabilitation Psychology* 49 (2): 172–179. Retrieved September 12, 2005, from the PsychINFO database.

Gray, S. L., J. E. Mahoney, and D. K. Blough. 2001. Medication adherence in elderly patients receiving home health services following hospital discharge. *Annals of Pharmacotherapy* 35:539–545.

Green, J. 1999. *Cultural Awareness in the Human Services: A Multi-Ethnic Approach.* Englewood Cliffs, N.J.: Prentice-Hall.

Grossman, A., A. R. D'Augelli, and S. L. Hershberger. 2000. Social support networks of lesbian, gay, and bisexual adults 60 years of age and older. *Journal of Gerontology: Psychological Sciences* 55B:P171–P179.

Gwyther, L. P. 1995. When "the family" is not one voice: Conflict in caregiving families. *Journal of Case Management* 4:150–155.

Hagen, B. 2001. Nursing home placement: Factors affecting caregivers' decisions to place family members with dementia. *Journal of Gerontological Nursing* 27 (2): 44–55.

Haggan, P. S. 1998. Counseling adult children of aging parents. *Educational Gerontology* 24 (4): 333–348.

Haley, W. E., R. S. Allen, S. Reynolds, H. Chen, A. Burton, and D. Gallagher-Thompson. 2002. Family issues in end-of-life decision making and end-of-life care. *American Behavioral Scientist* 46:284–298.

Hall, P., G. Stone, and V. J. Fiset. 1998. Palliative care: How can we meet the needs of our multicultural communities? *Journal of Palliative Care* 14 (2): 46–49.

Halverson J., and C. Chan. 2004. Screening for psychiatric disorders in primary care. *Wisconsin Medical Journal* 103:46–51.

Hanson, M., and I. A. Gutheil. 2004. Motivational strategies with alcohol-involved older adults: Implications for social work practice. *Social Work* 49:364–372.

Happ, M. B., M. D. Naylor, and P. Roe-Prior. 1997. Factors contributing to rehospitalization of elderly patients with heart failure. *Journal of Cardiovascular Nursing* 11:75–83.

Harrington, C., J. O'Meara, M. Kitchener, L. P. Simon, and J. F. Schnelle. 2003. Designing a report card for nursing facilities: What information is needed and why. *Gerontologist* 43 (Special Issue 2): 47–57.

Harris, E. C., and B. M. Barraclough. 1994. Suicide as an outcome for medical disorders. *Medicine* 73:281–296.

Harris, M. 1997. *Handbook of Home Health Care Administration.* Gaithersburg, Md.: Aspen.

Hash, K. 2003. Practice with caregivers: Individuals and groups. In M. J. Naleppa and W. J. Reid, *Gerontological Social Work: A Task-Centered Approach,* 203–234. New York: Columbia University Press.

Haupt, B. 1998. *An Overview of Home Health and Hospice Care Patients: 1996 National Home and Hospice Care Survey.* Advance Data from Vital and Health Statistics of the Centers for Disease Control and Prevention, No. 297. Hyattsville, Md.: National Center for Health Statistics.

Hayslip, B., Jr., S. L. McMurtry, J. K. King, P. L. Kaminski, and D. Graves-Oliver. In press. Older adults. In S. L. McMurtry, S. J. Rose, and R. A. Cisler, eds., *Guide to Brief Measures: Adult Mental Health and Personality.* New York: Guilford.

He, W., M. Sengupta, V. A. Velkoff, and K. A. DeBarros. 2005. 65+ in the United States: 2005. U.S. Census Bureau, Current Population Reports, P23–209. Washington, D.C.: U.S. Government Printing Office.

Healy, T. C. 1998 The complexity of everyday ethics in home health care: An analysis of social workers' decisions regarding frail elders' autonomy. Social Work in Health Care 27:19–37.

———. 1999. Community-dwelling cognitively impaired frail elders· An analysis of social workers' decisions concerning support for autonomy. Social Work in Health Care 30:27–47.

———. 2002. Culturally competent practice with elderly lesbians. Geriatric Care Management Journal 12 (3): 9–13.

———. 2003. Ethical decision making: Pressure and uncertainty as complicating factors. Health and Social Work 28:293–301.

Heffler, S., K. Levit, S. Smith, C. Smith, C. Cowan, H. Lazenby, and M. Freeland. 2001. Health spending growth up in 1999: Faster growth expected in the future. Health Affairs 20:193–203.

Heineken, J. 1998. Patient silence is not necessarily client satisfaction. Home Healthcare Nurse 16:115–121.

Heneghan, C. J., P. Glasziou, and R. Perera. 2006. Reminder packaging for improving adherence to self-administered long-term medications [Electronic version.] Cochrane Database of Systematic Reviews 1. Retrieved March 30, 2006.

Hepburn, K. W., J. Tornatore, B. Center, and S. W. Ostwald. 2001. Dementia family caregiver training: Affecting beliefs about caregiving and caregiver outcomes. Journal of the American Geriatrics Society 49:450–457.

Hobart, K. R. 2001. Death and dying and the social work role. Journal of Gerontological Social Work 38:181–192.

Hodge, D. 2003. The intrinsic spirituality scale: A new six-item instrument for assessing the salience of spirituality as a motivational construct. Journal of Social Service Research 30 (1): 41–61.

———. 2004. Working with Hindu clients in a spiritually sensitive manner. Social Work 49 (1): 27–38.

Hokanson, H. 2003a. Respite: Long term. In M. J. Naleppa and W. J. Reid, Gerontological Social Work: A Task-Centered Approach, 314–317. New York: Columbia University Press.

———. 2003b. Respite: Short-term. In M. J. Naleppa and W. J. Reid, Gerontological Social Work: A Task-Centered Approach, 317–320. New York: Columbia University Press.

———. 2003c. Caregiving: Burden on one family member. In M. J. Naleppa and W. J. Reid, Gerontological Social Work: A Task-Centered Approach, 312–314. New York: Columbia University Press.

Hooyman, N. R., and H. A. Kiyak. 2005. Social Gerontology: A Multidiscipliary Perspective. 7th ed. Boston: Allyn and Bacon.

Hopp, F. 2000. Preferences for surrogate decision makers, informal communication, and advance directives among community-dwelling elders. Results from a national study. Gerontologist 40:449–457.

Hopp, F., and S. A. Duffy. 2000. Racial variations in end-of-life care. Journal of the American Geriatrics Society 48:558–563.

Horvath, A. 2000. The therapeutic relationship: From transference to alliance. *Journal of Counseling Psychology* 56:163–173.

Howgego, I. M., P. Yellowlees, C. Owen, L. Meldrum, and F. Dark. 2003. The therapeutic alliance: The key to effective patient outcome? A descriptive review of the evidence in community mental health case management. *Australian and New Zealand Journal of Psychiatry* 37:169–183.

Hubble, M.A., B. L. Duncan, and S. D. Miller. 1999. Directing attention to what works. In M. A. Hubble, B. L. Duncan. and S. D. Miller, eds., *The Heart and Soul of Change*, 407–447. Washington, D.C.: American Psychological Association.

Hudson, M. F., W. D. Armachain, C. M. Beasley, and J. R. Carlson. 1998. Elder abuse: Two Native American views. *Gerontologist* 38 (5): 538–548.

Hudson, M. F., C. M. Beasley, R. H. Benedict, J. R. Carlson, B. F. Craig, and S. C. Mason. 1999. Elder abuse: Some African American views. *Journal of Interpersonal Violence* 14 (9): 915–939.

Hudson, R. 1996. Home and community-based care: Recent accomplishments and new challenges. *Journal of Aging and Social Policy* 7:53–69.

Hughes, C. M. 2004. Medication non-adherence in the elderly: How big is the problem? *Drugs and Aging* 21 (12): 793–811.

Hummert, M. L., T. A. Garstka, E. B. Ryan, and J. L. Bonnesen. 2004. The role of age stereotypes in interpersonal communication. In J. Nussbaum and J. Coupland, eds., *Handbook of Communication and Aging Research*, 91–114. Mahwah, N.J.: Lawrence Erlbaum.

Hummert, M.L., and M. Morgan. 2001. Negotiating decisions in the aging family. In M. L. Hummert and J. F. Nussbaum, eds., *Aging, Communication, and Health: Linking Research and Practice for Successful Aging*, 177–201. Mahwah, N.J.: Lawrence Erlbaum.

Hummert, M. L., J. M. Wiemann, and J. F. Nussbaum. 1994. *Interpersonal Communication in Older Adulthood: Interdisciplinary Theory and Research*. Thousand Oaks, Calif: Sage.

Imes, S., and D. Landry. 2002. Don't underestimate the power of culture. *Science of Nursing* 19 (4): 172–176.

Ingersoll-Dayton, B., M. E. Starrels, and D. Dowler. 1996. Caregiving for parents and parents-in-law: Is gender important? *Gerontologist* 36 (4): 483–491.

Institute of Medicine. 2002. *Unequal Treatment: Confronting Racial and Ethnic Disparities in Health Care*. Retrieved June 15, 2004, from www.iom.edu/iomhome.

——. 2005. *Complementary and Alternative Medicine in the United States*. Washington, D.C.: National Academies Press. Retrieved April 23, 2006, from fermat.nap.edu/books/0309092701/html/.

Jackson, L. E. 1993. Understanding eliciting and negotiating clients' alternative health beliefs. *Nurse Practitioner* 18:32–33, 37–43.

Jacobs, D. G., M. Brewer, and M. Klein-Benheim. 1999. Suicide assessment. In D. G. Jacobs, ed., *Medical School Guide to Suicide Assessment*, 3–39. San Francisco: Jossey-Bass.

Jacobs, P. E., and A. Lurie. 1984. A new look at home care and the hospital social worker *Journal of Gerontological Social Work* 7:87–99, 1984.

Jarrett, M. 1933. *Chronic Illness in New York City*. Vol. 2. New York: Columbia University Press.

Jette, A. M., S. Tennstedt, and S. Crawford. 1995. How does formal and informal community care affect nursing home use? *Journals of Gerontology* 50B (1): S4–S12.

Johnson, R. 1996. Risk factors associated with negative interactions between family caregivers and elderly care-receivers. *International Journal of Aging and Human Development* 43:7–20.

Johnson, R., and T. Tripp-Reimer. 2001. Relocation among ethnic elders: A review—Part 2. *Journal of Gerontological Nursing* 27:22–28.

Johnston, B. 2000. Exploring the frontier: Home care gets wired. *Caring* 19:6–10.

Kaakinen, J., E. Shapiro, and B. M. Gayle. 2001. Strategies for working with elderly clients: A qualitative analysis of elderly client/nurse practitioner communication. *Journal of the American Academy of Nurse Practitioners* 13:325–329.

Kadushin, G. 1996. Elderly hospitalized patients' perceptions of the interaction with the social worker during discharge planning. *Social Work in Health Care* 23:1–21.

——. 2004. Home health care utilization: A review of the research for social work. *Health and Social Work* 29:219–244.

Kadushin, G., and M. Egan. 2001. Ethical dilemmas in home health care: A social work perceptive. *Health and Social Work* 26:136–149.

——. 2004. An exploratory-descriptive study of home health social work practice under the Medicare Prospective Payment System. *Journal of Social Work in Long Term Care* 3:43–56.

——. 2006. Unmet patient need in home care under managed care. *Journal of Gerontological Social Work* 47:103–120.

Kadushin, A., and G. Kadushin. 1997. *The Social Work Interview*. New York: Columbia University Press.

Kahan, F. S., and B. E. C. Paris. 2003. Why elder abuse continues to elude the health care system. *Mount Sinai Journal of Medicine* 70 (1): 62–68.

Kaiser Family Foundation. 2005. *Medicare Chartbook*. Accessed September 15, 2007, at http://www.kff.org/medicare/upload/Medicare-Chart-Book-3rd-Edition-Summer-2005-Report.pdf.

——. 2006. *Medicare Fact Sheet: Low Income Assistance Under the Medicare Drug Benefit*. Accessed January 29, 2007, at www.kff.org.

Kane, C. 2000. African American family dynamics as perceived by family members. *Journal of Black Studies* 10 (5): 691–702.

Kane, R. A. 1995. Expanding the home care concept: Blurring distinctions among home care, institutional care, and other long-term-care services. *Milbank Quarterly* 73:161–186.

——. 1999. Goals of home care: Therapeutic, compensatory, or both? *Journal of Aging and Health* 11:299–321.

——. 2000. Assuring quality in care at home. In R. Binstock and L. Cluff, eds., *Home Care Advances*, 207–238. New York: Springer.

Kane, R A., and A. Caplan. 1993. *Ethical Conflicts in the Management of Home Care*. New York: Springer.

Kane, R. A., and R. L. Kane. 1987. *Long-Term Care: Principles, Programs, and Policies*. New York: Springer.

Kane, R. A., R. L. Kane, and R. Ladd. 1998. *The Heart of Long-Term Care*. New York: Oxford University Press.

Kane, R. A., J. Reinhardy, J. D. Penrod, and S. Huck. 1999. After the hospitalization is over: A different perspective on family care of older people. *Journal of Gerontological Social Work* 31 (1/2): 119–141.

Kane, R. L. 1999. Examining the efficiency of home care. *Journal of Aging and Health* 11:322–340.

Kassner, E. 2006. Home- and community-based long-term services and supports for older people. Accessed September 15, 2007, at http//assets.aarp.org/agcenter/il/fs90r_hcblt.pdf.

Kaye, L., and J. Davitt. 1999. *Current Practices in High-Tech Home Care*. New York: Springer.

Kaye, N. 2005. *Medicaid Managed Care: Looking Forward, Looking Back*. Portland, Me.: National Academy for State Health Policy.

Kayser, K., P. Hansen, and A. Groves. 1995. Evaluating social work practice in a medical setting: How do we meet the challenges of a rapidly changing system? *Research on Social Work Practice* 5 (4): 485–500.

Keenan, J., and J. Fanale. 1989. Home care: Past and present, problems and potential. *Journal of the American Geriatrics Society* 37:1076–1083.

Keenan, J., J. Fanale, C. Ripsin, and L. Billows. 1990. A review of federal home-care legislation. *Journal of the American Geriatrics Society* 38:1041–1048.

Kellett, U. M. 1999. Transition in care: Family carers' experience of nursing home placement. *Journal of Advanced Nursing* 29 (6): 1474–1481.

Kemper, K., and L. Barnes. 2003. Considering culture, complementary medicine, and spirituality in pediatrics. *Clinical Pediatrics* 42:205–208.

Kennedy, C. W., B. J. Polivka, and J. S. Steel. 1997. Psychiatric symptoms in a community-based medically ill population. *Home Healthcare Nurse* 15:431-441.

Kennedy, J. 2001. Unmet and undermet need for activities of daily living and instrumental activities of daily living assistance among adults with disabilities: Estimates from the 1994 and 1995 disability follow-back surveys. *Medical Care* 39 (12): 1305–1312.

Kethley, A., M. Herriott, and B. Pesznecker. 1982. Nurses and social workers in home health care: Identifying and resolving turf conflict. *Home Health Care Services Quarterly* 3:71–85.

King, J. 2003. Falls and accidents. In M. Naleppa and W. J. Reid, *Gerontological Social Work: A Task-Centered Approach*, 289–292. New York: Columbia University Press.

King, K. 1997. Psychological and social aspects of cardiovascular disease. *Annals of Behavioral Medicine* 19:264–270.

Kishi, H., R. G. Robinson, and J. T. Kosier. 2001. Suicidal ideation among patients with acute life-threatening physical illness. *Psychosomatics* 42: 382–390.

Kleinschmidt, K. C. 1997. Elder abuse: A review. *Annals of Emergency Medicine* 30:463–472.

Kolata, G. 2006. Medicare says it will pay, but patients say "no thanks." *New York Times*, March 3.

Komisar, H., and J. Feder. 1998. *The Balanced Budget Act of 1997: Effects on Medicare's Home Health Benefits and Beneficiaries Who Need Long-Term Care*. New York: Commonwealth Fund.

Kosloski, K., R. J. V. Montgomery, and J. G. Youngbauer. 2001. Utilization of respite services: A comparison of users, seekers, and nonseekers. *Journal of Applied Gerontology* 20 (1): 111–132.

Kosloski, K., J. P. Schaefer, D. Allwardt, R. J. V. Montgomery, and T. X. Karner. 2002. The role of cultural factors on clients' attitudes toward caregiving, perceptions of service delivery, and service utilization. *Home Health Care Services Quarterly* 21 (3/4): 65–88.

Krach, P. 1995. Assessment of depressed older prsons living in a home setting. *Home Healthcare Nurse* 13:61–64.

Kramer, B. J. 1997. Gain in the caregiving experience: Where are we! What next? *Gerontologist* 37 (2): 218–232.

Kraus, L., S. Stoddards, and D. Gilmartin. 1996. *Chartbook on Disability in the United States*. An InfoUse Report. Washington, D.C.: U.S. National Institute on Disability and Rehabilitation Research.

Kropf, N., and R. K. Grigsby. 1999. Telemedicine for older adults. *Home Health Care Services Quarterly* 17:1–11.

Kuhn, D. R. 1998. Caring for relatives with early stage Alzheimer's disease: An exploratory study. [Electronic version.] *American Journal of Alzheimer's Disease* 13 (4): 189–196. Retrieved September 12, 2005, from the PsychINFO database.

Kuo, T., and F. M. Torres-Gil. 2001. Factors affecting utilization of health services and home and community-based care programs by older Taiwanese in the United States. *Research on Aging* 23 (1): 14–36.

Lachs, M. S., and K. Pillemer. 1995. Abuse and neglect of elderly persons. *New England Journal of Medicine* 332 (7): 437–443.

——. 2004. Elder abuse. *Lancet* 364:1263–1272.

Lachs, M. S., C. Williams, S. O'Brien, L. Hurst, and R. Horwitz. 1997. Risk factors for reported elder abuse and neglect: A nine-year observational cohort study. *Gerontologist* 37 (4): 469–474.

Lachs, M. S., C. S. Williams, S. O'Brien, K. A. Pillemer, and M. E. Charlson. 1998. The mortality of elder maltreatment. *Journal of the American Medical Association* 280:428–432.

Landerman, R. L., G. G. Fillenbaum, C. F. Pieper, G. L. Maddox, D. T. Gold, and J. Guralnik. 1998. Private health insurance coverage and disability among older Americans. *Journals of Gerontology: Social Sciences* 53B: S258–S266.

LaPlante, M. P., C. Harrington, and T. Kang. 2002. Estimating paid and unpaid hours of personal assistance services in activities of daily living provided to adults living at home. *Health Services Research* 37:397–415.

LaPlante, M. P., S. H. Kaye, T. Kang, and C. Harrington. 2004. Unmet need for personal assistance services: Estimating the shortfall in hours of help and adverse consequences. *Journals of Gerontology* 59B:S98–S108.

La Viest, T. A. 1994. Beyond dummy variables and sample selection: What health services researchers ought to know about race as a variable. *Health Services Research* 29:1–16.

Lawrence, R. H., S. Tennstedt, and S. F. Assmann. 1998. Quality of the caregiver-care recipient relationship: Does it offset negative consequences of caregiving for family caregivers? *Psychology and Aging* 13:150–158.

Lawton, M. P. 1999. Environmental design features and well-being of older persons. In M. Duffy, ed., *Handbook of Counseling and Psychotherapy with Older Adults*. New York: John Wiley.

Lazarus, R., and S. Folkman. 1984. *Stress Appraisal and Coping*. New York: Springer.

Lebowitz, B. D., J. L. Pearson, L. S. Schneider, C. F. Reynolds, G. S. Alexopoulos, M. L. Bruce, Y. Conwell, I. R. Katz, B. S. Meyers, M. F. Morrison, J. Mossey, J. Niederehe, and P. Parmelee. 1997. Diagnosis and treatment of depression in late life: Consensus statement update. *Journal of the American Medical Association* 278: 1186–1190.

LeCroy, C. W., and E. Stinson. 2004. The public's perception of social work: Is it what we think it is? *Social Work* 49:164–174.

Ledoux, N. 2003. Connecting with the cognitively impaired: Dementia and Alzheimer's disease. *Caring* 22:30–32.

Lee J. S. 2002. Social work services in home health care: Challenges for the new prospective payment era. *Social Work in Health Care* 35:23–36.

——. 2006. Policies affecting health, mental health, and caregiving: Medicare. In B. Berkman and S. D'Ambrusoso, eds., *Handbook of Social Work in Health and Aging*, 847–858. New York: Oxford University Press.

Lee, J. S., and I. A. Gutheil. 2003. The older patient at home: Social work services and home health care. In B. Berkman and L. Harootyan, eds., *Social Work and Health Care in an Aging Society*, 73–95. New York: Springer.

Lee, J. S., and B. D. Rock. 2005. Challenges in the new prospective payment system: Action steps for social work in home health care. *Health and Social Work* 30:48–55.

Leff, E. W., and J. Sonstegard-Gamm. 2006. The home health care team approach to self-neglecting elders. *Home Healthcare Nurse* 24:249–257.

Leininger, M., and M. McFarland. 2002. *Transcultural Nursing Concepts, Theories, Research, and Practice.* 3rd ed. New York: McGraw-Hill.

Leipzig, R. M., R. G. Cumming, and M. E. Tinetti. 1999. Drugs and falls in older people: A systematic review and meta-analysis: I. psychotropic drugs. *Journal of the American Geriatrics Society* 47:30–39.

Leon, J., P. Neuman, and S. Parente. 1997. *Understanding the Growth in Medicare's Home Health Expenditures.* Washington, D.C.: Kaiser Family Foundation.

Lev, E. L., K. M. Daley, N. Conner, M. Reith, C. Fernandez, and S. V. Owen. 2001. An intervention to increase quality of life and self-care self-efficacy and decrease symptoms in breast cancer patients. *Scholarly Inquiry for Nursing Practice: An International Journal* 15:277–294.

Levande, D. L., S. W. Bowden, and J. Mollema. 1988. Home health services for dependent elders: The social work definition. *Journal of Gerontological Social Work* 11:5–17.

Leveille, S. G, E. H. Wagner, and C. Davis. 1998. Preventing disability and managing chronic illness in frail older adults: A randomized trial of a community-based partnership with primary care. *Journal of the American Geriatrics Society* 46:1191–1198.

Levenson, S. 1990. Evaluating competence and decision-making capacity in impaired older patients. *The Older Patient* (Winter): 11–16.

Levin, S. M., J. Kruger, and F. C. Blow. 2004. *Substance Abuse Among Older Adults: A Guide for Social Service Providers.* Washington, D.C.: U.S. Department of Health and Human Services, Substance Abuse and Mental Health Services Administration, Center for Substance Abuse Treatment.

Levine, C. 2000. Social functioning. In R. Kane and R. Kane, eds., *Assessing Older Persons,* 170–199. New York: Oxford University Press.

Li, H. 2006. Rural older adults' access barriers to in-home and community-based services. *Social Work Research* 30 (2): 109–118.

Li, H., L. A. Chadiha, and N. Morrow-Howell. 2005. Association between unmet needs for community services and caregiving strain. *Families in Society* 86 (1): 55–62.

Li, H., N. Morrow-Howell, and E. Proctor. 2004. Post-acute home care and hospital readmission of elderly patients with congestive heart failure. [Electronic version.] *Health and Social Work* 29 (4): 275–285. Retrieved September 11, 2005, from the Ovid database.

——. 2005. Assessing unmet needs of older adults receiving home and community-based services: Conceptualization and measurement. *Journal of Social Work in Long-Term Care* 3 (3/4): 103–120.

Lieberman, M. A., and L. Fisher. 1999. The effects of family conflict resolution and decision making on the provision of help for an elder with Alzheimer's disease. *Gerontologist* 39 (2): 159–166.

LifePlans. 1999. *A Descriptive Analysis of Patterns of Informal and Formal Caregiving Among Privately Insured and Non-Privately Insured Disabled Elders Living in the Community*. Final Report to the DHHS Office of Disability, Aging, and Long-Term Care Policy.

Lima, J. C., and S. M. Allen. 2001. Targeting risk for unmet need: Not enough help versus no help at all. *Journals of Gerontology* 56B:S302–S310.

Lipsman, R. 1996. Services and supports to the homebound elderly with mental health needs. *Journal of Long-Term Health Care* 15 (3): 24–38.

Liu, G. 2001. *Chinese Culture and Disability: Information for U.S. Service Providers*. Buffalo, N.Y.: Center for International Rehabilitation Research Information and Exchange.

Lorig, K. R. 2003. Self-management education: More than a nice extra. *Medical Care* 41 (6): 699–701.

Lorig, K. R., and H. R. Holman. 2003. Self-management education: History, definition, outcomes, and mechanisms. *Annals of Behavioral Medicine* 26 (1): 1–7.

Lorig, K. R., P. Ritter, and V. M. Gonzalez. 2003. Hispanic chronic disease self-management: A randomized community-based outcome trial. *Nursing Research* 52:391–369.

Lorig, K. R., P. Ritter, A. L. Stewart, D. S. Sobel, B. W. Brown, A. Bandura, V. M. Gonzalez, D. D. Laurent, and H. Holman. 2001. Chronic disease self-management program: Two-year health status and health care utilization outcomes. *Medical Care* 39:1217–1223.

Lotz, N. 1997. Home care. In T. Kerson, ed., *Social Work in Health Settings: Practice in Context*, 619–634. 2nd ed. New York: Haworth.

Lubben, J. E. 1988. Assessing social networks among elderly populations. *Family Community Health* 11:42–52.

Lubben, J., and M. Gironda. 2003. Centrality of social ties to the health and well-being of older adults. In B. Berkman and L. Harootyan, eds., *Social Work and Health Care in an Aging Society: Education, Policy, Practice, and Research*, 319–350. New York: Springer.

Lum, D. 2003. *Culturally Competent Practice: A Framework for Understanding Diverse Groups and Justice Issues*. 2nd ed. Pacific Grove, Calif.: Brooks/Cole.

Lum, Y., H. Chang, and M. Ozawa. 1999. The effects of race and ethnicity on use of health services by older Americans. *Journal of Social Service Research* 25 (4): 15–42.

Luna, I., E. de Ardon, Y. Lim, S. Cromwell, L. Phillips, and C. Russel. 1996. Relevance of familism in cross-cultural studies in family caregiving. *Western Journal of Nursing Research* 18 (3): 267–283.

Lustman, P. J., R. J. Anderson, K. E. Freedland, M. de Groot, R. M. Carney, and R. E. Clouse. 2000. Depression and poor glycemic control: A meta-analytic review of the literature. *Diabetes Care* 23:934–942.

Lyness, J. M., D. A. King, C. Cox, Z. Yoediono, and E. D. Caine. 1999. The importance of subsyndromal depression in older primary care patients: Prevalence and functional disability. *Journal of the American Geriatric Society* 47:647–652.

Lynn-McHale, D. J., and J. A. Deatrick. 2000. Trust between family and health care provider. *Journal of Family Nursing* 6:210–230.

Lyons, K. S., S. H. Zarit, A. G. Sayer, and C. J. Whitlatch. 2002. Caregiving as a dyadic process: Perspectives from caregiver and receiver. [Electronic version.] *Journals of Gerontology* 57B (3): 195–205. Retrieved September 11, 2005, from the ProQuest database.

Ma, G. 1999. Between two worlds: The use of traditional and Western health services by Chinese Americans. *Journal of Community Health* 24 (6): 421–437.

Mahoney, J. E., J. Eisner, T. Havighurst, S. Gray, and M. Palta. 2000. Problems of older adults living alone after hospitalization. *Journal of General Internal Medicine* 15 (9): 611–619.

Mahoney, J. E., M. Palta, J. Johnson, M. Jalaluddin, S. Gray, S. Park, and M. Sager. 2000. Temporal association between hospitalization and rate of falls after discharge. *Archives of Internal Medicine* 160:2788–2794.

Malinowski, R. 2002. Results of the 2001 home health social worker survey: Did social work practice change under PPS? *Home Health Care and Management* 14:372–377.

Marshall, C. E., D. Benton, and J. Brazier. 2000. Using clinical tools to identify clues of mistreatment. *Geriatrics* 55 (2): 42–53.

Martin, D. J., J. P. Garske, and K. Davis. 2000. Relation of the therapeutic alliance with outcome and other variables: A meta-analytic review. *Journal of Consulting and Clinical Psychology* 68:438–450.

Mastrian, K. G., and C. Dellasega. 1996. Helping families with long-term care decisions. *Caring* 15 (2): 68–72.

McAuley, W. J., S. S. Travis, and M. P. Safewright. 1997. Personal accounts of the nursing home search and selection process. *Qualitative Health Research* 7 (2): 236–254.

McCall, N., H. Komisar, A. Petersons, and S. Moore. 2001. Medicare home health before and after the BBA. *Health Affairs* 20:189–198.

McCallion, P., and R. W. Toseland. 1995. Supportive group interventions with caregivers of frail older adults. *Social Work with Groups* 18 (1): 11–25.

McCallion, P., R. W. Toseland, T. Gerber, and S. Banks. 2004. Increasing the use of formal services by caregivers of people with dementia. [Electronic version.] *Social Work* 49 (3): 440–450. Retrieved September 11, 2005, from the PubMed database.

McCusker, J., M. Cole, E. Keller, F. Bellavance, and A. Berard. 1998. Effectiveness of treatments of depression in older ambulatory patients. *Archives of Internal Medicine* 158:705–712.

McDonald, D. D., J. A. Deloge, N. Joslin, N. Petow, J. S. Severson, R. Votino, M. D. Shea, J. M. Drenga, M. T. Brennan, A. B. Moran, and E. Del Signore. 2003. Communicating end-of-life preferences. *Western Journal of Nursing Research* 25:652–666.

McEvoy, M. 2003. Culture and spirituality as an integrated concept in pediatric care. *American Journal of Maternal Child Nursing* 28 (1): 39–44.

McFarland, P., and S. Sanders. 2003. A pilot study about the needs of older gays and lesbians: What social workers need to know. *Journal of Gerontological Social Work* 40 (3): 67–80.

McFarlane, J., L. Greenberg, A. Weltge, and M. Watson. 1995. Identification of abuse in emergency departments: Effectiveness of a two-question screening tool. *Journal of Emergency Nursing* 21 (5): 391–394.

McInnis-Dittrich, K. 2005. *Social Work with Elders: A Biopsychosocial Approach to Assessment and Intervention.* 2nd ed. Boston: Pearson Education Company.

McNally, S., Y. Ben-Shlomo, and S. Newman. 1999. The effects of respite care on informal carers' well-being: A systematic review. *Journal of Disability and Rehabilitation* 21 (1): 1–14.

McNaughton, D. B. 2000. A synthesis of qualitative home visiting research. *Public Health Nursing* 17:405–414.

McNeal, G. 1998. Diversity issues in the homecare setting. *Critical Care Nursing Clinics of North America* 10 (3): 357–368.

MedPac. 1999. *Survey of Home Health Agencies*. Washington, D.C.: MedPac.

Mendes de Leon, C. F., T. Glass, L. A. Beckett, T. E. Seeman, D. A. Evans, and L. F. Berkman. 1999. Social networks in disability transitions across eight intervals of yearly data in the New Haven EPESE. *Journals of Gerontology* 54B: S162–S172.

Meredith, S. A., P. H. Feldman, D. Frey, K. Hall, K. Arnold, B. J. Brown, and W. A. Ray. 2001. Possible medication errors in home healthcare patients. *Journal of the American Geriatrics Society* 49:719–724.

Merrill, D. M. 1997. *Caring for Elderly Parents*. Westport, Conn.: Auburn House.

Millstein, G., M. L. Bruce, N. Gargon, E. Brown, P. J. Raue, and G. McAvay. 2003. Religious practice and depression among geriatric home care patients. *International Journal of Psychiatric Medicine* 33 (1): 71–83.

Mitchell, J., H. F. Mathews, L. M. Hunt, K. H. Cobb, and R. W. Watson. 2001. Mismanaging prescription medications among rural elders: The effects of socioeconomic status, health status, and medication profile indicators. *Gerontologist* 41: 348–356.

Monane, M., and J. Avorn. 1996. Medications and falls. *Clinics in Heriatric Medicine* 12:847–858.

Montgomery, R. 1999. The family role in the context of long-term care. *Journal of Aging and Health* 11:383–416.

Montoro-Rodriguez, J., K. Kosloski, and R. J. V. Montgomery. 2003. Evaluating a practice-oriented service model to increase the use of respite services among minorities and rural caregivers. *Gerontologist* 43 (6): 916–924.

Moon, A., and D. Benton. 2000. Tolerance of elder abuse and attitudes toward third-party intervention among African American, Korean American, and white elderly. *Journal of Multicultural Social Work* 8 (3/4): 283–303.

Moon, A., and T. Evans-Campbell. 1999. Awareness of formal and informal sources of help for victims of elder abuse among Korean American and Caucasian elders in Los Angeles. *Journal of Elder Abuse and Neglect* 11 (3): 1–23.

Moon, A., S. K. Tomita, and S. Jung-Kamei. 2001. Elder mistreatment among four Asian American groups: An exploratory study on tolerance, victim blaming, and attitudes toward third-party intervention. *Journal of Gerontological Social Work* 36 (1/2): 153–169.

Moon, A., and O. Williams. 1993. Perceptions of elder abuse and help-seeking patterns among African-American, Caucasian American, and Korean-American elderly women. *Gerontologist* 33 (3): 386–395.

Morgan, D. G., K. M. Semchuk, N. J. Stewart, and C. D'Arcy. 2002. Rural families caring for a relative with dementia: Barriers to use of formal services. *Social Science and Medicine* 55:1129–1142.

Morrison, J. 1995. *DSM-IV Made Easy*. New York: Guilford.

Morrison, R. S., L. H. Zayas, M. Mulvihill, S. A. Baskin, and D. E. Meier. 1998. Barriers to completion of health care proxies. *Archives of Internal Medicine* 158:2493–2497.

Morrow-Howell, N., E. K. Proctor, and P. Dore. 1998. Adequacy of care: Concept and its measurement. *Research on Social Work Practice* 8 (1): 86–102.

Morrow-Howell, N., E. Proctor, and P. Rozario. 2001. How much is enough?

Perspectives of care recipients and professionals on the sufficiency of in-home care. *Gerontologist* 41 (6): 723–732.

Mui, A. 1995a. Caring for frail elderly parents: A comparison of adult sons and daughters. *Gerontologist* 35:86–93.

——. 1995b. Multidimensional predictors of strain among older persons caring for frail elder spouses. *Journal of Marriage and the Family* 57:733–740.

Mulsant, B. H., and M. Ganguli. 1999. Epidemiology and diagnosis of depression in late life. *Journal of Clinical Psychiatry* 60:9–15.

Munson, M. L. 1999. Characteristics of elderly home health care users: Data from the 1996 National Home and Hospice Care Survey. Advance data from *Vital and Health Statistics Report*, no. 309. Hyattsville, Md.: National Center for Health Statistics.

Muran, J. C., and J. D. Safran. 1998. Negotiating the therapeutic alliance in brief psychotherapy. In J. D. Safran and J. C. Muran, eds., *The Therapeutic Alliance in Brief Psychotherapy*, 3–14. Washington, D.C.: American Psychological Association.

Murguia, A., R. Peterson, and M. Zea. 2003. Use and implications of ethnomedical health care approaches among Central American Immigrants. *Health and Social Work* 28 (1): 43–52.

Murguia, A., M. Zea, C. Reisen, and R. Peterson. 2000. The development of the Cultural Health Attributions Questionnaire. *Cultural Diversity and Ethnic Minority Psychology* 6 (3): 268–283.

Murtaugh, C. M., N. McCall, S. Moore, and A. Meadow. 2003. Trends in Medicare home health care use: 1997–2001. *Health Affairs* 22:146–156.

Naleppa, M. J. 1996. Families and the institutionalized elderly: A review. *Journal of Gerontological Social Work* 27 (1/2): 87–111.

Naleppa, M. J., and K. M. Hash. 2001. Home-based practice with older adults: Challenges and opportunities in the home environment. *Journal of Gerontological Social Work* 35:71–88.

Naleppa, M. J., and W. J. Reid. 2003. *Gerontological Social Work: A Task-Centered Approach*. New York: Columbia University Press.

National Association of Social Workers. 1987. NASW *Standards for Social Work in Health Care Settings*. Washington, D.C.: NASW.

——. 1995. NASW *clinical indicators for social work and psychosocial services in home health care*. Washington, D.C.: NASW.

——. 2000. *National Association of Social Workers Code of Ethics*. Retrieved July 5, 2006, from www.socialworkers.org/pubs.

——. 2001. *Standards for Cultural Competence in Social Work Practice*. Retrieved June 9, 2005, from www.socialworkers.org/sections/credentials/cultural_comp.asp.

National Commission on Chronic Illness. 1956. *Chronic Illness in the United States: Care of the Long-Term Patient*. Vol. 2. Cambridge, Mass.: Harvard University Press.

National Family Caregivers Association. 2001. *Survey of Self-Identified Family Caregivers*. Accessed September 15, 2007, at http://www.nfcacares.org/who_are_family_caregivers/care_giving_statstics.cfm#6.

National Gay and Lesbian Task Force Policy Institute. 1999. *Aging Initiative*. Washington, D.C.

National Institute of Mental Health. 2003. *Older Adults: Depression and Suicide Facts*. Retrieved May 20, 2007, from http://nimh.nih.gov/publicat/elderlydepsuicide.cfm.

National Institute on Aging. 2000. *Alzheimer's Disease: Unraveling the Mystery*. National Institutes of Health Publication No. 023782. Washington, D.C.: U. S. Department of Health and Human Services.

——. 2006. *Home Safety for People with Alzheimer's Disease*. Retrieved January 19, 2007, from http://www.nia.nih.gov/Alzheimers/Publicatioms/homesafety.htm.

National Institute on Alcohol Abuse and Alcoholism. 1995. *Alcohol Alert*, No. 27. January. Retrieved January 9, 2004, from www.niaaa.nih.gov/publications/aa27.htm.

National Institutes of Health. 2003. *New Prevalence Study Suggests Dramatically Rising Numbers of People with Alzheimer's Disease*. NIH News. Department of Health and Human Services, at http://www.nih.gov/news/pr/aug2003/nia-18,htm.

National Research Council. 2002. *Elder Maltreatment: Abuse, Neglect, and Exploitation in an Aging America*. Retrieved June 10, 2007, from www.nationalacademies.org/nrc/.

Navaie-Waliser, M., P. Feldman, D. Gould, C. Levine, A. Kuerbix, and K. Donelan. 2001. The experiences and challenges of informal caregivers: Common themes and differences among whites, blacks, and Hispanics. *Gerontologist* 41 (6):733–741.

Naylor, M. D. 2002. Transitional care of older adults. [Electronic version.] *Annual Review of Nursing Research* 20:127–147. Retrieved September 11, 2005, from the Ovid database.

Neal, J. L. 2001. Public awareness of home care. *Caring* 20:38–41.

Newcomer, R., M. Spitalny, P. Fox, and C. Yordi. 1999. Effects of the Medicare Alzheimer's Disease Demonstration on the use of community-based services. [Electronic version.] *Health Services Research* 34 (3): 645–670. Retrieved September 11, 2005, from the Ovid database.

Nezu, A. M., C. M. Nezu, S. H. Felgoise, K. S. McClure, and P. S. Houts. 2003. Project Genesis: Assessing the efficacy of problem-solving therapy for distressed adult cancer patients. *Journal of Consulting and Clinical Psychology* 71:1036–1048.

Nezu, A. M., C. M. Nezu, P. S. Houts, S. H. Friedman, and S. Faddis. 1999. Relevance of problem-solving therapy to psychosocial oncology. *Journal of Psychosocial Oncology* 16:5–26.

Nolan, M., and C. Dellasega. 2000. "I really feel I've let him down": Supporting family carers during long-term care placement for elders. [Electronic version.] *Journal of Advanced Nursing* 31 (4): 759–767. Retrieved July 29, 2005, from the Academic Search Elite database.

Nolan, M., G. Walker, J. Nolan, S. Williams, F. Poland, M. Curran, and B. C. Kent. 1996. Entry to care: Positive choice or fait accompli? Developing a more proactive nursing response to the needs of older people and their carers. *Journal of Advanced Nursing* 24:265–274.

Norlander, L., and K. McSteen. 2000. The kitchen table discussion: A creative way to discuss end-of-life issues. *Home Healthcare Nurse* 18 (8): 532–539.

Northouse, L. L., and P. G. Northouse. 1998. *Health Communication: Strategies for Health Professionals*. 3rd ed. Stamford, Conn.: Appleton and Lange.

Novick, J. G. 2001. The perils of underutilizing social work intervention in home care in the era of PPS. *Home Health Care Management and Practice* 13:134–141.

Nugent, W. R. 2000. Single case design visual analysis procedures for use in practice evaluation. *Journal of Social Service Research* 37 (4): 39–75.

Núñez, A. 2000. Transforming cultural competence intro cross-cultural efficacy in women's health education. *Academic Medicine* 75:1071–1080.

Nussbaum, J. F., M. L. Hummert, A. William, and J. Harwood. 1998. Communication and older adults. In B. R. Burleson and A. W. Kunkel, eds., *Communication Yearbook*, 19:1–47. London: Sage.

Nussbaum, J. F., L. L. Pecchioni, J. D. Robinson, and T. L. Thompson. 2000. *Communication and Aging*. Mahway, N.J.: Lawrence Erlbaum.

Oktay, J., and F. Sheppard. 1978. Home health care for the elderly. *Health and Social Work* 3:36–47.

Omi, M., and H. Winant. 2001. Racial formations. In P. Rothenberg, ed., *Race, Class, and Gender in the United States*, 11–20. New York: Worth.

Orange, J. B. 2001. Family caregivers, communication, and Alzheimer's disease. In M. L. Hummert and J. F. Nussbaum, eds., *Aging, Communication, and Health: Linking Research and Practice for Successful Aging*, 225–248. Mahwah, N.J.: Lawrence Erlbaum.

Orel, N. 2004. Gay, lesbian, and bisexual elders: Expressed needs and concerns across focus groups. *Journal of Gerontological Social Work* 43 (2/3): 57–77.

Ory, M., J. L.Yee, S. L. Tennstedt, and R. Schulz. 2000. The extent and impact of dementia care: Unique challenges experienced by family caregivers. In R. Schulz, ed., *Handbook on Dementia Caregiving: Evidence-Based Interventions for Family Caregivers*, 1–32. New York: Springer.

Osterberg, L., and T. Blaschke. 2005. Drug therapy: Adherence to medication. *New England Journal of Medicine* 353:487–497.

Ostwald, S.K., K. W. Hepburn, W. Caron, T. Burns, and R. Mantell. 1999. Reducing caregiver burden: A randomized psychoeducational intervention for caregivers of persons with dementia. *Gerontologist* 39 (3): 299–309.

Overeynder, J. 2003a. Advance planning: Power of attorney: Task menu. In William J. Reid and Mathias J. Naleppa, eds., *Gerontological Social Work: A Task-Centered Approach*, 262–265. New York: Columbia University Press.

Overeynder, J. 2003b. Home safety: Environmental assessment. In M. J. Naleppa and W. J. Reid, *Gerontological Social Work: A Task-Centered Approach*, 287–290. New York: Columbia University Press.

Ow, R., and D. Katz. 1999. Family secrets and the disclosure of distressful information in Chinese families. *Families in Society* 80 (6): 620–628.

Oxman T.E., and J. G. Hull. 1997. Social support, depression, and activities of daily living in older heart surgery patients. *Journals of Gerontology: Psychological Sciences* 52B:P1–P14.

Ozawa, M.N., and H. Tseng. 1999. Utilization of formal services during the 10 years after retirement. *Journal of Gerontological Social Work* 31 (1/2): 3–19.

Pachter, L., M. Cloutier, and B. Bernstein. 1995. Ethnomedical (folk) remedies for childhood asthma in a mainland Puerto Rican community. *Archives of Pediatric Adolescent Medicine* 149:982–988.

Palley, E., and P. A. Rozario. 2007. The application of the Olmstead decision on housing and eldercare. *Journal of Gerontological Social Work* 49:81–96.

Palmer, S., and T. A. Glass. 2003. Family function and stroke recovery: A review. *Rehabilitation Psychology* 48 (4): 255–265.

Panos, P., and A. Panos. 2000. A model for a culture-sensitive assessment of patients in health care settings. *Social Work in Health Care* 31 (1): 49–62.

Patterson, D., and R. Basham. 2006. Single system designs. In D. Patterson and R. Basham, *Data Analysis with Spreadsheets*, 123–145. Boston: Pearson/Allyn and Bacon.

Paveza, G. J., D. Cohen, C. Eisdorfer, S. Freels, T. Semla, J. W. Ashford, P. Gorelick, R. Hirschman, D. Luchins, and P. Levy. 1992. Severe family violence and Alzheimer's disease: Prevalence and risk factors. *Gerontologist* 32 (4): 493–497.

Pear, R. 2006. Renewed Worries on Medicare Drug Plans. *New York Times*, December 5.

Retrieved September 14, 2007, from http://www.nytimes.com/2006/12/05/washington/05medicare.html?ex=1189915200&en=da55532687b9bc5d&ei=5070.

Pearlin L. I., J. T. Mullan, S. J. Semple, and M. M. Skaff. 1990. Caregiving and the stress process: An overview of concepts and their measures. *Gerontologist* 30 (5): 583–594.

Pedlar, D. J., and D. E. Biegel 1999. The impact of family caregiver attitudes on the use of community services for dementia care. *Journal of Applied Gerontology* 18 (2): 201–221.

Peng, T. R., M. Navaie-Waliser, and P. H. Feldman. 2003. Social support, home health service use, and outcomes among four racial-ethnic groups. *Gerontologist* 43 (4): 503–513.

Penrod, J., and C. Dellasega. 1998. Caregivers' experiences in making placement decisions. *Western Journal of Nursing Research* 20 (6) : 706–732.

Pfeiffer, E. 1975. A short portable mental status questionnaire for the assessment of organic brain deficit in elderly patients. *Journal of the American Geriatric Society* 18:491–500.

Piette, J. D., M. Heisler, R. Horne, and G. C. Alexander. 2005. A conceptually based approach to understanding chronically ill patients' responses to medication cost pressures. *Social Science Medicine* 62 (4): 846–857.

Piette J. D., M. Heisler, and T. H. Wagner. 2004. Cost-related medication underuse among chronically ill adults: The treatments people forgo, how often, and who is at risk. *American Journal of Public Health* 94 (10): 1782–1787.

Pillemer, K., and J. J. Suitor. 1992. Violence and violent feelings: What causes them among family caregivers? *Journals of Gerontology* 47 (4): S165–S172.

Pinkson, E. M., G. R. Green, N. L. Linsk, and R. N. Young. 2003. A family eco-behavioral approach for elders with mental illness. In H. E. Briggs and K. Corcoran, eds., *Social Work Practice: Treating Common Client Problems*. Chicago: Lyceum.

Pinquart, M., and S. Sörensen. 2003. Associations of stressors and uplifts with caregiver burden and depressive mood: A meta-analysis. *Journals of Gerontology: Psychological Science* 58B (2): P112–P128.

——. 2004. Associations of caregiver stressors and uplifts with subjective well-being and depressive mood: A meta-analytic comparison. *Aging and Mental Health* 8 (5): 438–449.

——. 2005. Ethnic differences in stressors, resources, and psychological outcomes of family caregiving: A meta-analysis. *Gerontologist* 45 (1): 90–106.

——. 2006. Gender differences in caregiver stressors, social resources, and health: An updated meta-analysis. *Journals of Gerontology* 61B (1): P33–P45.

Poole, D. 1995. Health care: Direct practice. In *The Encyclopedia of Social Work* 2:1156–1167. Washington, D.C.: National Association of Social Workers.

Popple, P., and L. Leighninger. 1993. *Social Work, Social Welfare, and American Society*. New York: Allyn and Bacon.

Poss, J., and M. A. Jezewski. 2002. The role and meaning of *susto* in Mexican Americans' explanatory model of type 2 diabetes. *Medical Anthropology Quarterly* 16:360–377.

Proctor, E., N. Morrow-Howell, L. Hong, and P. Dore. 2000. Adequacy of home care and hospital readmission for elderly congestive heart failure patients. *Health and Social Work* 25 (2): 87–96.

Proctor, E., N. Morrow-Howell, and S. Kaplan. 1996. Implementation of discharge plans for chronically ill elders discharged home. *Health and Social Work* 21 (1): 30–40.

Quayhagen, M., M. P. Quayhagen, T. L. Patterson, M. Irwin, R. L. Hauger, and I. Grant. 1997. Coping with dementia: Family caregiver burnout and abuse. *Journal of Mental Health and Aging* 3 (3): 357–364.

Quinn, M. J., and S. K. Tomita. 1997. *Elder Abuse and Neglect: Causes, Diagnosis, and Intervention Strategies.* 2nd ed. New York: Springer.

Ratner, E., L. Norlander, and K. McSteen. 2001. Death at home following a targeted advance-care planning process at home: The kitchen table discussion. *Journal of the American Geriatrics Society* 49:778–781.

Raudonis, B. M., and J. M. Kirschling. 1996. Family caregivers' perspectives on hospice nursing care. *Journal of Palliative Care* 12:14–19.

Raue, P. J., E. L. Brown, and M. L. Bruce. 2002. Assessing behavioral health using OASIS. Part 1: Depression and suicidality. *Home Healthcare Nurse* 20 (3): 154–161.

Raue, P. J., E. L. Brown, C. F. Murphy, and M. L. Bruce. 2002. Assessing behavioral health using OASIS: Part 2: Cognitive impairment, problematic behaviors, and anxiety. *Home Healthcare Nurse* 20 (4): 230–235.

Reamer, F. G. 1998. *Ethical Standards in Social Work.* Washington, D.C.: NASW Press.

——. 1999. *Social Work Values and Ethics.* New York: Columbia University Press.

——. 2001. *Tangled Relationships: Managing Boundary Issues in the Human Services.* New York: Columbia University Press.

——. 2003. Boundary issues in social work: Managing dual relationships. *Social Work* 48:121–133.

Reay, A. M. C., and K. D. Browne. 2001. Risk factor characteristics in carers who physically abuse or neglect their elderly dependants. *Aging and Mental Health* 5 (1): 56–62.

Reinhardy, J. 1992. Decisional control in moving to a nursing home: Post-admission adjustment and well-being. *Gerontologist* 32:96–101.

——. 1995. Relocation to a new environment: Decisional control and the move to a nursing home. *Health and Social Work* 20:31–38.

Reinhardy, J., and R. A. Kane. 1999. Choosing an adult foster home or a nursing home: Residents' perceptions about decision making and control. *Social Work* 44:571–585.

Reis, M., and D. Nahmiash. 1998. Validation of the indicators of abuse (IOA) screen. *Gerontologist* 38 (4): 471–480.

Rempusheske, V. F., and A. C. Hurley. 2000. Advance directives and dementia. *Journal of Gerontological Nursing* 26:27–34.

Reuss, G. F., S. L. Dupuis, and K. Whitfield. 2005. Understanding the experience of moving a loved one to a long-term care facility: Family members' perspectives. *Journal of Gerontological Social Work* 46 (1): 17–46.

Reverby, S. 1987. *Ordered to Care.* Cambridge: Cambridge University Press.

Rinehart, B. H. 2002. Senior housing: Pathway to service utilization. *Journal of Gerontological Social Work* 39 (3): 57–75. [Electronic version.] Retrieved September 11, 2005, from the Ovid database.

Ringham, K. 2001. The family meeting in the home: A benchmark of high-quality geriatric care. Paper presented at the annual meeting of the American Network of Home Health Care Social Workers, Rosemont, Illinois.

Rizzo, V., and A. Abrams. 2000. Utilization review: A powerful social work role in health care settings. *Health and Social Work* 25 (4): 264–269.

Roberts, J., G. Browne, C. Milne, L. Spooner, A. Gafni, M. Drummond-Young, et al. 1999. Problem-solving counseling for caregivers of the cognitively impaired: Effective for whom? *Nursing Research* 48 (3): 162–172.

Robinson, B. C. 1983. Validation of a caregiver strain index. *Journal of Gerontology* 38 (3): 344–348.

Robinson, C. A. 1996. Health care relationships revisited. *Journal of Family Nursing* 2:152–173.

Robinson, K. M., K. C. Buckwalter, and D. Reed. 2005. Predictors of use of services among dementia caregivers. *Western Journal of Nursing Research* 27:126–140.

Roby, J. L., and R. Sullivan. 2000. Adult protection service laws: A comparison of state statutes from definition to case closure. *Journal of Elder Abuse and Neglect* 12 (3/4): 17–51.

Rodgers, B. 1997. Family members' experiences with nursing home placement of an older adult. *Applied Nursing Research* 10:57–63.

Roe, B., M. Whattam, H. Young, and M. Dimond. 2001. Elders' perceptions of formal and informal care: Aspects of getting and receiving help for their activities of daily living. *Journal of Clinical Nursing* 10:398–405.

Rolland, J. 1998. Beliefs and collaboration in illness: Evolution over time. *Families, Systems, and Health* 16:7–25.

——. 1999. Chronic illness and the family life cycle. In B. Carter and M. McGoldrick, eds., *The Expanded Family Life Cycle*, 492–511. Needham Heights, Mass.: Allyn and Bacon.

Rosenberg, G. 1994. Social work, the family, and the community. *Social Work in Health Care* 20:7–20.

Rosenfeld, D. 1999. Identity work among lesbian and gay elderly. *Journal of Aging Studies* 13 (2): 121–144.

Rosenfeld, K. E., N. S. Wenger, and M. Kagawa-Singer. 2000. End-of-life decision making: A qualitative study of elderly individuals. [Electronic version.] *Journal of General Internal Medicine* 15 (9): 620–625. Retrieved July 4, 2004, from the Ovid database.

Ryan, A. A. 1999. Medication compliance and older people: A review of the literature. *International Journal of Nursing Studies* 36:153–162.

Ryan, A. A., and H. F. Scullion. 2000. Nursing home placement: An exploration of the experiences of family carers. *Journal of Advanced Nursing* 32 (5): 1187–1195.

Ryan, E. B., S. D. Meredith, M. J. MacLean, and J. B. Orange. 1995. Changing the way we talk with elders: Promoting health using the communication enhancement model. *International Journal of Aging and Human Development* 41:89–107.

Salamon, M., and G. Rosenthal. 2004. *Home or Nursing Home: Making the Right Choices.* 2nd ed. New York: Springer.

Salvatore, T. 2000. A preventable tragedy. *Caring* 19:34–37.

Salzman, C. 1995. Medication compliance in the elderly. *Journal of Clinical Psychiatry* 56:18–22.

Sattin, R. W., J. G. Rodriguez, C. A. DeVito, P. A. Wingo, and the Study to Assess Falls Among the Elderly (SAFE) Group. 1998. Home environmental hazards and the risk of fall injury events among community-dwelling older persons. *Journal of the American Geriatrics Society* 46:669–676.

Schaughnessy, P. W. 2000. Shaping home care by measuring outcomes. In R. Binstock and L. Cluff, eds., *Home Care Advances: Essential Research and Policy Issues*, 163–190. New York: Springer.

Schilder, A., C. Kennedy, I. Goldstone, R. Ogden, R. S. Hogg, and M. V. O'Shaughnessy. 2001. "Being dealt with as a whole person." Care seeking and adherence: The benefits of culturally competent care. *Social Science and Medicine* 52:1643–1659.

Schillinger, D., K. Grumbach, J. Piette, F. Wang, D. Osmond, C. Daher, J. Palacios, G. D. Sullivan, and A. B. Bindman. 2002. Association of health literacy with diabetes outcome. *JAMA* 288:475–482.

Schneider, A., K. Hyer, and M. Luptak. 2000. Suggestions to social workers for surviving in managed care. *Health and Social Work* 25 (4): 276–279.

Schneider, M. K. 2003. Adult day care. In M. J. Naleppa and W. J. Reid, *Gerontological Social Work: A Task-Centered Approach,* 320–322. New York: Columbia University Press.

Schneider, R. L., N. P. Kropf, and A. J. Kisor. 2000. *Gerontological Social Work.* Belmont, Calif.: Wadsworth/Thomson Learning.

Schoenberg, N. E., and R. T. Coward. 1998. Residential differences in attitudes about barriers to using community-based services among older adults. *Journal of Rural Health* 14:295–304.

Schofield, M. J., and G. D. Mishra. 2003. Validity of self-report screening scale for elder abuse: Women's health Australia study. *Gerontologist* 43 (1): 110–120.

Schofield, M. J., R. Reynolds, G. D. Mishra, J. R. Powers, and A. J. Dobson. 2002. Screening for vulnerability to abuse among older women: Women's health Australia study. *Journal of Applied Gerontology* 21 (1): 24–39.

Schonfeld, L., R. G. Larsen, and P. G. Stiles. 2006. Behavioral health services utilization among older adults identified within a state abuse hotline database. *Gerontologist* 46:193–199.

Schulberg, H. C., P. S. Pilkonis, and P. Houck. 1998. The severity of major depression and choice of treatment in primary care practice. *Journal of Consulting and Clinical Psychology* 66:932–938.

Schulz, R. 2000. *Handbook on Dementia Caregiving: Evidence-Based Interventions in Family Caregiving.* New York: Springer.

Schulz, R., A. O'Brien, S. Czaja, M. Ory, R. Norris, L. M. Martire, et al. 2002. Dementia caregiver intervention research: In search of clinical significance. [Electronic version.] *Gerontologist* 42 (5): 589–602. Retrieved September 12, 2005, from the Ovid database.

Schulz, R., and S. R. Beach. 1999. Caregiving as a risk factor for mortality: The caregiver health effects study. *JAMA* 282:2215–2219.

Schulz, R., L. Burton, C. Hirsch, and J. Jackson. 1997. Health effects of caregiving: The Caregiver Health Effects Study: An ancillary study of the Cardiovascular Health Study. *Annals of Behavioral Medicine* 19:110–116.

Schumacher, K., C. A. Beck, and J. M. Marren. 2006. Family caregivers: Caring for older adults, working with their families. *American Journal of Nursing* 106 (8): 40–49.

Schur, D., and C. J. Whitlatch. 2003. Circumstances leading to placement: A difficult caregiving decision. *Lippincott's Case Management* 8 (5): 187–195.

Schwarz, K. A., and C. E. Blixen. 1997. Does home health care affect strain and depressive symptomatology for caregivers of impaired older adults? *Journal of Community Health Nursing* 14 (1): 39–48.

Schwarz, K. A., and B. L. Roberts. 2000. Social support and strain of family caregivers of older adults. *Holistic Nursing Practice* 14 (2): 77–90.

Semple, S. J. 1992. Conflict in Alzheimer's caregiving families: Its dimensions and consequences. *Gerontologist* 32:648–655.

Sevast, P. A. 2007. Advancing leadership in health care social work: home health and hospice intensive: cms and medical social work—current issues and future plans. Paper presented at the Society for Social Work Leadership in Healthcare 42nd National Conference, Philadelphia.

Shaefor, B. W., and C. R. Horejsi. 2006. *Techniques and Guidelines for Social Work Practice*. 7th ed. Boston: Allyn and Bacon.

Shaughnessy, P. W. 2000. Shaping home care by measuring outcomes. In R. Binstock and L. Cluff, eds., *Home Care Advances: Essential Research and Policy Issues*, 163–190. New York: Springer.

Sidell, N. 1997. Adult adjustment to chronic illness: A review of the literature. *Health and Social Work* 22:5–11.

Sienkiewicz, J. 2001. How using social work can save money under PPS. *Home Healthcare Nurse* 19:408–415.

Simmons, J. 1994. Community based care: The new health social work paradigm. *Social Work in Health Care* 20:35–46.

Singer, P. A., D. K. Martin, J. V. Lavery, E. C. Thiel, M. Kelner, and D. C. Mendelssohn. 1998. Reconceptualizing advance care planning from the patient's perspective. *Archives of Internal Medicine* 158:879–884.

Sirey, J., M. L. Bruce, G. S. Alexopoulos, D. A. Perlick, P. Raue, S. J. Friedman, and B. S. Meyers. 2001. Perceived stigma as a predictor of treatment discontinuation in young and older outpatients with depression. *American Journal of Psychiatry* 158 (3): 479–481.

Small, J. A., S. Kemper, and K. Lyons. 1997. Sentence comprehension in Alzheimer's disease: Effects of grammatical complexity, speech rate, and repetition. Psychology and Aging 12:1–11.

Smerglia, V. L., and G. T. Deimling. 1997. Care-related decision-making satisfaction and caregiver well-being in families caring for older members. [Electronic version.] *Gerontologist* 37 (5): 658–665. Retrieved September 11, 2005, from the Ovid database.

Smith, G., J. O'Keefe, L. Carpenter, P. Doty, G. Kennedy, B. Burwell, R. Mollica, and L. Williams. 2000. *Understanding Medicaid Home and Community Services: A Primer*. Washington, D.C.: George Washington University, Center for Health Policy Research.

Smyth, K. A., and M. K. Milidonis. 1999. The relationship between normative beliefs about help seeking and the experience of caregiving in Alzheimer's disease. *Journal of Applied Gerontology* 18 (2): 222–238.

Sörensen, S., P. Duberstein, D. Gill, and M. Pinquart. 2006. Dementia care: Mental health effects, intervention strategies, and clinical implications. *Lancet Neurology* 5:961–973.

Sörensen, S., M. Pinquart, and P. Duberstein. 2002. How effective are interventions with caregivers? An updated meta-analysis. *Gerontologist* 42 (3): 356–372.

Soskis, C. W. 1997. End-of-life decisions in the home care setting. *Social Work in Health Care* 25:107–116.

Spaid, W. M., and A. S. Barusch. 1994. Emotional closeness and caregiver burden in the marital relationship. *Journal of Gerontological Social Work* 21 (3/4): 197–211.

Sperling, R., and C. Humphrey. 1999. *OASIS and OBQI: A Guide for Education and Implementation*. Philadelphia: Lippincott, Williams, and Wilkins.

Spohn, P., L. Bergthold, and C. Estes. 1988. From cottages to condos: The expansion of the home health care industry under Medicare. *Home Health Care Services Quarterly* 8:25–55.

St. Pierre, M., and W. Dombi. 2000. Home health care PPS: New payment system, new hope. *Caring* 19:6–15.

Stanford Patient Education Research Center Web site. Accessed January 1, 2006, at www.patienteducation.stanford.edu.

Stark, D. 1997. Social work practice in home health care: Predictors of job satisfaction among home health social workers. Ph.D. diss., University of Pittsburgh.

Starrels, M. E., B. Ingersoll-Dayton, D. W. Dowler, and M. B. Neal. 1997. The stress of caring for a parent: Effects of the elder's impairment on an employed adult child. *Journal of Marriage and the Family* 59 (4): 860–872.

Steffen, A. M., and S. Berger. 2000. Relationship differences in anger intensity during caregiving-related situations. *Clinical Gerontologist* 21:3–19.

Steinman, M. A., L. P. Sands, and K. E. Covinsky. 2001. Self-restriction of medications due to cost in seniors without prescription coverage. *Journal of General Internal Medicine* 16 (12):793–799.

Stevens, R., and R. Stevens. 1974. *Welfare Medicine in America*. New York: Free Press.

Strawbridge, W. J., and M. I. Wallhagen. 1991. Impact of family conflict on adult child caregivers. *Gerontologist* 31:770–771.

Stuart, B., B. A. Briesacher, D. G. Shea, B. Cooper, F. S. Baysac, and M. R. Limcangco. 2005. Riding the rollercoaster: The ups and downs in out-of-pocket spending under the standard Medicare drug benefit. *Health Affairs (Millwood)* 24 (4): 1022–31. Erratum in *Health Affairs (Millwood)* 24 (5): 1380.

Stuart, B., L. Simoni-Wastila, and D. Chauncey. 2005. Assessing the impact of coverage gaps in the Medicare Part D drug benefit. *Health Affairs (Millwood)*, January–June, Supplement Web Exclusives, W5-167–W5-179.

Stulginsky, M. M. 1993. Nurses' home health experience. *Nursing and Health* 14:476–485.

Sudha, S., and E. Multran. 2001. Race and ethnicity, nativity, and issues of health care. *Research on Aging* 23 (1): 3–13.

Suitor, J. J., and K. Pillemer. 1996. Sources of support and interpersonal stress in the networks of married caregiving daughters: Findings from a two-year longitudinal study. *Journals of Gerontology* 51B:S297–S305.

Szanto, K., A. Gildengers, B. H. Mulsant, G. Brown, G. S. Alexopoulos, and C. F. Reynolds. 2002. Identification of suicidal ideation and prevention of suicidal behavior in the elderly. *Drugs and Aging* 19:11–24.

Tappen, R. M., C. Williams-Burgess, J. Edelstein, T. Toughy, and S. Fishman. 1997. Communicating with individuals with Alzheimer's disease: Examination of recommended strategies. *Archives of Psychiatric Nursing* 11:249–256.

Tatara, T. 1999. *Understanding Elder Abuse in Minority Populations*. Philadelphia: Taylor and Francis.

Tauer, C. 1993. Risks and choices: When is paternalism justified? In R. Kane and A. Caplan, eds., *Ethical Conflicts in the Management of Home Care: The Case Manager's Dilemma*, 45–52. New York: Springer.

Taylor, S. E., and D. A. Armor. 1996. Positive illusions and coping with adversity. *Journal of Personality* 64:873–897.

Tebb, S. 1995. An aid to empowerment: A caregiver well-being scale. *Health and Social Work* 20 (2): 87–92.

Thobaben, M. 2002. Racial and ethnic disparities in health care. *Community-Based Health Care Management and Practice* 14 (6): 479–481.

Thomas, C. P., and C. M. M. Payne. 1998. Home alone: Unmet need for formal support services among home health clients. *Home Health Care Services Quarterly* 17 (2): 1–20.

Thompson, E. H., Jr., A. M. Futterman, D. Gallagher-Thompson, J. M. Rose, and S. B. Lovett. 1993. Social support and caregiving burden in caregivers of frail elders. *Journals of Gerontology* 48 (5): S245–S254.

Thompson, S. C., M. Galbraith, C. T. Thomas, J. Swan, and S. Vrungos. 2002. Caregivers of stroke patient family members: Behavioral and attitudinal indicators of overprotective care. *Psychology and Health* 17:297–312.

Tinetti, M. E. 2003. Preventing falls in elderly persons. *New England Journal of Medicine* 348:42–48.

Tomita, S. 1999. Conditions for mistreatment among Japanese: An exploratory study. In T. Tatara, ed., *Understanding Elder Abuse in Minority Populations*, 119–139. Philadelphia: Brunner/Mazel.

———. 2006. Mistreated and neglected elders. In B. Berkman and S. D'Ambruso, eds., *Handbook of Social Work in Health and Aging*, 219–230. New York: Oxford University Press.

Toseland, R. W., P. McCallion, T. Gerber, and S. Banks. 2002. Predictors of health and human services use by persons with dementia and their family caregivers. *Social Science and Medicine* 55:1255–1266.

Toseland, R. W., P. McCallion, T. Gerber, C. Dawson, S. Gieryic, and V. Guilamo-Ramos. 1999. Use of health and human services by community-residing people with dementia. [Electronic version.] *Social Work* 44 (6): 535–548. Retrieved September 12, 2005, from the PubMed database.

Trief, P., J. Sandberg, R. Greenberg, K. Graff, N. Catronova, M. Yoon, and R. Weinstock. 2003. Describing support: A qualitative study of couples living with diabetes. *Families, Systems, and Health* 21:57–67.

Trojan, L., and O. Yonge. 1993. Developing trusting, caring relationships: Home care nurses and elderly clients. *Journal of Advanced Nursing* 18.1903 1910.

Tseng, C. W., R. H. Brook, E. Keeler, W. N. Steers, and C. M. Mangione. 2004. Cost-lowering strategies used by Medicare beneficiaries who exceed drug benefit caps and have a gap in drug coverage. *Journal of the American Medical Association* 292 (8): 952–960.

Tsuji, I., S. Whalen, and T. E. Finucane. 1995. Predictors of nursing home placement in community-based long-term care. *Journal of the American Geriatrics Society* 43:761–766.

University of Washington. 2005. Culture clues "tip sheets." Retrieved July 1, 2005, from http:/depts.washington.edu/pfes/cultureclues.html.

Unützer, J., W. Katon, M. Sullivan, and J. Miranda. 1999. Treating depressed older adults in primary care: Narrowing the gap between efficacy and effectiveness. *Milbank Quarterly* 77 (2): 225–243.

U.S. Department of Health and Human Services. 1999. *Social Services Block Grant Program Annual Report on Expenditures and Recipients*. Washington, D.C.: U.S. Department of Health and Human Services.

———. 2000. *Understanding Medicaid Home and Community-Based Services: A Primer*. Washington, D.C.: U.S. Department of Health and Human Services.

———. 2001. *Diabetes Fact Sheet*. Retrieved September 21, 2004, from www.ahrq.gov.

———. 2002. *Healthy People 2010 Fact Sheet*. Washington, D.C.: DHHS. Retrieved September 8, 2004, from www.healthypeople.gov.

U.S. Department of Health and Human Services. Administration on Aging. 2003. *The Older Americans Act National Family Caregiver Support Program Compassion in Action*. Accessed September 15, 2007, at http://www.aoa.gov/prof/aoaprog/caregiver/overview/NFCSP_Exec_Summary_FULL_03.pdf.

———. 2004. *The Older Americans Act National Family Caregiver Support Program*. Retrieved August 29, 2004, from http://www.aoa.gov/aoa/pages/state.html.

———. 2005. *Celebrate Long-Term Living: Annual Report 2005*. www.aoa.gov.

U.S. Department of Health and Human Services. Centers for Medicare and Medicaid Services. 2001a. *Medicare and Home Health Care*. Washington, D.C.: U.S. Department of Health and Human Services.

———. 2001b. *Medicare and You 2002*. Washington, D.C.: U.S. Department of Health and Human Services.

———. 2005a. *Medicaid at-a-Glance*. Accessed August 10, 2006, at cms.hhs.gov.

———. 2005b. *Medicare Benefits Policy Manual*. Publication 102. Chapter 7, Section 50.3. www.cms.hhs.gov/manuals, 07/01/06.

———. 2006. *Medicare and Your Mental Health Benefits*. Accessed September 22, 2007, at http://www.medicare.gov/publications/pubs/pdf/mental.pdf.

———. 2007. *Medicare and You*. No. 10050. Retrieved June 1, 2007, from www.medicare.gov/publications.

U.S. Department of Health and Human Services. Health Care Financing Administration. 1999. Medicare and Medicaid Programs: Comprehensive assessment and use of the OASIS as part of the conditions of participation for home health agencies. (42 CFR Part 484). *Federal Register* 64 (15): 3764–3784.

U.S. Department of Health and Human Services. Office of Minority Health. 2001. *National Standards for Culturally and Linguistically Appropriate Service in Health Care: Final Report*. Retrieved September 14, 2003, from www.omhrc.gov/CLAS/index/htm.

U.S. Department of Labor. Bureau of Labor Statistics. 1998. *Basic Statistics About Home Care*. http://www.nahc.org/Consumer/hcstats.html.

———. 2006-07. *Occupational Outlook Handbook*. Accessed September 30, 2007, at http://www.bls.gov/oco/ocos060.htm.

U.S. Department of Veterans Affairs. 1998. *National Home and Community-Based Care Strategy*. Washington, D.C.: Veterans Health Administration.

———. 2005. *VA Long Term Care: Fact Sheet*. January. Accessed August 10, 2006, at www.va.gov.

———. 2006. *Federal Benefits for Veterans and Dependents*. Accessed August 11, 2006, at www1.va.gov.

U.S. General Accounting Office. 1998. *Long-term care: Baby boom generation presents financing challenges*. Accessed September 15, 2007, at http://www.gao.gov/archive/1998/he98107t.pdf.

———. 2000a. *Medicare Home Health Care: Prospective Payment System Could Reverse Recent Declines in Spending*. Accessed September 15, 2007, at http://www.gao.gov/new.items/he00176.pdf.

———. 2000b. *Mental Health Parity Act: Employers' Mental Health Benefits Remain Limited Despite New Federal Standards*. Accessed September 15, 2007, at http://www.gao.gov/archive/2000/he00113t.pdf.

U.S. Office of Strategic Planning. Health Care Financing Administration. 1999. *A Profile of Medicare Home Health: Chartbook*. http://www.hcfa.gov/stats/cbookhha.pdf.

Van de Laar, K. E. W., and J. J. Van der Bijl. 2001. Strategies enhancing self-efficacy in diabetes education: A review. *Scholarly Inquiry for Nursing Practice* 15 (3): 235–248.

Van Hook, M., B. Hugen, and M. Aguilar. 2001. *Spirituality Within Religious Traditions in Social Work Practice*. Pacific Grove, Calif.: Brooks/Cole.

Van Wormer, K., J. Wells, and M. Boes. 2000. *Social Work with Lesbians, Gays, and Bisexuals: A Strengths Perspective*. Boston: Allyn and Bacon.

Vandeweerd, C., G. J. Paveza, and T. Fulmer. 2006. Abuse and neglect in older adults with Alzheimer's disease. *Nursing Clinics of North America* 41:43–55.

Verbugge, L., and A. M. Jette. 1994. The disablement process. *Social Science and Medicine* 38 (1): 1–14.

Villaume, W. A., M. H. Brown, and R. Darling. 1994. Presbycusis, communication, and older adults. In M. L. Hummert, J. J. Wieman, and J. F. Nussbaum, eds., *Interpersonal Communication in Older Adulthood*, 83–105. Thousand Oaks, Calif.: Sage.

Vincent, P., and J. Davis. 1987. Functions of social workers in a home health agency. *Health and Social Work* 12:213–219.

Vitaliano, P. P., H. M. Young, and J. Russo. 1991. Burden: A review of measures used among caregivers of individuals with dementia. *Gerontologist* 31 (1): 67–75.

Vivian, B. G. 1996. Reconceptualizing compliance in home health care. *Nursing Forum* 31:5–13.

Vivian, B. G., and J. R. Wilcox. 2000. Compliance communication in home health care: A mutually reciprocal process. *Qualitative Health Research* 10 (1): 103–116.

Vladeck, B., and N. Miller. 1994. The Medicare home health initiative. *Health Care Financing Review* 16:7–16.

Vladescu, D., K. Eveleigh, J. Ploeg, and C. Patterson. 1999. An evaluation of a client-centered case management program for elder abuse. *Journal of Elder Abuse and Neglect* 11 (4): 5–22.

Voss, R., V. Douville, A. Soldier, and G. Twiss. 1999. Tribal and shamanic-based social work practice: A Lakota perspective. *Social Work* 44 (3): 228–241.

Wagner, Donna L. 2003. *Workplace Programs for Family Caregivers: Good Business and Good Practice*. San Francisco: Family Caregiver Alliance, National Center on Caregiving.

Waldfogel, J. 2001. Family and medical leave: Evidence from the 2000 surveys. *Monthly Labor Review* 124 (9): 17–23.

Waldrop, J., S. M. Stern, and U.S. Census Bureau. 2003. *Disability Status: 2000. U.S. Census Brief*. Washington, D.C.: U.S. Department of Commerce.

Wallace, S., L. Levy-Storms, R. Kington, and R. Andersen. 1998. The persistence of race and ethnicity in the use of long-term care. *Journals of Gerontology: Social Sciences* 53B:S104–S112.

Walters, K., S. Iliffe, S. Tai, and M. Orrell. 2000. Assessing needs from patient, carer, and professional perspectives: The Camberwell Assessment of Need for Elderly people in primary care. *Age and Aging* 29 (6): 505–510.

Wang, P. S., R. L. Bohn, E. Knight, R. J. Glynn, H. Mogun, and J. Avorn. 2002. Noncompliance with antihypertensive medications: The impact of depressive symptoms and psychological factors. *Journal of General Internal Medicine* 17:504–511.

Wasik, B. H., and D. M. Bryant. 2001. *Home Visiting: Procedures for Helping Families*. 2nd ed. Newbury Park, Calif.: Sage.

Weaver, F. M., L. Perloff, and T. Waters. 1998. Patients' and caregivers' transition from hospital to home: Needs and recommendations. *Home Health Care Services Quarterly* 17 (3): 27–48.

Weaver, H. 2003. *Voices of First Nations People*. Binghamton, N.Y.: Haworth.

———. 2005. Cultural identity: Theories and implications. In *Explorations in Cultural Competence: Journeys to the Four Directions*, 25–46. Belmont, Calif.: Thomson/Brooks/Cole.

Weaver, H., and B. White. 1997. The Native American family circle: Roots of resiliency. *Journal of Family Social Work* 2 (1): 67–79.

Weiner, D. K., J. T. Hanlon, and S. A. Studenski. 1998. Effects of central nervous system polypharmacy on falls liability in community-dwelling elderly. *Gerontology* 44 (4): 217–221.

Welch, H. G., D. Wennberg, and W. P. Welch. 1996. The use of Medicare home health care services. *New England Journal of Medicine* 335:324–329.

Welfel, E. R., P. R. Danzinger, and S. Santoro. 2000. Mandated reporting of abuse/maltreatment of older adults: A primer for counselors. *Journal of Counseling and Development* 78 (3): 284–292.

Wendt, D. 1996. Building trust during the initial home visit. *Home Healthcare Nurse* 14:91–98.

White, T., A. Townsend, and M. Stephens. 2000. Comparisons of African American and White women in the parent care role. *Gerontologist* 40 (6): 718–728.

Wilber, K. H., and S. L. Reynolds. 1996. Introducing a framework for defining financial abuse of the elderly. *Journal of Elder Abuse and Neglect* 8:61–80.

Willen, S. B., S. M. Harman, and D. Alexander-Israel. 1997. Home care and the Alzheimer's disease patient: An educational imperative. *Caring* 16:44–49.

Williams, B. 1994. Comparison of services among different types of home health agencies. *Medical Care* 32:1134–1152.

Williams, B., S. Mackay, and J. Torner. 1991. Home health care: Comparison of patients and services among three types of agencies. *Medical Care* 29:583–587.

Williams, S., and P. Dilworth-Anderson. 2002. Systems of social support in families who care for dependent African American elders. *Gerontologist* 42 (2): 224–236.

Williams, S., and C. Wilson. 2001. Race, ethnicity, and aging. In R. Binstock and L. George, eds., *Handbook of Aging and the Social Sciences*, 160–178. 4th ed. San Diego: Academic Press.

Wills, E. M. 1996. Nurse-client alliance. *Home Healthcare Nurse* 14:455–459.

Wolf, D. 1999. The family as provider of long-term care: Efficiency, equity and externalities. *Journal of Aging and Health* 11: 360–382.

Wolf, R. 1999–2000. Emotional distress and elder abuse. Retrieved June 11, 2007, from www.elderabusecenter.org.

———. 2000. Risk assessment instruments. [Electronic version]. *National Center on Elder Abuse Newsletter* 3 (1). Retrieved December 31, 2006, from http://www.elderabusecenter.org.

Worcester, M., and S. Hedrick. 1997. Dilemmas in using respite for family caregivers of frail elders. *Family and Community Health* 19 (4): 31–48.

Wright, D. L., and W. S. Aquilino. 1998. Influence of emotional support exchange in marriage on caregiving wives' burden and marital satisfaction. *Family Relations* 47 (2): 195–204.

Yaffe, K., P. Fox, R. Newcomer, L. Sands, K. Lindquist, K. Dane, and K. E. Covinsky. 2002. Patient and caregiver characteristics and nursing home placement in patients with dementia [Electronic version.] *JAMA* 287 (16): 2090–2097.

Yates, M. E., S. Tennstedt, and B.-H. Chang. 1999. Contributors to and mediators of psychological well-being for informal caregivers. *Journals of Gerontology: Psychological Sciences* 54B (1): P12–P22.

Yeates, C., J. M. Lyness, P. Duberstein, C. Cox, L. Seidlitz, A. DiGiorgio, and E. Caine. 2000. Completed suicide among older patients in primary care practices: A controlled study. *Journal of the American Geriatrics Society* 48:23–29.

Yesavage, J. A., T. L. Brink, T. L. Rose, O. Lum, V. Huang, M. Adey, and V. Leirer. 1983. Development and validation of a geriatric depression screening scale: A preliminary report. *Journal of Psychiatric Research* 17:37–49.

Yin, T., Q. Zhou, and C. Bashford. 2002. Burden on family members: Caring for frail elderly—a meta-analysis of interventions. *Nursing Research* 51 (3): 199–208.

Yordi, C., R. DuNah, A. Bostrom, P. Fox, A. Wilkinson, and R. Newcomer. 1997. Caregiver supports: Outcomes from the Medicare Alzheimer's Disease Demonstration. [Electronic version.] *Health Care Financing Review* 19 (2): 97–117. Retrieved September 11, 2005, from the Ovid database.

Young, H. M., V. M. McCormick, and P. P. Vitaliano. 2002. Attitudes toward community-based services among Japanese American families. [Electronic version.] *Gerontologist* 42 (6): 814–825. Retrieved September 11, 2005, from the PubMed database.

Zarit, S. H., M. A. P. Stephens, A. Townsend, R. Greene, and S. A. Leitsch. 1999. Patterns of adult day care service use by family caregivers: A comparison of brief versus sustained use. *Family Relations* 48 (4): 355–361.

INDEX